The Little Palm Book

Corbin Collins

Peachpit Press • Berkeley, California

The Little Palm Book

Corbin Collins

Peachpit Press
1249 Eighth Street
Berkeley, CA 94710
(510) 524-2178
(800) 283-9444
(510) 524-2221 (fax)

Find us on the World Wide Web at: http://www.peachpit.com
Peachpit Press is a division of Addison Wesley Longman

Editor: Marjorie Baer
Technical Editor: Michael Bergen
Production/Interior Design Coordinator: Amy Changar
Interior Design: Robin Williams
Graffiti font courtesy of Jeff Carlson
Compositor: Maureen Forys
Cover Design: John Tollett with Mimi Heft
Cover Illustration: Trish Booth
Indexer: Karin Arrigoni

Photographs of Palm devices and accessories courtesy of Palm Computing, Inc., a 3Com company.

ISBN 0-201-69954-0

9 8 7 6 5 4 3 2 1

Printed and bound in the United States of America.

Acknowledgments

This book wouldn't be anything close to what it is without the help and support of many people. I want to thank:

Marjorie Baer, for being such a wonderful colleague, calming influence, wise editor, and generous driver.

Nancy Ruenzel, for her ironclad commitment to Peachpit and marvelous leadership.

Amy Changar, for her command of production issues and flexibility when it came to this book.

Maureen Forys, for her mastery of layout and quick volunteer work on the icons.

Michael Bergen, for his sharp-eyed technical editing, for his infectious excitement about these devices, for starting the SFPUG, for being so nice to me when I turned up at a meeting out of the blue, and for adding so much to the quality of this book.

Marty Cortinas, for being willing to step into the brink at the drop of a hat, and for noticing and handling so much stuff.

Trish Booth, for the lovely image that graces the front cover.

Mimi Heft, for her capable cover design and production.

Cliff Colby, for going on burrito runs on a moment's notice and telling me Lincoln stories.

Mara Winokur of Palm Computing, for being so helpful to a lowly author trying to get stuff from her.

To the rest of the editorial team at Peachpit for supporting me when I got to do this.

To family and friends who didn't complain when I disappeared for three grumpy months.

Dedication

To Tracy, for thinking of it, for seeing the sense in it, for having faith that I could do it, for talking me into it over three pints at Magnolia's on Haight Street, for understanding the sacrifices involved in the creation of it, for wanting to move to Ireland, for being colorful in a black-and-white world, for continuing to put up with me, for unlocking my heart.

Table of Contents

PART 2 The Built-In Palm Applications 59

Chapter 4 Date Book 61

Chapter 5 Address Book 79

Chapter 6 To Do List 91

PART 3 Connecting with
Your Computer   123

Chapter 9 Windows HotSync
and Palm Desktop   125

PART 4 Connecting with the Net 193

Foreword

I have to begin with a disclaimer. I'm extremely biased, and I hope that bias comes through in this foreword. To put it plainly, I love the Palm. I was so excited when I first started using the Palm that I founded and became president of the San Francisco Palm/Pilot User Group. My friends stop me midsentence when I start going on about how cool Palms are, and my wife calls me The First Evangelist of the Church of Palm. When strangers see me using mine and they ask me about it, they never quite seem prepared for the fervor with which I answer their questions.

Palm connected organizers are more than just Personal Digital Assistants, they're one of the most enabling technologies I know of. I know Palm users who range from geeks who write computer code in their heads for fun to people whose VCRs still blink 12:00. I've seen Palms deployed in major corporations, college campuses, and nonprofit organizations. Is this because they're small, inexpensive, easy-to-learn devices that keep all of your information at hand? Yes, partly. They're also really fun! On more than one occasion I've surprised someone by pulling my trusty Palm out of my pocket to answer a question, make a phone call or figure out the tip for a meal (just because I'm a computer expert doesn't mean I can do math in my head!).

The excitement and enthusiasm surrounding the Palm reminds me very much of the early days of the Apple Macintosh, when we knew we had the better computer system and wanted to share that knowledge with everyone. The market, however, had different ideas, and the Apple Macintosh never had a huge market share. The Palm on the other hand, does. As of this writing the Palm controls 78 percent of the handheld market, with over four million units out there.

So what can you do with these little things? As you'll read in this book, they're Personal Digital Assistants with some built-in programs that work perfectly fine right out of the box. But if you want to customize your Palm, and add hardware and software to precisely serve your needs, then the sky's the limit.

The great thing is their versatility. I used mine to plan my wedding, much to the amusement of my friends and colleagues. I noticed that as the date got closer, and they saw how organized I was, their amusement turned to envy (for the record, I am not usually a very organized person). I used all four of the main built-in programs: Memo Pad to keep lists of invitees, gifts, vendors, music, ring sizes, questions for the caterers, etc. I used the To Do List to track tasks by date, category (ceremony, reception, shower, bachelor party) and priority. The Address Book kept all of our guests' addresses for invitations and thank-you cards, as well as all of our vendors' contact information. And, of course, Date Book had all of our key dates. I planned my honeymoon much the same way.

If you're worried about handwriting, you have no excuse for not being able to write in the Palm's special language, Graffiti. If I can scrawl in such a way that the Palm can understand me, so can you. In fact, Graffiti is one of the original neat things about the Palm. It's actually how the Palm got invented—Jeff Hawkins developed Graffiti, and then a device on which to use it! It'll look strange at first, but don't be put off, it really is quite easy to learn and use. The only problem may be that you'll find it so easy and convenient that you'll want to use it as your regular writing—I've seen graffiti on whiteboards in conference rooms throughout Silicon Valley, sort of as geek chic!

I encourage you to read this book, learn from it and enjoy it. Don't stop here, though. Look at the Web sites in the appendix, and go to your local user group meeting, if there's one near you. Hopefully, you'll soon get to the point where instead of thinking "What can this thing do?," you'll think "What do I want this thing to do?," and you'll find the resources to make it happen.

Happy Palm-ing!

Mic Bergen
President, San Francisco Palm/Pilot User Group
president@sfpug.org

Introduction

Welcome to *The Little Palm Book!* This book aims to intro-
duce you to the wonderful world of Palm handheld devices,
without bogging you down with a bunch of extraneous, fancy
information. I'm sticking to the facts here. I know you're busy.
I don't try to talk about everything—I only cover the most useful and helpful things for you to know, and that's how I kept
the book so little.

Quietly, Palm handheld computers have invaded the workplace,
campus, and home. Suddenly there are all these affordable,
cool devices that are excellent at doing a few things: accept-
ing, storing, and retrieving your addresses and phone numbers, schedules, to-do lists, and memos. They let you read and
reply to your email while you're on the bus. They simplify getting all that information into and out of your regular computer.
And they make it easy to keep all the information updated,
whether you change it on your Palm or on your computer. The
Palm does not claim to do much more than that (even though
software developers have figured out *lots* more for them to do,
as you'll see).

The Palm is not a replacement for your computer—it's an extension of it.

Who Should Read This Book

I assume you are an intelligent person who happens to be new to the Palm world and who doesn't have a lot of time. You are interested in these devices, but not obsessively—you want them to be fun and useful, not take over your life. You are at least familiar with computers, and you almost certainly have a PC or Mac at work or at home. You've used email, and you've been on the Web. I assume you want to know how to start actually using your Palm as fast as possible.

How This Book Is Organized

The book is arranged into fifteen chapters, grouped in four parts. Each chapter and part build on the knowledge gained from the preceding one. So the book is best read straight through from the beginning, although it is still useful as a reference—just look up what you want to know about in the Table of Contents or Index and flip straight to that page.

Almost everything in this book applies to all Palm models, from III through VII. Chapter 15, which covers the special Palm VII programs, is an exception.

Part I

I start at the very beginning—opening the box. From there I acquaint you with the Palm and how it operates, teach you how to set it up to work for you, and show you how to enter data into it using the onscreen keyboards and the Palm hand-writing system called Graffiti.

Part II

Here is where you'll learn how to use the main built-in programs that ship with every Palm: Date Book, Address Book, To Do List, Memo Pad, Expense, Security, and Calculator. These programs form the primary use of the Palm for most users, so they are covered in considerable detail.

Part III

The Palm is not an island unto itself—part of its enormous success lies in the ease with which it synchronizes its data with your regular computer (PC or Mac). You'll learn how to use the computer version of your Palm programs (called Palm Desktop) and how to HotSync (synchronize between Palm and computer).

Part IV

Amazingly, you can also use your Palm to connect to your Internet Service Provider, check and reply to your email, and surf the Web. And if you have a Palm VII, you can do all that—*plus* you get to use the Palm VII's wireless transmitter to access online information you Palm.Net account. Finally, the appendix points the way toward building on the Palm knowledge you gained in this book.

Elements of This Book

You'll notice icons throughout this book. They are as follows:

The Note icon accompanies text that is not essential but may be interesting or useful nonetheless.

The Tip icon flags important, timesaving tricks that you would do well to learn.

The Warning icon alerts you to something bad that could happen.

The Palm III icon notifies you of information relevant to the Palm III only.

The Palm IIIe icon notifies you of information relevant to the Palm IIIe only.

The Palm IIIx icon notifies you of information relevant to the Palm IIIx only.

The Palm V icon notifies you of information relevant to the Palm V only.

The Palm VII icon notifies you of information relevant to the Palm VII only.

The Palm OS 3.3 icon points out material relating to the Palm OS 3.3 upgrade, which should be available from Palm Computing by the time this book hits the shelves. This upgrade fulfills Palm's promise to offer Flash ROM upgrades for the Palm models III through VII. Check out www.palm.com to see if it's out yet. It may be available for download or you can probably order it on a CD-ROM for a nominal fee.

Are They Palms or PalmPilots?

They used to be called *Pilots*, but then the Pilot Pen company got mad. Then they were called *PalmPilots*, but even that didn't entirely clear up the matter. Then 3Com gave them the clunkier moniker *Palm connected organizers*. You'll hear them referred to as *hand-held computing devices* or *personal digital assistants* (PDAs), which are true enough as terms but include other products besides Palm devices. So in this book, for simplicity's sake, I call them *Palms*. It's just easier. And besides, you know exactly what I mean when I talk about *your Palm,* so why confuse things?

All right. Enough preliminaries! Let's get started figuring out what these things are, how they work, and what you can do with them.

part one

Palm Basics

This part of the book takes you from opening the box your Palm was shipped in to mastering the Graffiti writing system. I take you on a tour of your new device in Chapter 1 to familiarize you with all its buttons and other parts. Chapter 2 tells you how to set up your Palm and gives an overview of what's in it and how the Palm operating system works. Finally, in Chapter 3 you'll learn all about how to get information into your Palm using the Graffiti writing system and the onscreen keyboards.

Getting Acquainted

It's so exciting when you first get a brand-new new toy—er, productivity-enhancing personal computing device—isn't it? If you're like me, you cleared some space on the floor, ripped off the plastic shrink-wrap, eagerly flipped open the box, and spread all the goodies around you in a frenzy of techno-lust.

A new Palm device will affect you that way. And before you know it, you'll be pulling out your Palm everywhere you go. But first you need to get acquainted with the basics.

What Kind Did You Get?

This book covers the Palm III, Palm IIIx, Palm IIIe, Palm V, and Palm VII devices. It does not cover the older Pilots or Palm-Pilots (unless you have upgraded them to Palm III status). The differences among the models are actually more cosmetic than substantive (except for the Palm VII, which is also a wireless communication device).

All Palms come with the same set of basic programs (applications), run at roughly the same speed, provide super-cool infrared (IR) beaming, and come with plenty of memory.

Palm III

This model, introduced in 1998, is the oldest one covered in this book, but in almost every way it's just as robust and feature-filled as its fancier younger siblings (see **Figure 1.1**), and much cheaper. It can store 6000 addresses, 3,000 appointments (five years' worth), 1,500 To Do items, 1,500 memos, and 200 email messages. The Palm III has 2MB of memory, infrared capability, comes with Palm OS 3.0, and includes a flip cover to protect the screen. At the time of this writing (summer 1999), you can buy a Palm III for around $175.

Some users complain that the Palm III screen is hard to read and end up pining for one of the later models, which feature an improved screen. And it's true, there is a degree of graininess to the Palm III screen. If you're shopping for a Palm, be sure to try out different models and look closely at the screen display quality. On the other hand, the backlight feature on the Palm III is better than on the Palm V.

Palm IIIe

The Palm IIIe is the newest Palm model. Aimed at students and other people who don't need the fancy conduit software that syncs a Palm with programs such as Microsoft Outlook, the stripped-down Palm IIIe was introduced in July 1999 as a lower-priced version of the Palm III. It includes all the main built-in programs that come with other Palms. In fact, in all aspects the Palm IIIe has the same features as the Palm III except that it lacks the Outlook conduit software (which comes bundled with the other models) and the memory configuration is different, which means it is not upgradeable with the Flash ROM updates periodically released by 3Com). On the other hand, it has the new, sharper screen found on the IIIx. You can buy a Palm IIIe for as little as $150.

Upgrading to Palm OS 3.3

For a long time, 3Com touted the Flash ROM upgradeability of the Palm, but the problem was there didn't seem to be any upgrades available. Finally, there is a Flash ROM upgrade called Palm OS 3.3. Flash ROM means you can upgrade the operating system with software only—that is, without installing new hardware.

Palm IIIx

The *x* is for *expandable*. The Palm IIIx is similar to the Palm III except the screen is sharper, it has twice the memory (4MB), and it has a different internal memory setup that allows for greater expansion possibilities in the future (see **Figure 1.2**). A Palm IIIx can store 12,000 addresses, 6,000 appointment (a decade's worth), 3,000 To Do items, 3,000 memos, and 400 email messages. It comes with Palm OS 3.1 installed. A Palm IIIx will cost you around $300 at the time of this writing. If you're looking for maximum handheld power and upgradeability, this is probably the model you want.

> *Most people love the clarity of the IIIx's screen…until they notice the screen streak problem. Screen streaks are faint lines that appear on the Palm IIIx's screen next to vertical lines in many Palm programs. They only appear in some applications. Supposedly, 3Com has fixed the problem in new releases of the IIIx and may fix or replace the screen streak problem if it's bothering you (call 3Com at 1-800-881-7256 to find out).*

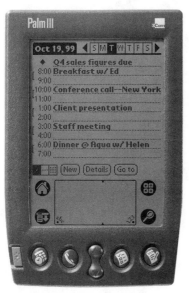

Figure 1.1 The Palm III is the oldest model covered in this book.

Figure 1.2 The Palm IIIx is the most expandable and memory-rich of the bunch.

Palm V

The Palm V (see **Figure 1.3**) is roughly the same as a Palm III, except it is smaller—I don't think you'd *want* a handheld computer smaller than a Palm V. It has an attractive, brushed metal case that flares out at the bottom instead of in, comes with Palm OS 3.1, and does not use regular batteries. Instead, it comes with a built-in lithium ion battery that you keep charged by simply placing it in its cradle, which has an AC adapter you plug into a wall outlet. A few minutes a day will keep your Palm V fully charged.

> *Because of its smaller, "flared out" design, the Palm V does not fit the regular Palm modems and cradles that fit the Palm III and VII models. So, if you have a Palm III modem and cradle, you can't use them with your Palm V. The Palm V has its own line of accessories and peripherals.*

A Palm V has 2MB of memory, can store the same amount of data as the Palm III, and costs roughly $450 at the time of this writing.

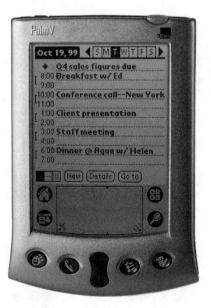

Figure 1.3 The Palm V is a lean, mean, handheld machine.

Palm VII

The much-ballyhooed Palm VII is like a Palm III with built-in wireless access via an antenna that sticks out the top (see **Figure 1.4**). Because of its special wireless features, the Palm VII comes with Palm OS 3.2. You use Palm Computing's Palm.Net service to connect online without a modem or phone line and retrieve your email and a host of customized information from various service providers and Web sites, a process 3Com calls *Web clipping*. The special Palm VII programs that use the wireless feature are called *query applications*.

Antenna

The Palm VII is the most expensive device of them all, debuting in mid-1999 for $550. The Palm.Net service costs extra, too, either $9 per month or $29 per month, depending on how much you plan to use it (see Chapter 15 for a lot more on the Palm VII's special features and applications).

The Palm VII has 2MB of memory and can store the same amount of data as the Palm III and V.

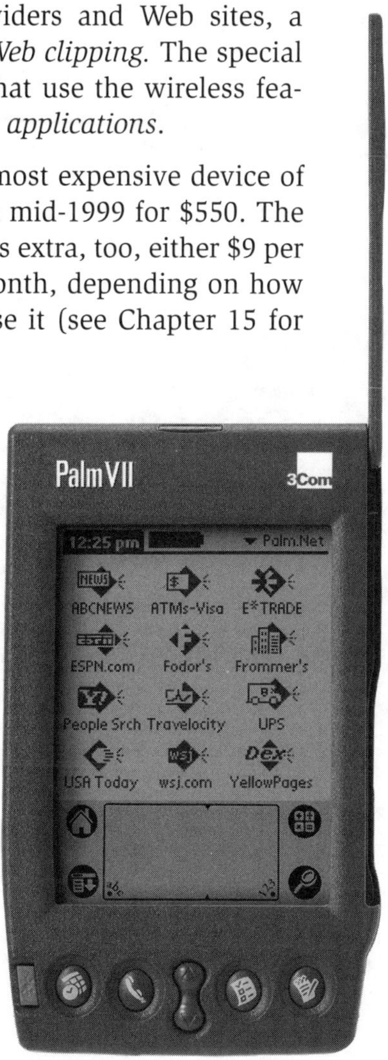

Figure 1.4 The Palm VII adds wireless connectivity and online services, but be prepared to shell out for it.

Other "Palm" devices

Palm isn't the only company that makes handheld machines that run the Palm OS. IBM offers virtually identical devices, called WorkPads. The different WorkPad models are the WorkPad (which is the same as a Palm IIIx) and the WorkPad C3 (which is a Palm V): The only difference between WorkPads and their Palm-ish counterparts are the colors of the cases and buttons. Otherwise, they are precisely the same machines.

IBM also makes a product confusingly called the WorkPad X50, which is actually more of a notebook PC than a handheld device (it's bigger and has a keyboard). More importantly, the WorkPad X50 does not run the Palm OS— it runs Windows CE, a competing operating system for handheld machines.

Where to buy Palm devices

Most consumer electronics stores and office supply shops sell Palms, but you may pay more than you need to. Several online outlets sell them cheaper, even factoring in shipping. Web sites such as www.buy.com and www.outpost.com sell Palm devices, software, and peripherals for rock-bottom prices and offer numerous shipping options, including next-day service. If you don't mind the idea that someone else's palm once held your Palm, you can find used devices quite cheap at auction sites such as eBay (www.ebay.com), OnSale (www.onsale.com), and Yahoo Auctions (auctions.yahoo.com). Auction sites offer some level of mediation and assurance of quality. Or try your local paper's classified section. See the appendix for a list of more Palm resources, online and offline.

A Trip Around Your Palm

For such an amazing, powerful, and versatile machine, your Palm device has a relatively simple interface. The following are the main elements of the Palm device interface (they are discussed in detail in the following paragraphs): See **Figure 1.5** for an illustration of these things.

1. Power/backlight button

2. IR port

3. Application buttons

4. Scroll button

5. Contrast wheel

6. Printed icons

7. Liquid Crystal Display (LCD) screen

8. Graffiti area

9. Serial port

10. Reset button

Figure 1.5 The Palm interface is elegant and relatively simple.

The Palm VII, of course, also has an antenna for wireless connection to the Internet (back in **Figure 1.4** you can see this antenna).

The Palm V has no contrast wheel. Instead, it has a button on top that causes an onscreen contrast control to appear onscreen. You change the contrast by sliding the control with the stylus.

Power/backlight button

This little green button is how you turn the device on and off. On the Palm V the button is located at the top of the device. If you press it down and hold it for a second or two, the screen will suddenly glow green. This is known as *backlighting*, and it makes using your Palm in dim light a joy. There is something comfortable and cozy when you are all alone and the little screen is glowing up at you. I can't explain it, but I love the backlight. The Palm V's backlight is not quite as vivid, because it reverses the pixels.

All good things come at a cost: The backlight is a battery hog. The more you use it, the sooner you'll be replacing (or recharging) the batteries.

Application buttons

The four plastic application buttons located along the bottom of your Palm are an easy way to launch the four main, built-in Palm applications (pressing them also turns on your Palm if it is off, saving you that step):

 Date Book: You can plan your schedule for the next few years using Date Book. It features day, week, and month views. See Chapter 4 for more on Date Book.

Address Book: This is a great way to have all your phone numbers, email addresses, addresses, and other contact info one button away. See Chapter 5 to learn about Address Book.

 To Do List: Here's where you keep your list of things you have to do. It's so satisfying to check off or delete tasks as you accomplish them. Chapter 6 has the scoop on To Do List.

 Memo Pad: You can read and write documents using Memo Pad. See Chapter 7 for more.

You don't have to accept 3Com's default programs for these buttons. You can reprogram any button to launch any application you want (more on this in Chapter 2).

Scroll button

The scroll button provides an easy way to move quickly through documents. When you press the bottom or top of the scroll button, the screen contents shift up or down by one screenful. It's often much faster to use the scroll button to shift the screen up or down than it is to tap the scrollbars that appear on the right side of the screen in many Palm applications (more about scrollbars in Chapter 2).

Memo Pad is nice, but many add-on Palm applications (those created by people other than 3Com) have improved how you can read and write long documents, even entire books, on your Palm. The scroll button makes reading a one-button pleasure with these applications, which are known as Doc programs. Chapter 11 discusses programs that will turn your Palm into an electronic book.

Printed icons

The four silkscreen icons that are permanently printed at the four corners of the Graffiti writing area on your Palm are kind of like the physical buttons, in that they are always right there and available, no matter what icons are onscreen. See **Figure 1.6** to learn what each one is called.

Menu   Applications   Calculator   Find

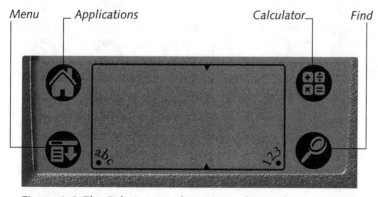

Figure 1.6 The Palm's printed icons are always there, waiting for you to tap them.

Inconveniently, Palm changed the printed icons slightly while I was in the middle of writing this book. The new icons are somewhat better than the old ones, especially the Applications icon, which used to be a big arrow and now looks like a house (home base). On the other hand, Palm removed the icon labels so that you can't read to tell what they are anymore. Ah, progress.

Applications: Tap this icon, and you can see all the programs on your Palm. That's why I call it home base. Tap it again, and the Palm cycles through its application categories (All, Games, Main, Systems, Utilities, and Unfiled). You'll learn more about applications and categories in Chapter 2. See **Figure 1.7** to see what the Applications icon shows you when you tap it.

Menu: On your computer, you are used to accessing program menus by clicking on them. For example, to save a file you click File > Save. The Menu icon is where menus are on the Palm (see **Figure 1.8**). Palm menus take some getting used to, as the Menu button is located at the bottom of the screen rather than the top, as you're accustomed to it. Chapter 2 tells you all about using menus.

Figure 1.7 Home base: the Applications screen shows you what programs are installed on your Palm.

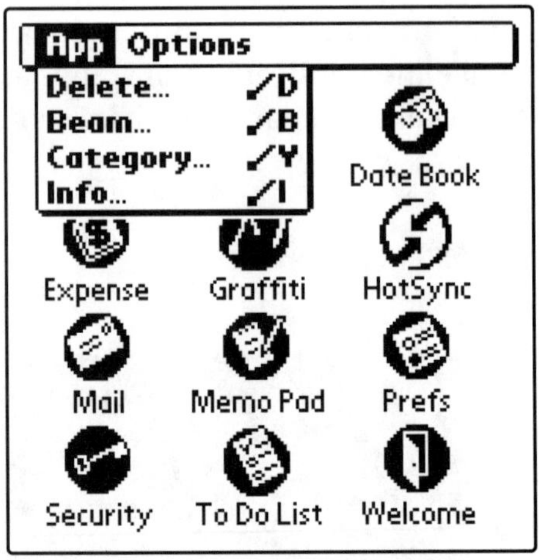

Figure 1.8 You use menus on your regular computer, and here's what they look like on the Palm.

There is no need to save files on the Palm, by the way— everything is always saved the moment you create or change it. You don't have to even think about it.

There is an add-on Palm program called MenuHack that lets you access Palm menus by tapping the title bar located at the top of many programs, which feels more intuitive to computer users. Chapter 11 talks more about Menu Hack.

Calculator: This icon is a bit of an anomaly, because it doesn't provide any quick operating system function. Instead, it launches the Palm Calculator, which is very simple and straightforward (see **Figure 1.9**). Chapter 8 goes into more calculating detail.

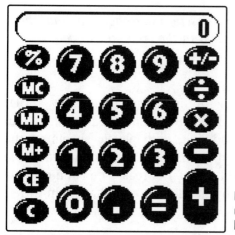

Figure 1.9 Look familiar? You use the Palm calculator just like you do any calculator.

Find: Tap the Find button at any time to quickly look up any piece of information that is stored anywhere in your Palm. A little dialog box pops up and asks you to enter some text to search for (see **Figure 1.10**). After you enter a word or two and tap OK, Find reports back what it found (**Figure 1.11**).

Figure 1.10 Use the stylus to write some text into the Graffiti writing area, and Find races off to find everything in your Palm that contains that text.

Find

Find: burrito

OK   Cancel

Figure 1.11 Here's what
Find found.

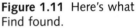
If you highlight some text onscreen and then tap Find, that text is automatically entered in the Find box for you.

The screen

You're probably familiar with liquid crystal display (LCD) screens. Lots of modern gadgets and gizmos feature them. An LCD screen is really a sandwich, with plastic sheets on the outside and gooey liquid on the inside. The Palm activates the liquid so that it makes light and dark areas. The Palm can use the light and dark areas to form letters and shapes, in different shades of gray.

The screen is also sensitive to physical touch. When you touch someplace on the screen with the stylus (or any other dull, small, rounded-end implement—even your finger, but that smudges it), the Palm executes whatever function is called for (see **Figure 1.12**). If you tap a program icon, the Palm starts that program. If you tap in the middle of some text in Memo Pad, the Palm figures that you want to place the cursor there and does so. Tap a button called Cancel, and whatever was about to happen will be canceled. And so on. It's very intuitive—what you think will happen when you tap something probably *will* happen.

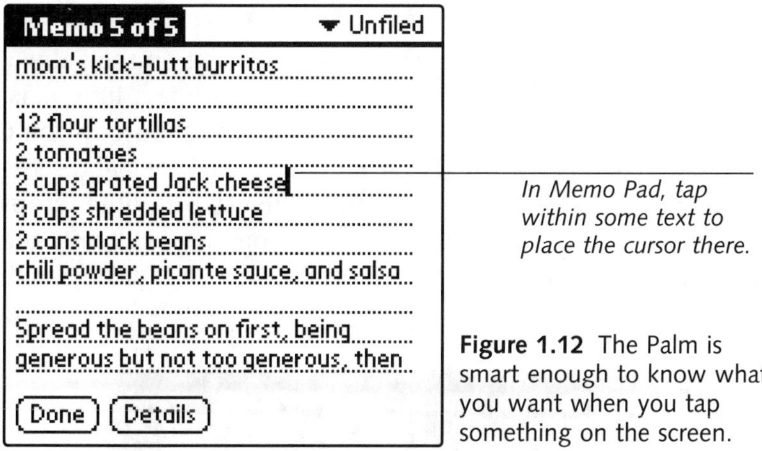

Memo 5 of 5   ▼ Unfiled

mom's kick-butt burritos

12 flour tortillas
2 tomatoes
2 cups grated Jack cheese
3 cups shredded lettuce
2 cans black beans
chili powder, picante sauce, and salsa

Spread the beans on first, being
generous but not too generous, then

(Done) (Details)

In Memo Pad, tap within some text to place the cursor there.

Figure 1.12 The Palm is smart enough to know what you want when you tap something on the screen.

Graffiti area

Using the stylus, you can write on the Graffiti area, and the Palm interprets your letters, numbers, and punctuation and shows them on the screen. This is quite a feat. Computer manufacturers have been trying to develop a system like this for some time. At least a couple efforts failed by trying to have the machine learn about how you write, notably Apple's Newton MessagePad.

The Palm engineers reversed that and decided that it's easier and more accurate to teach *you* a simple writing system that the Palm already understands. Therefore, the Palm has a preconceived notion of the way letters, numbers, and punctuation marks are to be formed (see **Figure 1.13**). This extremely well-designed system is called Graffiti, it's quickly learned, and you'll find out all you need to know about it in Chapter 3.

Figure 1.13 The Graffiti writing area, where you write characters that the Palm can understand and display.

Serial port

Look at the bottom of your Palm device. Except on the Palm V (whose serial port is naked to the world) there is a little plastic door that slides up and down, and when you slide it up you'll see ten little copper strips. These strips make up the Palm's serial port (see **Figure 1.14**). The strips connect with other strips on other devices (such as the cradle) to complete a circuit, and the result is that the two devices can talk electronically with each other.

Figure 1.14 Slide the door up to reveal the Palm's serial port.

The cradle isn't the only thing you can connect to the Palm's serial port. Modems (see Chapter 12) and other devices, such as the GoType keyboard (see Appendix A), can also hook up to it.

IR port

The IR feature is one of the most fun and amazing things about Palm devices. The IR port at the top of the device sends and receives information right through the air. In the process known as *beaming*, you point one Palm device at another and beam stuff back and forth. You can beam *almost* anything: Documents, Address Book entries, emails—even applications and games.

You can also use the IR port for other things, such as printing to IR-ready printers and using your Palm as your TV and stereo remote control. See Chapter 11 for programs that use the IR port in interesting ways.

Contrast wheel

If you turn your Palm over, you'll see a little control wheel along the side. This controls the contrast on the screen. Fiddle with it so that the screen looks good to you. The Palm V's contrast button, located at the top of the device, lets you control the contrast onscreen.

Reset button

On the back of your Palm you'll notice a tiny hole somewhere near the middle. Through that hole lies the reset button. If your Palm ever freezes up or crashes, you will have to use the reset button—but don't try it until then. (You press the reset button using a paperclip or the reset pin, which you'll find if you unscrew the back end of the stylus.) Actually, three different levels of reset are possible with the Palm.

> *Resetting can be dangerous: Depending on which type you employ, you can lose all your data when you reset. You learn how to reset in Chapter 2.*

What Comes with Your Palm

Before we move on to the next chapter to actually begin learning to use your Palm, you should familiarize yourself with all the stuff that came with it. Palm devices are shipped with the following:

- The HotSync cradle
- At least one stylus
- A cover
- Documentation

- Software for your PC on CD-ROM (Mac users note: You have to buy this software separately)
- Batteries

Macintosh users, unfortunately, cannot use the free Palm Desktop software and must purchase the Palm MacPac 2 software separately. 3Com and other vendors sell the MacPac 2 for $14.95.

The HotSync cradle

The HotSync cradle is the little holding stand that connects to your desktop or notebook computer (see **Figure 1.15**). It's also where the Palm V recharges its built-in battery. You place your Palm in the cradle and push the button on its face to begin a HotSync session, in which the data on your computer and your Palm are *synchronized,* or brought up to date with each other.

HotSyncing sounds complicated, but it's actually a very easy and handy way of doing all sorts of things, such as inputting a lot of data into your Palm without having to write it on the screen using Graffiti, and outputting data you have stored on your Palm for printing or using in other programs on your computer. I talk about HotSyncing a lot in this book. See Chapter 9 for lots more on HotSyncing.

 The Palm V's HotSync cradle also plugs into a wall outlet and recharges your Palm V's internal lithium ion battery.

Figure 1.15 The Hot-Sync cradle is where your Palm sits during a Hotsync session.

The stylus

The stylus is the little black pen-like implement you use to tap buttons and write with on the Palm screen using the Graffiti handwriting system. When you're not using it, the stylus slides neatly into the stylus channel at the top of the unit.

In the old days, 3Com used to include a cheap, lightweight stylus that many Palm users found unsatisfactory and replaced with fancier, more expensive models sold by a variety of third parties. The squeaky wheels finally got their oil because all models starting with the Palm III come with better, heavier styli.

Still, if 3Com's stylus leaves you wanting something even better, you have plenty of others to choose from.

> *Never use any kind of regular ink pen to write on your Palm's screen because you can permanently damage the screen if you do. Some Palm users report scratches on the screen, leading many to recommend using a screen protector, such as WriteRights by Concept Kitchen.*

The cover

You can't just throw your naked Palm in your briefcase or backpack and expect it to last very long because the screen would get scratched. So your Palm comes with a cover (see the cover on the Palm III in Figure 1.1). The Palm III and IIIx come with detachable flip covers that make you feel like you're in a Star Trek outtake. (I'm sure they designed it to appeal to the legions of Trekkies out there.)

The Palm V, on the other hand, has a nice little leather cover that slides into either the right or left stylus channel (a blessing for lefties) and flips over sideways.

The Palm VII comes with a little leather case and no flip cover (at least my field test model didn't come with a cover), although it does have indentations on the case that suggest the existence somewhere of Palm VII flip covers.

As with most things in the Palm universe, the cover has inspired many companies to create more elegant alternatives.

The documentation

In your Palm's box, you'll find a handy "Getting Started" fold-out card, which is a spare but quick and easy reference to use to figure out how to put in batteries, hook up your cradle to your computer's serial port, and install the Palm Desktop software. It also includes some pictures of Palm screens and Graffiti letters. Palm includes a helpful accessory catalog (do you need an "I sync, therefore I am" T-shirt?) and registration card (you get a free extra stylus if you register). You can also register online at Palm's Web site (www.palm.com).

All Palms come with *Handbooks*. These are useful as references in a pinch, but they are not what you'd call fun or friendly, and they are not exactly all that well organized. It can be hard to find what you're looking for with these manuals, and if you take them to bed with you be sure to set your alarm clock first. To be fair, it should be noted that 3Com does a better job than most in the documentation department, but like most computer companies, writing books is just not its forte. And why should it be? Engineering ingenious little devices isn't mine.

Third parties are on the case

One thing your Palm didn't come with is a case, and as you might imagine, a host of Palm device cases are available for sale by 3Com and other companies (see the slick Accessories Catalog that came in your box). They range from rich, Corinthian leather portfolios with slots for your Platinum Card to zippered vinyl Palm-shaped bags to cases with belt clips and everything in between. A case is one accessory you would do well to acquire, especially if you do much traveling with your Palm. It can be messy trying to cram the Palm, a cradle, a Palm modem, and whatever other paraphernalia you may start collecting into your suitcase. Palm devotees are fond of debating which cases are the best.

The software

Every Palm comes with at least one CD-ROM containing the Palm Desktop software you need to install on your computer in order to HotSync your Palm and your PC. Sadly, Mac users may as well throw away the Windows CD-ROM they find in the box, because they have to purchase their Palm software, called Mac-Pac 2, separately for $15 (more on this in a minute). Palm III and IIIx devices include a Bonus Pack CD-ROM too.

Here's a quick inventory of what's on your CD-ROM. See Chapters 9 through 11 for details on using Palm-related software.

Palm Desktop Organizer Software CD-ROM: 3Com's free Windows CD-ROM contains the following software and support material:

- The Palm Desktop software you need to run on your computer in order to HotSync (see Chapter 10 to learn about using the Palm Desktop).
- Quick Tour, a slick Macromedia Director presentation complete with musical score and animated Palms flying around.
- Help Notes (if you have trouble with your computer's COM ports or setting up the Mail application, read the Help Notes).
- A very good ReadMe file with lots of helpful setup information
- Five games: Hardball, Mine Hunt, Sub Hunt, Puzzle, and Giraffe.

If you don't have a CD-ROM drive, you can order 3.5-inch floppy disks by calling 3Com at 1-800-881-7256 in the U.S., 1-800-891-6342 in Canada.

The Bonus Pack: The Palm III models also come with another CD-ROM, called the Bonus Pack, compiled by Macmillan Digital Publishing. It contains:

- Lite versions of three Palm applications: FCPlus, World-FAQ, and TealPaint.
- Four games: Hardball, Mine Hunt, Sub Hunt, and Puzzle...which already were on the other CD-ROM.
- Snap! Online and AvantGo, two Web-based applications (more on these in Chapter 11).
- Conduits for Outlook and Act! (Conduits are "bridges" between software on your PC and the Palm Desktop software.)

The MacPac 2 CD-ROM: To order the MacPac 2 CD-ROM, call 3Com at 1-800-881-7256 in the U.S., 1-800-891-6342 in Canada. Once you indignantly shell out the $15 and open the CD-ROM box, you'll find that you also get a Getting Started Guide and a Macintosh adapter (to connect the HotSync cradle to your Mac's printer port or modem port).

Incredibly, if you have an original iMac or G3, you still have one more hurdle to leap. Those machines don't have regular serial ports like the old Macs do (some of the later ones do). Instead, they have USB ports, which are not currently supported by Palm cradles. You'll have to buy a USB-to-serial adapter at your local computer store, Radio Shack, or online shop before you can HotSync with your serial-less Mac. If you have a PowerBook or iMac with IrDA (an infrared port), you can HotSync your Palm to your Mac via the Palm's infrared port if you install the Palm OS 3.3 upgrade. See Chapter 9 for more on HotSyncing with your Macintosh and Appendix B for more on the Palm OS 3.3 upgrade.

Here's what you'll find on the MacPac 2 CD-ROM:

- Palm MacPac installer (which installs Palm Desktop software 2.1, HotSync Manager, and QuickTour (a multimedia presentation about your Palm)

- Read Me First! (a helpful file containing late-breaking news)

- Palm Extras (Extra software, including software that lets you transfer your email between your Palm if you use Eudora Light or Eudora Pro on your computer, and Adobe Acrobat Reader so you can read additional online documentation in Acrobat format). See Chapter 13 for more on Palm email.

- Documentation (in Adobe Acrobat format)

The batteries

If you have a laptop computer, you're used to batteries draining away to nothing within hours. Not so with the Palm. You'll be pleased to discover that a set of batteries will last you two to four weeks, depending on how much you use your Palm, how much you use the backlight feature, whether you play many games, and so on.

It's a good idea to buy a lot of batteries and keep them around at all times. The battery indicator at the top of many screens shows you how much power you have left.

If you ignore the indicator and let the batteries actually run out of power (your Palm won't turn on), they still have enough juice to hold your data for as much as a week, but you should install fresh batteries as soon as you can to be safe.

Two Duracell AAA batteries are included with your Palm (unless you have a Palm V, which doesn't need batteries). Install these into the clip door in the back of the unit.

You can use your Palm VII as soon as you insert the batteries, except that you have to wait for 70 minutes after installing the batteries before you can activate the wireless services. This time period is necessary for the batteries to fully charge up the wireless transmitter. When the Palm VII starts up for the first time, the first screen asks you if you want to activate the device. Tap the Cancel button to check out the rest of your Palm's applications and features while you wait for the transmitter to charge.

Charging the Palm V battery

The Palm V's built-in lithium ion battery must be charged for three hours before you can use it. To charge the Palm V's battery, unpack everything from the plastic wrapping and follow these steps:

1. Make sure your computer (your PC, not just your Palm) is off.

2. Find the AC adapter and plug the skinny end of its cord into the hole in the back of the cradle connector. The cradle connector is at the end of the cord attached to the cradle.

3. Plug the cradle connector into a free serial port on your computer. If your computer doesn't have a free

serial port, you may have to first plug the cradle connector into the included adapter, which will probably fit one of your other ports.

4. Plug the AC adapter into a wall outlet.

5. Set your Palm V gently into the cradle, right-side up and face out. If the stylus holder on the cradle is emitting a green light, your Palm V is charging. If there is no green light, make sure all your connections are tight and that the AC adapter is plugged in.

Not having to worry about buying batteries is a very cool benefit of owning a Palm V. However, the Palm V's lithium ion battery won't last forever, and I can't help but wonder what happens when it finally dies. You can probably send the unit back to 3Com to have the battery replaced, but what would happen to your Palm's data during that trip is unclear. Of course, if you regularly HotSync, you should have no problem because your Palm data for your built-in programs is on your PC, ready to replenish your Palm when you HotSync after a battery replacement.

For backing up the data held in your add-on programs, consider buying Backup Buddy, an add-on program that saves all your Palm's data in case of a data-wiping disaster (see Chapter 11 for more on Backup Buddy).

Which batteries are the best?

Opinions vary. Some swear by the Duracell Ultra. Others love those that power the Energizer Bunny, while others claim that cheaper batteries actually last longer. Still others use rechargeable batteries, which may save money in the long run, although rechargeables degrade faster, even if they just sit on a shelf, and when they start to die, they die fast (I wouldn't use rechargeable batteries in a Palm). Regular alkaline batteries discharge their power at an even rate, making the battery guage more accurate when you're using them. It's probably best for you to try some different kinds and see which you like best.

Setting Up
Your Palm

Every computer has an operating system, and the Palm is no different. Your desktop or laptop computer's operating system is probably Windows 95 or Windows 98. If you have a Macintosh, its operating system some version of the Mac OS. The Palm's operating system is called the Palm OS.

Operating systems provide the under-the-hood number crunching on top of which your programs, or applications, run. An operating system sits between a program, such as Microsoft Word, and the computer's circuitry, translating commands and actions back and forth. Modern operating systems like Windows and the Mac OS provide what is known as a *graphical user interface*, or GUI (pronounced "gooey").

A GUI means that instead of having to type in commands on an ugly black screen (ever seen MS-DOS?), you are treated to a pleasant, visual field on the screen that tries to make accomplishing tasks as easy and intuitive as possible. The Palm OS is as GUI as the Mac OS and Windows.

The Stylus Is Your New Mouse

In Windows and the Macintosh, you use the mouse to move the mouse pointer around the screen, which lets you point at, select, drag, click, and double-click on icons and buttons in your programs. On the Palm, you tap directly on icons, buttons, and text with the stylus to get things done.

There is no "double-tapping" built into the Palm, so get used to just tapping once on stuff. Add-on Palm programs— created by third parties (anyone but 3Com)—allow you to multi-tap to select a word or paragraph, for example. I talk about add-on programs in Chapter 11.

You can select text by pressing the stylus onto some text and dragging through it to select as much as you want. Once you get the hang of it, which takes about ten seconds, tapping and dragging will be as natural to you as clicking is now.

The other wonderful thing you can do with the stylus is write text, numbers, punctuation, and ShortCut commands in the Graffiti area. You also have the option of calling up a couple of onscreen keyboards, where you tap the "keys" to enter characters into your Palm. Chapter 3 covers Graffiti and the onscreen keyboards.

The Setup Process

When you first turn on your Palm, you are immediately greeted by the Palm Computing Welcome screen (see **Figure 2.1**), which disappears after a few seconds and is replaced by the Setup screen (see **Figure 2.2**).

If you have a Palm VII and you raised the antenna (and who wouldn't?), you'll see an Activation screen urging you to activate the Palm.Net service. Tap the Cancel button for now (you should learn basics first, but we will come back to Palm.Net in Chapter 15).

Figure 2.1
The first thing your Palm shows you is the Palm Computing logo.

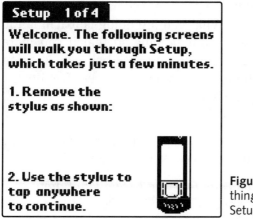

Setup 1 of 4

Welcome. The following screens will walk you through Setup, which takes just a few minutes.

1. Remove the stylus as shown:

2. Use the stylus to tap anywhere to continue.

Figure 2.2 The second thing you see is the first Setup screen.

Note the lack of mechanical groans or the whirr of disk drives spinning! There is no long startup process, and there is no disk drive—everything in the Palm is in memory and ready for you the second you turn it on.

The Setup process only happens automatically when you turn on the Palm for the first time and after resetting (more on resetting later in this chapter). You can bring back the Setup any time you want later by clicking on the Welcome icon in the Applications screen.

Follow the instructions you see—take out the stylus and tap on the screen. The Palm will show you what it calls a *target* in the second Setup screen (see **Figure 2.3**). Tap anywhere on the screen with the stylus to continue (see **Figure 2.4**).

Setup 2 of 4

In the following screen, you will be asked to tap the center of the target as shown below. This ensures accurate stylus entry.

Use the stylus to tap anywhere to continue.

Figure 2.3 Tap anywhere to get to the next screen.

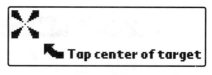

Tap center of target

Figure 2.4 This is where you calibrate your taps to make sure the Palm is registering them properly.

Do what it says, carefully tap on what seems to you to be the exact center of the target. What you are doing is teaching the Palm the idiosyncrasies of your tapping so that it can more accurately calibrate the screen to you. It'll ask you to tap a few more targets in different places on the screen. Eventually, you'll see Setup screen 3 shown in **Figure 2.5**. Here you will set your country, time, and date.

If you live anywhere but the U.S., tap the drop-down arrow (the little triangle) next to Country to get to the screen in **Figure 2.6**.

As you work with the Palm OS, you'll see a lot of drop-down arrows like the one in Figure 2.5. These arrows signify that if you tap them, more choices are underneath waiting for you to tap on them. The concept should be familiar to you from using Windows or the Mac.

Tap on the clock to set the time, and the date to set the date (see **Figures 2.7** and **2.8**). Tap Next to go to the final Setup screen.

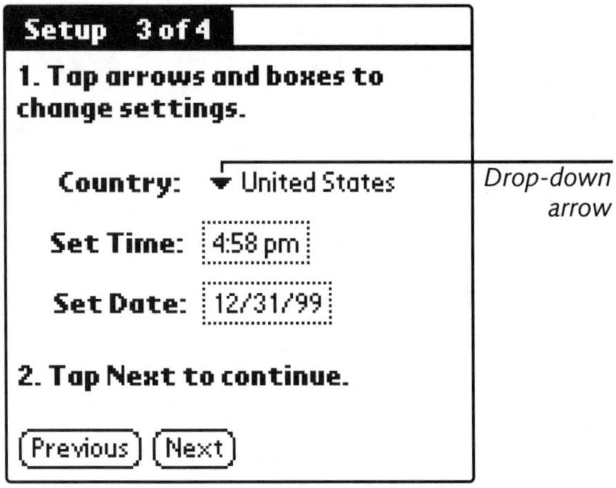

Figure 2.5 Choose your country, set the time, and pick today's date.

Figure 2.6 Choosing a different country.

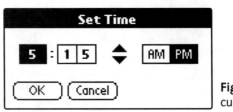

Figure 2.7 Setting the current time.

Set Date

◀ **1999** ▶

Jan	Feb	Mar	Apr	May	Jun
Jul	Aug	Sep	Oct	Nov	Dec

S	M	T	W	T	F	S
			1	2	3	4
5	6	7	8	9	10	11
12	13	14	15	16	17	18
19	20	21	22	23	24	25
26	27	28	29	30	(31)	

(Cancel) (Today)

Figure 2.8 Picking today's date.

In **Figure 2.9**, you see an invitation to learn about entering text on your Palm. It's talking about the Graffiti writing system, which I discuss in detail in Chapter 3. If you want to skip ahead and learn Graffiti now, tap Next and flip to Chapter 3. Otherwise, tap Done. I recommend holding off on learning Graffiti until you learn the basics of the operating system (fear not, it's a small operating system).

Your Palm is all set up now and ready to go! What you see now is where your Palm adventures begin: the Applications screen (**Figure 2.10**).

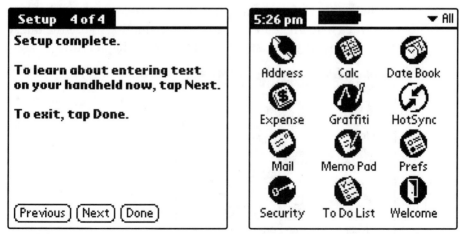

Setup 4 of 4

Setup complete.

To learn about entering text on your handheld now, tap Next.

To exit, tap Done.

(Previous) (Next) (Done)

Figure 2.9 Tap Done to finish Setup.

5:26 pm ▼ All

Address　Calc　Date Book

Expense　Graffiti　HotSync

Mail　Memo Pad　Prefs

Security　To Do List　Welcome

Figure 2.10 The Applications screen is where you can see all the programs installed on your Palm.

The Applications Screen: Home Base

On Windows 95 and 98, you start up your computer and, after a few minutes of whirring, whizzing, and beeping, you find yourself at the Windows desktop, your computer's home base. Here is where you can see the Start button and the rest of the Start bar across the bottom of the screen, including a clock and little buttons, and icons for your programs floating in a background.

Palm OS versions

The Palm III comes with Palm OS 3.0. The Palm IIIx and Palm V come with Palm OS 3.1. And Palm VII comes with Palm OS 3.2. Recently, 3Com announced the Palm OS 3.3 flash upgrade. This upgrade is available for all four models (and the Work-Pad models).You can download it for free or order the CD-ROM and pay a nominal fee for the convenience.

On the Mac OS, you see pretty much the same thing. This home base environment is a computer's metaphor for the place where you can see most of your stuff and where you get work done.

The Palm's home base is the Applications screen, seen in **Figure 2.10**. On a new Palm, you will see 12 icons for the 12 built-in Palm applications (programs) that are accessible from home base.

You can get back to the Applications screen at any time, no matter where you are in your Palm, by tapping the Applications screen icon.

 The Palm VII's Applications screen contains several more icons than the other Palms do (see **Figure 2.11**). These are called query applications. If your Palm VII is your first Palm, it's probably a good idea to learn Palm basics before attempting to use the query applications. If you just can't wait, flip to Chapter 15.

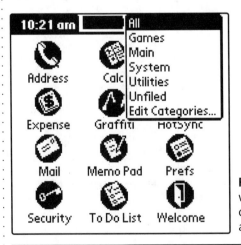

Figure 2.11 Because of its wireless feature, the Palm VII comes with applications that are unique to that model.

Categories

Once you start installing add-on programs, there will be more program icons than can fit on the screen at once. At that point, scroll bars will pop up and you'll have to scroll up and down the screen to find your programs. Luckily, you don't have to have all your programs onscreen at once. You can organize them into categories so that only one category at a time is onscreen.

At the top right of the Applications screen, you see a drop-down arrow with the word All next to it. Tap that arrow, and down comes a category box (see **Figure 2.12**), indicating six categories you can put your applications in, plus a seventh option called Edit Categories. Tap Main or System, and you see that some of the applications you saw under All are also in Main, and some are in System. On your new Palm, you won't have any application icons under Games, Utilities, or Unfiled.

Figure 2.12 The Palm's built-in application categories drop down.

The built-in categories aren't all that helpful, in my opinion. System, Main, and Utilities sound very similar to me. So, the Palm lets you edit the names of the categories. Tap Edit Categories, and you'll see the Edit Categories box (**Figure 2.13**), where you can delete them, rename them, or add new ones. (There's no need to actually do that until and unless you have a need to.)

Note that little "i" within a circle at the top right in **Figure 2.13**. That's an Information button. Information buttons contain additional information about a screen. Tap the Information button, and you'll see a screen similar to **Figure 2.14**. Tap Done when you're done reading it, and then tap OK to get back to home base (the Applications screen).

Figure 2.13 You can add, delete, and rename categories for your applications.

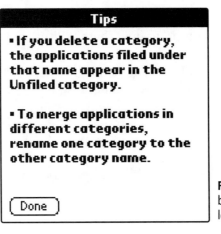

Figure 2.14 Information buttons, not surprisingly, lead to information.

Home base menus

On your "real" computer, you're used to using menus to issue commands, and those menus are always along the top of the screen. Typical menus are File, Edit, View, Options, Help, and so on. Same with the Palm—menus are also at the top of the screen. So how come you don't see them? Because they are hidden under the Menu icon.

 To save screen space (at 2⅜ inches square, every millimeter is at a premium), the Palm's interface designers decided that you'd have to tap something to make the menus pop up. At home base, tap the Menu icon, and you'll see two menus, App and Options, appear at the top of your screen (see **Figure 2.15**).

App menu

Thoughtfully, the App menu is already dropped down for you— so there at least you get your extra tap back. Under the App menu, you see the choices Delete, Beam, Category, and Info.

Menu choices, slashes, and dots

If a menu choice has three dots after it, it means that it leads to another box where you will choose to issue one or more commands. If it doesn't have dots after it, the next screen *is* the command. This is just like menus work on Mac and Windows. Note also the funny slashes with dots followed by letters on many menu choices. Those are Graffiti commands, which let you access menu choices in an even faster way.

Menu

Menu choice

Graffiti
command

Figure 2.15 Palm menus are there, just like on your computer—you just have to tap the Menu icon to get to them.

Delete: Tap Delete, and you are shown the Delete screen (**Figure 2.16**), where you can delete applications that you are tired of or never use. Another reason you'd want to delete programs would be to release the memory they are taking up. Every program takes up some space in your Palm, leaving less space for everything else. In **Figure 2.16**, you can see that the Delete screen also shows you how much free memory your Palm currently has and how much each memory application is consuming (in kilobytes, shortened to K).

To delete something, tap it to select it and then tap Delete. I've installed some games that I could delete (Chapter 11 tells you how you can install add-on software, including these games on the Windows CD-ROM). But I don't want to delete them, because they are fun, especially HardBall—before Hard-Ball, I used to read books in my spare time. Tap Done and then tap the Menu icon to drop down the App menu again.

Figure 2.16 You can delete these programs and also check to see how much of your Palm's memory they are consuming.

You can't delete the main built-in Palm programs, like Date Book, To Do List, Memo Pad, Address Book, and so on. They are permanently etched into the machine's circuits. Which means they don't take up any of the Palm's memory anyway, so there would never be a need to delete them.

Beam: Tap Beam, and you're presented with a list of programs that you can *beam* to another Palm device (**Figure 2.17**). If you tap one of the applications to select it and then tap Beam, your Palm searches for another Palm device in the vicinity (within three feet) and sends that program to the other device through thin air. It's pretty amazing. Several chapters in this book discuss beaming.

Those little icons that look like locks beside some programs mean those programs are unbeamable. Every Palm has those programs permanently built-in anyway, so there's no reason to beam them.

You probably don't have another Palm device to try out beaming right now, so tap Done and tap the Menu icon to drop down the App menu again.

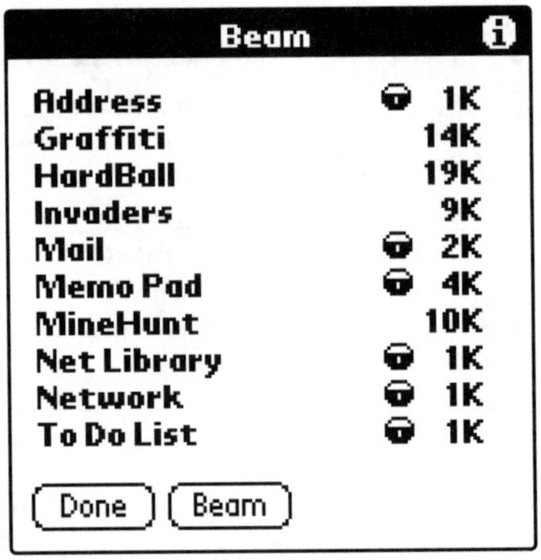

Beam		ⓘ
Address	⊖	1K
Graffiti		14K
HardBall		19K
Invaders		9K
Mail	⊖	2K
Memo Pad	⊖	4K
MineHunt		10K
Net Library	⊖	1K
Network	⊖	1K
To Do List	⊖	1K

(Done) (Beam)

Figure 2.17 A list of programs you could send to another Palm device via the IR port.

Category: Tap Category to see the list of your programs along with their categories (**Figure 2.18**). Here you can use the drop-down arrows to change which categories your programs are in. Tap Done and then tap the Menu icon to bring up the App menu one more time.

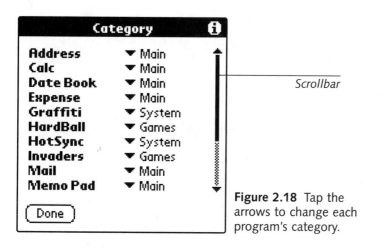

Scrollbar

Figure 2.18 Tap the arrows to change each program's category.

See the scroll bar along the right side of the screen? It works just like scroll bars do in Windows and the Mac. You can tap the bottom and top arrows to move the list up or down one item, you can tap in the grayed out part to move one screenful, or you can press down on the darkened bar with the stylus and drag it as far as you like.

Info: Tap Info to get to the Info screen, which just lists some various pieces of information about each of your programs. You get to these pieces of info by tapping the three boxes, Version, Records, and Size. These are pretty boring, except maybe Records.

The Records box (**Figure 2.19**) tells you how many items are in your Palm of whatever type of record you create in each program. **Figure 2.19** shows that on this new Palm, I have two records in Address Book (both pre-entered by 3Com), one in Mail (one email, guess who from?), four in Memo Pad (four memos... from the helpful folks at 3Com), and so on. As you start adding addresses, memos, appointments, and to do items, the number of records for each will grow rapidly.

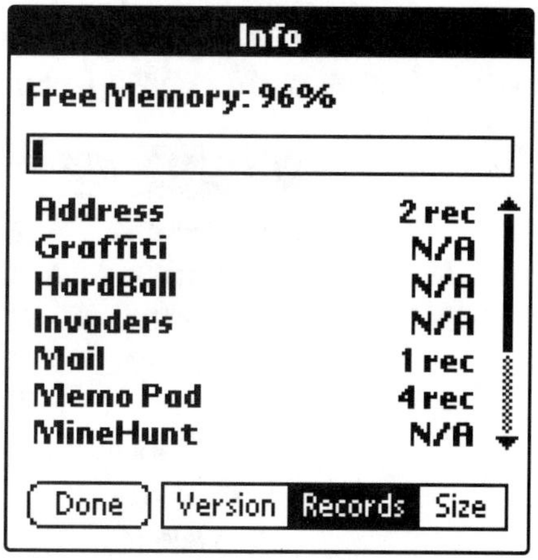

Figure 2.19 As you use your Palm, you will start racking up lots more records than these pitiful numbers.

Options menu: Tap Done to return to home base. Tap Menu again and then tap Options to drop down the Options menu. You'll see two meager choices: Preferences and About Applications. Tap Preferences to get to the Options Preferences box shown in **Figure 2.20**.

Figure 2.20 The Options Preferences box lets you change the view and decide what the Palm remembers.

The checkbox next to Remember Last Category means that, if it's checked, the Palm will remember which category of applications was open last time you had the Palm turned on and show that category the next time you turn on your Palm.

Checkboxes on the Palm work just like they do in Windows and on the Mac. To check or uncheck a checkbox, tap it.

The other part of the Options Preferences box in **Figure 2.20** is revealed when you tap the View By drop-down arrow. Your two choices are Icon and List. Icon is the default option, the one you're already used to seeing, and it just means the Palm will show you those nice big icons in home base. If you tap List and then tap OK, you'll see the Applications screen scrunched up with tiny icons (see **Figure 2.21**).

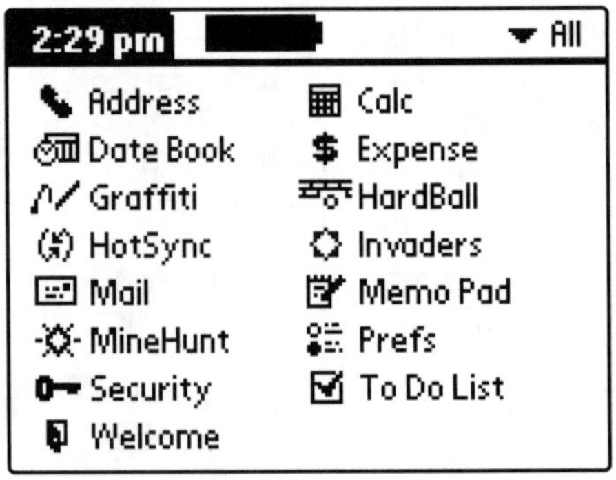

Figure 2.21 View By List shrinks down the icons in the Applications screen.

Menus within programs

Now you know about the menus available from the Applications screen. Just as programs do in Windows and on the Mac, most Palm programs also offer additional menus while you're running them (many of which you're used to: Undo, Cut, Copy, Paste, Select All). You'll learn more about using these menus in the chapters devoted to the built-in applications (Chapters 4 through 8).

Setting Your Preferences

Okay, go back to home base by tapping the Menu icon. Tap on the Preferences icon. You should see a screen like the one shown in **Figure 2.22**. At the top right, you'll see that the Preferences screen has opened so that the General drop-down arrow is selected. Underneath that arrow are eight choices, and each one brings up its own Preferences screen.

General

In General Preferences, shown in **Figure 2.22**, you can set the following options:

Set Time: This works just like it did when you went through the initial Setup process. Tap the little clock to make changes.

Set Date: Again, it's just like it was during Setup. Tap the date to make changes.

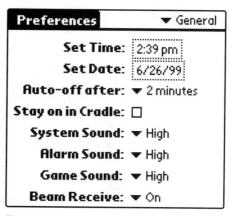

Figure 2.22 Here are your options in the General Preferences screen.

Auto-off after: This power-saving option controls how long your Palm will stay on and wait for you to do something. Your choices are one, two, or three minutes. Setting this to one minute will make your batteries last longer, but you'll be pressing the Power button more often to turn on your narcoleptic Palm.

Stay on in Cradle: This option makes your Palm V stay awake all the time whenever you keep it charging in its cradle.

System Sound: The little beeps you hear when you tap around can be turned up, down, or off. They are not very loud, which is probably why Palm sets the default to High.

Alarm Sound: You'll learn about setting alarms in Chapter 4. The Palm's alarm is not very loud. You may as well keep it set to High (the default).

Game Sound: Different Palm games produce different bleeps and noises, and you can turn them down or off here.

Beam Receive: This makes it so that your Palm is always ready to receive a beam from another Palm device. Keeping Beam Receive on means never having to think about whether your Palm is ready to get beamed; however, it also uses up battery power by making your Palm spend energy listening for IR transmissions.

Buttons

Tap the drop-down arrow at the top right on the General Preferences screen to drop down the list of different Preference screens. Tap Buttons to open the Button Preferences screen (see **Figure 2.23**).

Figure 2.23 The Buttons Preferences screen lets you reprogram the Palm's buttons.

Buttons Preferences is where you can reprogram the buttons on the face of the Palm to launch any application you want. Just tap the arrow next to the application whose button you want to reprogram and select the new application from the list that pops up.

In addition to the buttons, there is one printed, Graffiti-area icon you can reprogram: Calculator.

Default: If you reprogram a few buttons and then change your mind, just click Default to set the buttons back to the way 3Com intended them to be.

Pen: Tap the Pen button at the bottom of the Buttons Preferences screen to access a really useful feature (see **Figure 2.24**). A Palm command can be issued by pressing the stylus on the Graffiti area and drawing a line straight up to the top of the screen. And here is where you can set up what the "Big Line" command will mean on your Palm. Your choices are:

- *Backlight.* The Big Line you draw will turn the backlight on or off.

- *Keyboard.* The line will call up an onscreen keyboard (see Chapter 3 for more on onscreen keyboards).

- *Graffiti Help (the default).* The Big Line will bring up some screens that remind you how to write Graffiti characters.

- *Turn Off & Lock.* The Big Line will shut down your Palm and lock it so that no one else can use it without entering a password (see Chapter 8 for more on the Palm's Security program).

- *Beam Data.* The Big Line will start the beaming process.

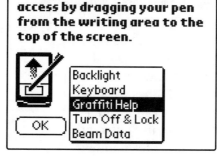

Figure 2.24 You can draw a Big Line up the entire screen and make one of these things happen.

It's fun to play with the Pen, or "Big Line," feature. I recommend you leave the setting on the default Graffiti Help for now. As you'll find out in the next chapter, when you blank on the stroke for a Graffiti character, it's nice to know that help is just a stylus swipe away. After you master Graffiti, you may want to change the Big Line feature to Turn Off & Lock.

HotSync: You can reprogram the HotSync button on the cradle to launch a different program with this option, but that seems silly to me. Leave this one set as is.

Digitizer

Tap the drop-down arrow at the top right on the Buttons Preferences screen to drop down the list of different Preference screens again. Tap Digitizer to open the Digitizer screen. You've already seen this screen. During Setup, this is where you had to tap in the center of targets to calibrate your stylus tapping to your Palm.

If your taps ever seem to be acting weird, as in not registering correctly, try to make your way to the Digitizer screen to correct the calibration.

Formats

Tap the drop-down arrow at the top right on the Digitizer screen to drop down that Preferences list again. Tap Formats to open the Formats Preferences screen (see **Figure 2.25**). This screen lets you make changes in minute preferences in the details of how numbers, dates, and times will display in the Palm. Different cultures use different date, time, and number formats.

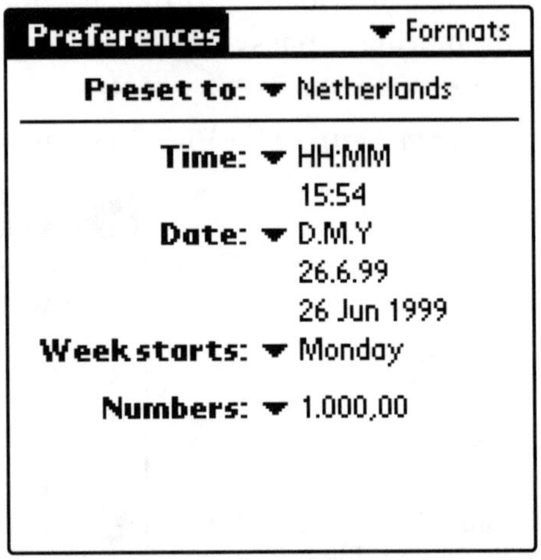

Preferences	▼ Formats
Preset to: ▼ Netherlands	
Time: ▼ HH:MM	
15:54	
Date: ▼ D.M.Y	
26.6.99	
26 Jun 1999	
Week starts: ▼ Monday	
Numbers: ▼ 1.000,00	

Figure 2.25 The Palm can be cosmopolitan when it comes to how dates, times, and numbers will display on your Palm.

Really, all you have to do here is tap Preselect to: and pick your country. The Palm knows how your people write these things.

Modem

Tap that drop-down arrow at the top right on the Formats Preferences screen to drop down that Preferences list yet again (don't worry, you won't wear it out). Tap Modem to open the Modem Preferences screen. Take a brief peek if you like and dream of the day when you hear those comforting modem shrieks coming from the palm of your hand. But you probably don't have a modem or haven't set it up yet. To learn how to set up your modem, see Chapter 12.

Network

Tap the drop-down arrow at the top of the screen and tap Network. Network Preferences control how your Palm deals with network connections, such as when you dial into your Internet Service Provider. Same deal with Network Preferences as with Modems: the details are in Chapter 12.

Owner

Tap the drop-down arrow at the top of the screen and tap Owner. This is where you inform people who find your Palm where they should send it. Okay, stop laughing—it *could* happen. Write your contact information here using Graffiti (see **Figure 2.26**).

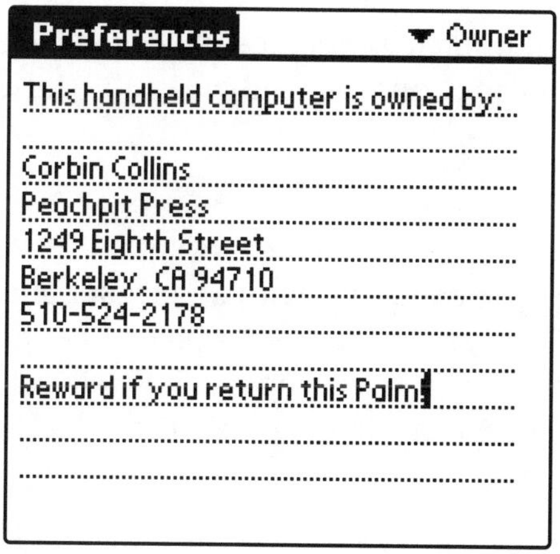

Preferences   ▼ Owner

This handheld computer is owned by:

Corbin Collins
Peachpit Press
1249 Eighth Street
Berkeley, CA 94710
510-524-2178

Reward if you return this Palm|

Figure 2.26 It might not ensure your machine's safe return, but at least it'll make you feel slightly better if you put your contact info in the Owner's Preferences screen.

ShortCuts

Tap the drop-down arrow at the top of the screen and tap Short-Cuts. **Figure 2.27** shows the ShortCuts Preferences screen, where you can take note of the built-in ShortCuts that Palm supplied with your device. ShortCuts are part of Graffiti, which is covered in the next chapter.

Basically, Graffiti ShortCuts are a way for you to save time and carpal tunnel doctor bills by allowing you to create abbreviations for longer words or phrases. For example, you could create a ShortCut that writes out your name when you write your initials. You'll learn how to do that in the next chapter.

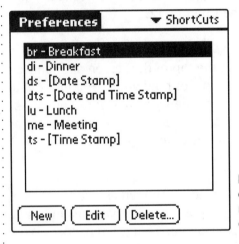

Figure 2.27 ShortCuts can save you time by not having to write out commonly used words.

Wireless

Palm VII owners have one additional Preferences screen, called Wireless. Don't worry about that one right now. You'll learn about it in Chapter 15.

Resetting Your Palm

The Palm is a fairly simple little computer with an elegant and robust operating system. Even so, sometimes a piece of software will make it go haywire and freeze up, or it'll tell you that it's encountered a "Fatal Error" and just sit there, mute and helpless. You'll try pressing all the buttons, including the power button, and nothing will happen. It won't turn off or restart. It won't do anything. Now what?

You have to reset it. There are three kinds of reset on the Palm: soft, semisoft, and hard. If you find that you have to reset your Palm, you should always first try a soft reset. If that doesn't work, try a semisoft reset. If that fails, you will have to do a hard reset.

On the back of your Palm, find the small round hole some-where near the middle of the case. That's the reset hole. You can't get to it with the regular end of the stylus. In fact, in the old days of the Pilot and PalmPilot, you had to straighten a paper clip and use that to reset your Palm. Nowadays many of the Palm styli come with a special reset pin. Unscrew the back end of the stylus to reveal the reset pin. If yours doesn't have a reset pin, you'll have to find a paper clip.

Soft reset

A soft reset is just another way of forcing your Palm to shut down and turn back on again. It will not harm your data. Most of the time, a soft reset will cure a frozen Palm. Just insert the reset pin or paperclip firmly into the hole once and remove it. Your Palm will start up again and open up to the General Pref-erences screen. If it doesn't start right up, or if the problem you were having is still there, try a semisoft reset.

Semisoft reset

A semisoft reset is just like a soft reset except that it avoids starting any system extensions that are built into or added to the Palm with add-on software. It also blocks any OS updates you may have added. To do a semisoft reset, hold down the up scroll button while you insert the reset pin into the reset hole. Your Palm should start up and open to the General Pref-erences screen. If it doesn't, you are down to your last resort: the hard reset.

Hard reset

A hard reset will fix virtually any problem your Palm may be having.

A hard reset will also erase everything in your Palm and take it back to the state it was in the first time you turned it on. Only do a hard reset when soft and semisoft resets have not solved the problem your Palm is having.

To do a hard reset, hold down the power button while you insert the reset pin into the reset hole. Your Palm will start up, having forgotten all about its recent troubles—(and everything else too). It will be like a brand-new device.

The good news is that you can now HotSync your Palm and bring its data back up to the point it was at during your last HotSync. The Palm Desktop software has all your Palm's data safely backed up. So, the lesson of the hard reset is to Hot-Sync often. Just be sure to use the "Desktop overwrites Palm" option when you HotSync to restore after a hard reset. See Chapter 9 (Windows users) or 10 (Mac people) for more on HotSyncing.

The Palm Desktop software comes to your rescue with a Hot-Sync after a hard reset, true, but bear in mind that it only backs up the data in the Palm's built-in applications (Address Book, Date Book, etc.). It does not back up add-on software. Because of that, if you plan to run a lot of add-on software, I recommend that you purchase Backup Buddy, which is possibly the best $19.95 you can spend on your Palm. During a HotSync, Backup Buddy backs up everything, including add-on software, that is on your Palm (see Chapter 11 for more on Backup Buddy).

Graffiti and the Onscreen Keyboards

A seamless way for humans and computers to communicate has long been the Holy Grail of information technology. Science fiction tells us that we will soon be conversing with our computers like old school chums. And wouldn't it be nice to arrive at work in the morning, tell your machine in your normal voice what you want done, and then go have a coffee while it does your job?

Unfortunately, that sweet little scenario is still quite a ways off. People and computers are vastly different, and it's a struggle to get one to understand anything generated by the other. Simply getting an affordable machine to understand your handwriting turns out to be not at all simple. Apple's Newton was one of the more notable handwriting-recognition failures and was famous for misreading what you wrote. If you wrote, "Hi my name is Bob" the Newton might understand it as "Hit my mane you slob."

That's why the Palm's successful Graffiti writing system is so smart: it doesn't try to bring the mountain to Mohammed. In other words, instead of trying to teach the Palm to recognize the idiosyncratic way *you* write letters and numbers in your normal handwriting, the Graffiti system asks that you learn a simple alphabet that is almost exactly like the one you already know.

Graffiti is the primary way of inputting your writing and data into your Palm, but it isn't the only game in town. Two onscreen keyboards are built into your Palm, one for letters and one for numbers. The keyboards are great in a pinch, especially when you need an extended or accented character, and they are always only one tap away.

The third way of entering text and other data into your Palm is to type it into your regular computer and then HotSync. You'll learn more about that in Chapters 9 and 10.

And actually, there are still other ways to get stuff into your Palm: the $79.99 GoType keyboard is one. And add-on programs like Jot! that let you use the whole Palm screen as the Graffiti area are another—more on these in Chapter 11.

Learning Graffiti

With Graffiti, you can use the stylus to enter any character found on a standard keyboard. If you write your characters precisely the way Graffiti wants you to, you will be able to write text, punctuation, and numbers into your Palm with 100 percent accuracy. Learning basic Graffiti letters and numbers is easy and fast. Mastering punctuation and extended characters takes a bit longer.

I already mentioned it but it bears repeating: Never use an ink pen or anything else with a hard tip to write on the Graffiti screen. If you can't find your stylus, in a pinch you can use a toothpick (which will also work as a reset pin— and you can store it in your battery door).

At home base—the Applications screen—tap the Graffiti icon to call up the Graffiti practice program (see **Figure 3.1**). The screen that appears shows a representation of the Graffiti writing area, divided into the letters side and the numbers side. In Graffiti, you write letters on the left side of the little marks, and numbers on the right.

It may seem counterintuitive at first to have to split up numbers and letters, but doing so simplifies the strokes for you and makes it easier for the Palm to understand what you're writing. How? Well, think about how you'd make write the letter "i" and the number "1." Because any Graffiti character should be as simple as possible, a simple downstroke on the screen should be enough to signify an "i" or a "1"—but unless the Palm knows one is a number and one is a letter, you'd have to come up with a slightly different strokes, which would make them harder to remember, which would make the whole system less useful.

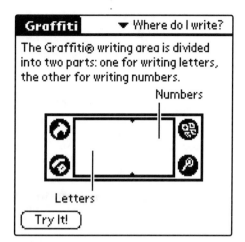

Figure 3.1 The Graffiti practice program starts off by explaining the two sides of the Graffiti area.

Tap the Try It! button to get to the screen shown in **Figure 3.2.**

Read the screen and tap Next to get to the next screen, where you actually *can* try it (see **Figure 3.3**).

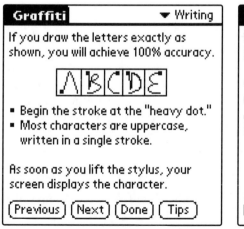

Figure 3.2 Some beginning tips and a peek at the first five characters in the Graffiti alphabet.

Figure 3.3 Here's where you can practice your Graffiti skills by writing letters.

Note the drop-down arrow at the top right of your screen. Each screen in the Graffiti practice program has a name, and you can go directly to any of them by tapping on that arrow and then tapping your selection.

Letters

On your Palm, in the Graffiti area, practice writing the letters one by one, trying to make your strokes exactly the way you see them in the "ideal characters" reference table onscreen. Start where you see the dot and write each letter in one stroke (except for "x," which does take two separate strokes).

As you write them, the moment you lift the stylus from the screen, the Palm shows you exactly the stroke you made in the blank area on the left side of the screen. That gives you a way to fine-tune the way you stroke your letters by seeing how far off you are each time (see **Figure 3.4** for an example of a failed "a"). When your stroke is off, the Palm sometimes reads what you wrote as a different letter, or it refuses to even speculate and prints nothing onscreen.

Figure 3.4 This lame attempt at a letter "a" was far enough off that the Palm couldn't tell it was supposed to be an "a," so it printed nothing onscreen.

Notice the strokes for inserting a space (a single line drawn to the right), a backspace (a single line drawn to the left), and a Return (an angle going down from upper right to lower left). If you mess up a letter and want to erase what you did, just write a backspace (line to the left). In fact, a backspace will erase anything you write in Graffiti.

If you make a letter close enough to the ideal, the Palm rewards you by printing the desired letter onscreen (see **Figure 3.5**). As you practice, you'll get faster, and there seems to be no limit to Graffiti-writing speed except your own skill—that is, there's no lag time waiting for the Palm to think about things, and you can never get going faster than the Palm. It lets you know immediately whether each character is recognized.

Graffiti strokes for letters

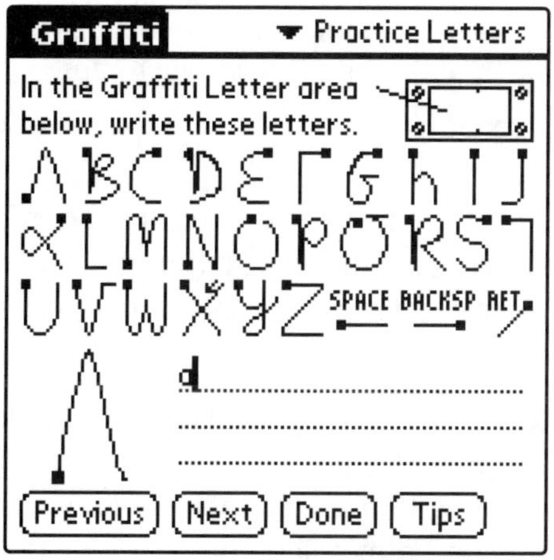

a	$\wedge$	n	N
b	B	o	O
c	C	p	p
d	D	q	O
e	$\mathcal{E}$	r	R
f	$\lceil$	s	S
g	G	t	$\rceil$
h	h	u	U
i	I	v	V
j	J	w	W
k	$\prec$	x	X
l	L	y	y
m	M	z	Z

Figure 3.5 Much better—a big sharp stroke made an "a" the Palm immediately recognized.

Almost all Graffiti strokes are pretty much one-stroke versions of the uppercase version of each letter (the sole exception is h), so start gearing your mind toward all capital letters. Note that some Graffiti characters, such as f, k, and t, are only partially formed uppercase letters.

Capitals

Tap Next when you're done practicing your lowercase letters. Or tap the drop-down arrow at the top right and select Practice Capitals. Either way, on your Palm you should see a screen like **Figure 3.6**. Capital (uppercase) letters in the Graffiti system are just like small (lowercase) letters except that they begin with the Caps Shift stroke, which is a line drawn straight up in the Graffiti area.

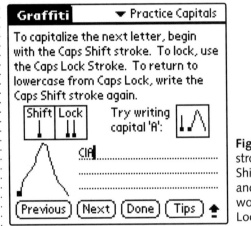

Figure 3.6 The Caps Shift stroke works just like the Shift key on your keyboard, and the Caps Lock stroke works just like your Caps Lock key.

The Caps Shift stroke simulates the Shift key on your keyboard. Draw the Caps Shift stroke once, and the next letter you write will be capitalized, whereas the letter after that is lowercase again.

What if you want every letter to be capitalized? The Caps Lock stroke (two successive lines drawn straight up) works like your keyboard's Caps lock key, meaning that all characters you write from then on will appear on the Palm's screen as uppercase, until you turn it off. To turn off Caps Lock, draw another Caps Shift line. The Caps Shift and Caps Lock strokes work on both sides of the Graffiti area.

I had the most trouble writing the letter v, which always ended up onscreen as u. It's hard to remember, but if you can get in the habit of writing it backward (right to left), you'll be rewarded with a perfect v every time.

Numbers

Tap Next when you're done with capitals, or tap the drop-down arrow at the top right and select Practice Numbers (**Figure 3.7**). You write numbers on the right side of the Graffiti area. Most people have no trouble with numbers. The 4 is sometimes tricky—try making the angle sharper.

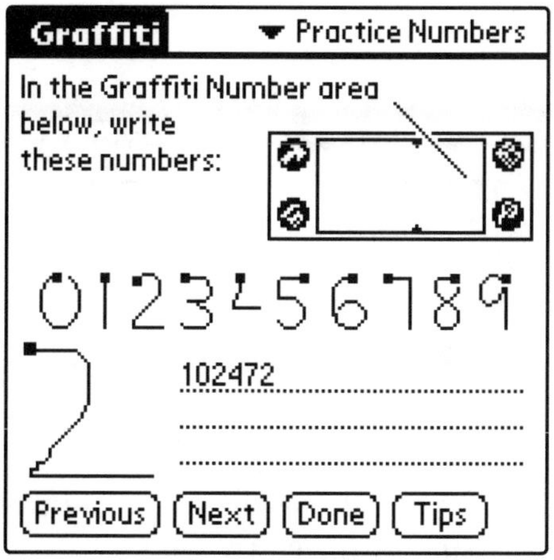

Figure 3.7 Numbers are cake and look just like the Arabic numerals you're used to, except the 4.

Most people have no trouble learning basic rules of writing letters and numbers in Graffiti. If you practice for ten or twenty minutes, you'll pretty much have things down. However, you'll be writing along thinking "this is easy," and all of a sudden you need & or $ or @ or # or even ! or ?—what do you do then? Keep reading.

Punctuation

Tap the Previous button twice, or tap the drop-down list and choose Practice Letters again. You're going to practice punctuation marks and symbols. All punctuation marks and symbols begin with a punctuation shift, which is a single dot—one tap.

On your Palm, go ahead and just tap once anywhere in the Graffiti area (both the number and letter sides work for punctuation) to invoke the punctuation shift. You should see a large dot appear in the lower right corner of your screen (see

Graffiti strokes for numbers	
1	l
2	2
3	3
4	L
5	5
6	6
7	7
8	8
9	9
0	0

Figure 3.8 The large dot in the lower right corner reveals that the Palm is ready to accept a punctuation or symbol character.

Graffiti strokes for punctuation

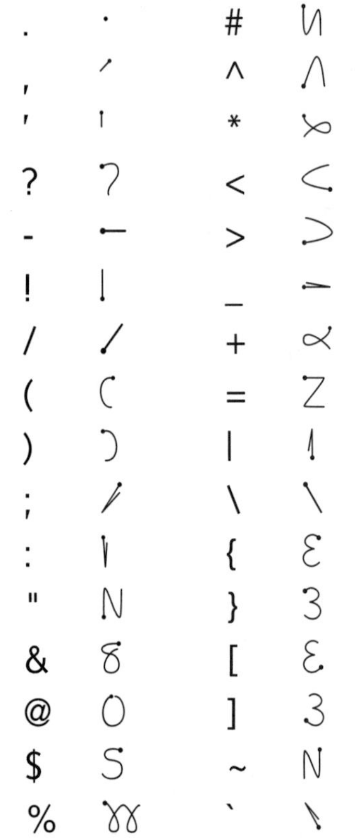

.	·	#	ʯ
,	∕	^	∧
'	⌐	*	❊
?	?	<	⊂
-	⏄	>	⊃
!	⌐	_	⌐
/	╱	+	∝
(	(	=	Z
)	)	|	⎮
;	╱	\	⟍
:	⎮	{	ε
"	N	}	3
&	δ	[	ε
@	О	]	3
$	S	~	N
%	ᴤᴤ	`	⟍

Figure 3.8). That's the sign that you are now in punctuation mode.

Practice punctuation and symbols as long as you like, concentrating on the ones you use most. As you look at them all, you'll probably murmur, "But I'll never remember all of those!" And you're right, you won't. Which is why there is the Big Line command.

Graffiti Help from the Big Line: You may recall the Big Line from Chapter 2. It's the command that you invoke by drawing a single big line up the entire face of your Palm, starting in the Graffiti area. By default, the Palm is set up to make the Big Line call up Graffiti Help.

Go ahead and invoke the Big Line now. If you don't see a screen like **Figure 3.9**, it means you probably changed the Big Line's settings in Chapter 2. To fix that, tap the Applications icon, tap Prefs, tap the drop-down arrow and choose Buttons, tap Pen, and select Graffiti Help from the drop-down arrow—now you can do the Big Line.

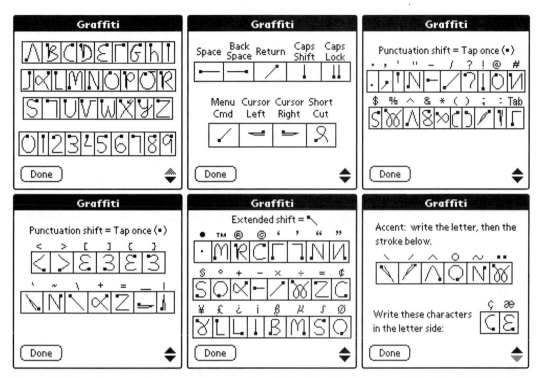

Figure 3.9 Don't worry if you can't remember all the Graffiti strokes—all this Graffiti Help is only a stylus swipe away.

Tap the drop-down arrow in Graffiti Help to work your way through the different screens, all shown in **Figure 3.9**. Graffiti Help isn't so much an application as an onscreen reference. Once you find the stroke for the character you want, tap Done, the button that appears on every screen in Graffiti Help, and you will be returned to wherever you were before you drew the Big Line.

Graffiti has strokes for many more characters, as shown in **Figure 3.9**. To access the extended characters, you write the Extended shift stroke, which is a diagonal line from upper left to lower right. After Extended shift is invoked, you write the stroke for the extended character. The Extended shift only lasts for one character, after which the Palm immediately reverts to normal Graffiti mode.

Graffiti tips

- Write as large as you can while staying within the boundaries of the Graffiti area. You can actually write so big you go outside the area a bit, and it's still okay.

- Don't write too slowly. Write at the quick rate you normally would.

- Write straight up and down, not at an angle.

- In the box your Palm came in, there was a white folding card with Graffiti characters and some very handy gray Graffiti reference stickers. Two stickers fit perfectly on the inside of the flip cover on the Palm III and V models.

- When you get stuck, remember the Big Line—Graffiti Help always there and ready for you.

- You'll learn letters and numbers in no time. Concentrate on learning the punctuation and symbols.

- See your Palm's *Handbook* for more tips and tables of alternative strokes you can try.

Figure 3.10 Here's where you see the list of all available ShortCuts on your Palm.

Graffiti ShortCuts

A timesaving feature called Graffiti ShortCuts lets you write something once and then assign a ShortCut to it. You may have used a similar technique on your PC's word processor, where it's probably called a macro. A Short-Cut can contain up to 45 characters. To invoke a ShortCut, you write the ShortCut stroke (a little loop, like a cursive lowercase "L") and then write the character(s) you already assigned as the shortcut. For example, you could make a ShortCut for your name.

Tap Prefs and from the drop-down arrow at the upper right select ShortCuts. You should see a screen like **Figure 3.10**. There you have a list of the built-in ShortCuts that came with your Palm.

You can see that you already have ShortCuts for the words *breakfast* (br), *dinner* (di), *lunch* (lu), and *meeting* (me). You also have ShortCuts that will insert today's date (ds, for "date stamp"), the current time (ts, for "time stamp"), and the current date and time (dts). Let's create a new ShortCut that will insert your name when you invoke it.

Creating a ShortCut for your name: Tap New. Under Short-Cut Name, enter your initials (using Graffiti, of course). Under ShortCut Text, write out your name (see **Figure 3.11**). Tap OK if you are pleased with what you've done. From now on, when you have to write your name on your Palm, just write the Short-Cut loop followed by your initials.

Figure 3.11 Making it simple to write out your whole name with just a few letters.

If your initials are the same as one of the built-in shortcuts, you might add your middle initial.

Everyone has a unique writing style, and you probably tend to use many of the same words over and over. Pay attention as you're writing in your Palm to words that crop up again and again and then make ShortCuts for them.

Giraffe

On your Windows CD-ROM, you'll find a game called Giraffe. Look for a file called giraffe.prc, and install that from the Palm Desktop (see Chapter 11 for how to install software). After it's installed, Giraffe shows up in the Applications screen as an icon.

Giraffe is like a deck of children's Flash cards—something educational disguised as a game (see **Figure 3.12**). In Giraffe, characters fall from the sky, and you have to write the Graffiti strokes for each one you see before it hits the ground. If the Palm recognizes the stroke, the character disappears. As the game progresses, everything speeds up, and more obscure characters start falling.

> *Giraffe should be in the Add-Ons folder on the CD-ROM. If you can't find your CD-ROM or if you have the MacPac 2, which doesn't include Giraffe, you can supposedly download the file giraffe.prc for free from www.palm.com, but I was unable to find the file. (Mac users may have to resort to getting it beamed to them.)*

Figure 3.12 The Giraffe game is a terrific way to have fun under the auspices of practicing your Graffiti.

The Onscreen Keyboards

When you're first learning Graffiti, you may get intimidated or discouraged, and you'll be longing for a keyboard. The Palm has three onscreen keyboards (letters, numbers, and international), and at first you may regard them as your salvation. But all too soon, as you discover just how slow it is to poke along tapping teeny tiny keys on that itty bitty screen, you'll finally admit to yourself that Graffiti is faster for routine text entry. Much faster, actually.

Still, for everything there is a season, and the onscreen keyboards have their place, especially the international one. When you forget your Graffiti, it can be just as fast to bring up an onscreen keyboard, find your character, tap it, and return to wherever you were as it is to write the Big Line, find the Graffiti stroke, and then write the stroke.

You can access the onscreen keyboards any time you can enter data—that is, any time you see a blinking text cursor on the screen. There are two main ways you can access the keyboards. In most applications, the Edit menu has a choice called Keyboard. And in the Graffiti area on your Palm's screen, in the two bottom corners, you'll see two dots, one surrounded by "abc" and the other by "123" (see **Figure 3.13**). You can tap those to call up the keyboards as well (**Figure 3.14**).

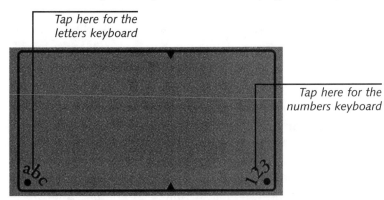

Tap here for the letters keyboard

Tap here for the numbers keyboard

Figure 3.13 Tap the "abc" and "123" dots in the Graffiti area to call up the onscreen keyboards.

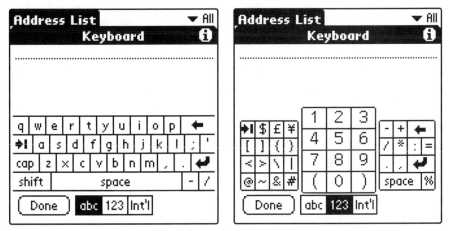

Figure 3.14 The text keyboard (left) and the numerical keyboard (right).

The numerical keyboard contains many of the punctuation marks you need when typing text.

Once you have a keyboard onscreen, you can tap Int'l to bring up the third and probably most useful keyboard: the international keyboard (see **Figure 3.15**). Use this keyboard if you need to correctly write accented characters. Let's face it: you probably won't remember how to write the accented characters in déjà vu or Mötley Crüe. Words like those are excellent opportunities to call up the international keyboard.

When you're done with a keyboard, tap Done to return to wherever you were.

3.3 If you have installed the Palm OS 3.3 upgrade, the international keyboard has an additional character for the Euro, the new European common currency.

If you have a lot of text to enter into your Palm, such as all your addresses and contact info, or if you need to write a long memo or email, using the onscreen keyboard would be like digging a grave with a toothpick. And even Graffiti isn't going to be fast enough for you for long stretches of data. In those cases, you are much better off using the Palm Desktop software on your computer. That software, which you'll learn about in Chapters 9 and 10, duplicates the Palm's primary built-in programs on your regular computer, where you are quick as lightning on your real keyboard. After you write your memo or email or enter all your addresses or whatever, you simply perform a HotSync, and voilà—the data is transferred to your Palm (more on HotSync in Chapter 9).

Gentle reader, you deserve congratulations! If you've read Part I of this book, you understand the basics of your Palm device, how to set it up, and how to enter data into it. Now you are ready to actually *do* something with your knowledge. In Part II, you'll learn how to use the Palm's built-in programs to get organized, keep track of everything, and look very cool doing so.

part two

The Built-In Palm Applications

This part covers the four main, built-in Palm programs: Date Book, Address Book, To Do List, and Memo Pad. The final chapter in this part covers Expense, Security, and Calculator. (You already learned about the basic built-in programs in Part I, including the Graffiti practice program, Prefs, and Welcome in Part I. Rounding out the built-in programs are Mail and HotSync, which are covered in Part III.) Rather than waste these pages and your time repeating information on menus, options, and preferences that work the same across all four primary programs, I selected the Date Book chapter to cover these things in detail. Read Chapter 4 first, and then, having learned how to use the menus, set up options, and choose preference, move on to the rest of the applications.

Date Book

Date Book, the first button on your Palm, is your calendar. It's where you schedule *events* and manage your appointments, meetings, dates—anything that is going to happen and that you need to remember. Once you start using Date Book, you'll have no more excuses to miss anything.

You can set alarms to remind you to do something or that something is about to happen. You can set repeating events, such as a weekly 10 A.M. meeting, and events with dates but no particular times, like birthdays and anniversaries. You can make appointments from now until the year 2031. In short, you can keep track of your schedule as never before, because it will all be in your Palm.

Date Book Basics

Press the Date Book button or tap the Date Book icon in home base (the Applications screen). You should see a screen very much like **Figure 4.1**. That's what today looks like to your Palm, from 8 A.M. to 6 P.M. Whenever you open Date Book, it opens to show you today. At the top of the screen are the days of the week. If you tap them, the Palm shows you that day. The scroll bars beside the days of the week move you one week in whichever direction you tap.

The three views

Notice the three little boxes at the bottom of the screen. Those are for day view (which is where you are now), week view, and month view.

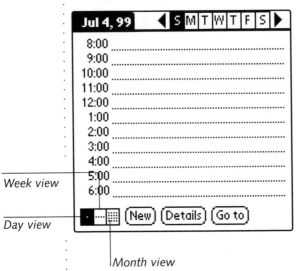

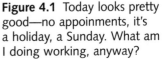

Figure 4.1 Today looks pretty good—no appoinments, it's a holiday, a Sunday. What am I doing working, anyway?

Tap the middle button to see the week view (**Figure 4.2**). Now today has shrunk to one column among seven, and you can see this whole week in one glance. Today happens to be Sunday, July 4, 1999, which is why the S and the 4 are bold. I have the Palm set up for United States date formatting (we set Preferences in Chapter 2), which means weeks always start on Sunday. The scroll bars at the top still scroll in one-week chunks.

Now tap the month view button to bring up the month view (**Figure 4.3**). Today has shrunk to a little box among all the others in July. At the top, you scroll by months. Tap on whatever today is for you, and Date Book returns to the day view.

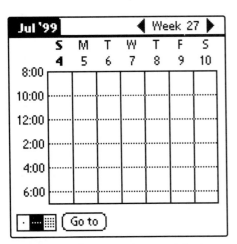

Figure 4.2 The upcoming week looks like smooth sailing too.

The power of Go to

After you return to day view, tap the Go to button at the bottom of the screen. The Go to Date screen appears (**Figure 4.4**). This is a handy way to zero in on any day from January 1, 1904 to December 31, 2031. Tap the Today button to go back to the day view.

Figure 4.3 The whole darned month is free of appointments—I'll be fixing that momentarily.

Figure 4.4 Go to makes it easy to visit any day within 127 years, such as this one.

The power of Find

You can find any event in Date Book quickly by tapping the Find icon and writing some text that you know appears in the event's description (also called the *time line*). Chapter 2 has more information about Find.

Entering Events

It's time to start adding events in Date Book. With Date Book open to today, in day view, tap the New button (or enter the Graffiti command /N). The Set Time screen appears (**Figure 4.5**). The Set Time screen is where you set up the time details of the event you want to schedule.

It's the Fourth of July, and we're going to a barbecue. It starts at 3 and will be over by 10. Tap the Start Time box and then tap on 3 in the hour column to enter 3:00 P.M. as the start time. Tap the End Time box and tap 10 (note you have to scroll by tapping the arrow) to enter 10:00 P.M. as the end time (see **Figure 4.6**) If the event starts at 3:30 or any other time besides on the hour, tap the hour and then tap in the minutes column to select the number of minutes after the hour (in five-minute increments). When you have the correct times entered, tap OK.

You are brought back to day view. The cursor is blinking patiently at the line where you need to write a description of the event. Use Graffiti to write a description (see **Figure 4.7**).

Another way to add an event is to simply tap on the line closest to the time the event starts, write the event's description, and then tap on the event's start time in day view to open the Set Time screen, where you can adjust the end time. In **Figure 4.7**, I tapped on the 12:00 noon time line and now the cursor is there, waiting for me to write a description for a new event.

 Date Book automatically assumes each event will last an hour. And if your event does last an hour, you don't have to do anything except tap on a start time line and write a description. If it lasts for less or more than an hour, access the Set Time screen by tapping on the event's start time and correct your schedule Event Details

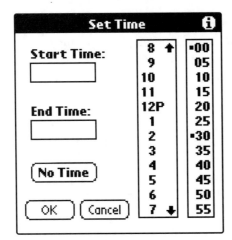

Figure 4.5 What times does your event start and end?

Figure 4.6 Tap numbers to select the start and end times.

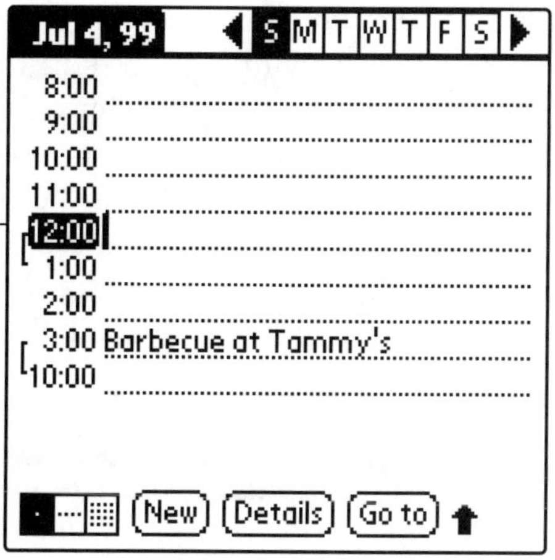

```
┌─────────────────────────────────────┐
│ Jul 4, 99   ◀ S M T W T F S ▶       │
│ 8:00 ............................... │
│ 9:00 ............................... │
│ 10:00 .............................. │
│ 11:00 .............................. │
│ ▐12:00▌ ............................ │
│  1:00 .............................. │
│  2:00 .............................. │
│  3:00 Barbecue at Tammy's ......... │
│ 10:00 .............................. │
│                                      │
│                                      │
│ ■ · ▦ (New) (Details) (Go to) ↑     │
└─────────────────────────────────────┘
```

Tap on a time line to put the cursor there and write a new event's description.

Figure 4.7 Now the event has a description, too.

Tap somewhere in your event's description on its time line and tap the Details button. Date Book shows you the Event Details screen (**Figure 4.8**). In this screen, you can do any of the following:

- Reschedule the event by tapping in the Time or Date boxes

- Set an alarm for the event

- Make the event a repeating event

- Mark an event as private

- Delete the event

Rescheduling an event

It's easy to reschedule an event. Suppose the barbecue is rained out and postponed till the next day. Tap anywhere in the description, tap Details, tap in the Date box, choose the new date (the next day), and tap OK. You have just rescheduled the barbecue. You could also have moved it any number of hours within the same day by tapping in the Time box.

```
┌─────────────────────────────────────┐
│ Jul 4, 99   ◀ S M T W T F S ▶       │
│ 8:00 ............................... │
│ 9:00                                 │
│ ┌─────────────────────────────────┐ │
│ │ Event Details              ⓘ    │ │
│ │   Time:  3:00 pm - 10:00 pm     │ │
│ │   Date:  Sun 7/4/99             │ │
│ │  Alarm:  ☐                      │ │
│ │ Repeat:  None                   │ │
│ │ Private: ☐                      │ │
│ │ (OK) (Cancel) (Delete...) (Note)│ │
│ └─────────────────────────────────┘ │
└─────────────────────────────────────┘
```

Figure 4.8 If you need to change anything about an event, tap Details.

Another way to reschedule an event to sometime in the same week is to simply drag it there in week view. Tap on the week view button at the bottom left on the screen, so that you see the week view screen, which shows events as gray boxes within the column for that day. Press the stylus on the gray box, keep it pressed down on the screen, and drag it straight over to the next day (**Figure 4.9**). Dragging with the stylus works just the way dragging with the mouse pointer does on your computer.

See the description box at the top of Figure 4.9? That's there because in week view, when you tap on a gray box, the event's description appears at the top of the screen. The description box changes on the fly as you drag to reflect the new time or date. Another thing to notice is that you can scroll to see later hours after 6 P.M. by tapping the drop-down arrows.

You can reschedule an event to a different time in the same day by dragging it up or down. Date Book assumes the event will still last the same amount of time, shown as a gray box— a block of time. In **Figure 4.10**, I dragged the barbecue event to start at 9 A.M., and Date Book moved its end time to 4 P.M.

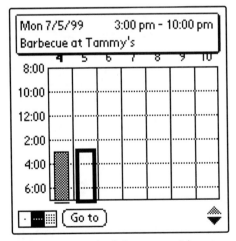

Figure 4.9 Reschedule an event by dragging it from one day to the next.

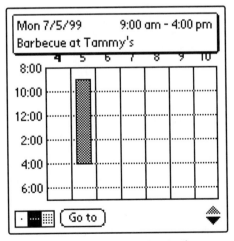

Figure 4.10 Sometimes nine in the morning is as good a time as any for beer and chicken.

Simultaneous events

Suppose Mom and Dad are supposed to call me from a boat in Indiana at 4 to wish me a happy Fourth of July. If I enter the new event, you can see in **Figure 4.11** how Date Book brackets it within the surrounding barbecue event. And if I tap on week view, it squeezes down the fat gray block to make room for two skinny gray blocks of time side by side (**Figure 4.12**).

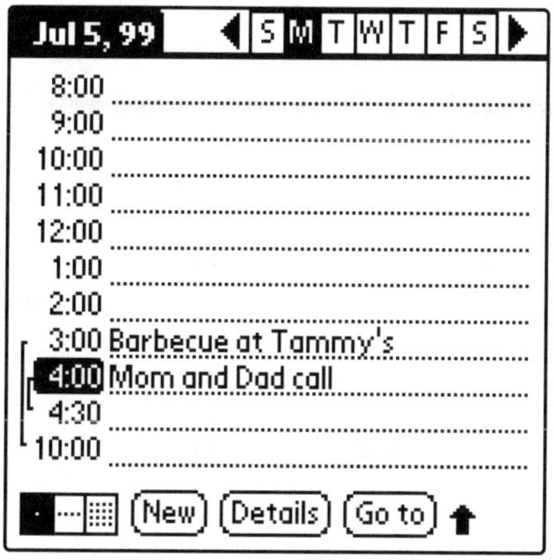

Figure 4.11 Date Book brackets simultaneous events in day view.

Figure 4.12 In week view, two skinny blocks replace one fat one to show events happening at the same time.

Setting an alarm for an event

On Tuesday morning, I'm rushed. I have again put off writing my weekly status report, and I know I'll be working on it right up until the editorial meeting. It might have been a good idea for me to set an alarm to go off a few minutes before the meeting, so that I could wrap up my status report beforehand, email it, compose myself, and stride into the meeting pretending everything is fine.

I tap on the Editorial meeting time line so that the cursor is blinking in it (you can see the cursor in **Figure 4.13**). The cursor there

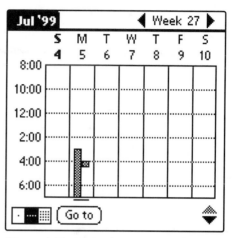

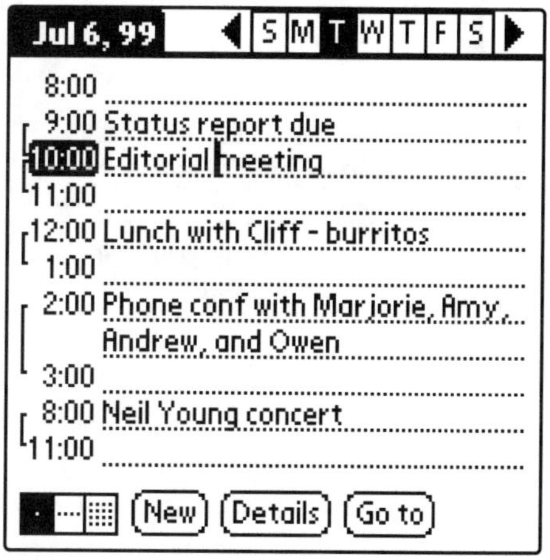

Figure 4.13 The morning looks rushed—better set an alarm to warn me of the meeting.

means that that particular event is selected. Now I can tap Details to bring up the Event Details screen.

To set the alarm, I put a check mark in the Alarm checkbox (see **Figure 4.14**). When I do, Date Book tells me the alarm will go off 5 minutes before the event. I can change it if I want by changing the number 5 to whatever. Ten minutes makes me more comfortable, so I change it to 10.

If you tap the drop-down arrow beside Minutes, you discover that you could make the alarm go off hours or days before an event. That wouldn't do much good in this case, but if the event were someone's birthday, you could set the alarm days in advance.

After you set an event to set off the alarm, Date Book adds a little alarm icon to the end of its time line in the day view (see **Figure 4.15**).

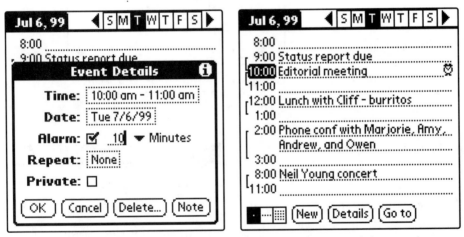

Figure 4.14 Setting the alarm for ten minutes prior to the event.	**Figure 4.15** Date Book lets you know visually that the event has an alarm set for it.

So, what happens when the alarm goes off? A screen like the one in **Figure 4.16** appears on your Palm and doesn't go away until you tap OK. And if you have your Palm's alarm sound set to anything but Off, you'll hear a little "deedledeet...deedledeet...deedledeet" to accompany the Reminder screen. By default, the Palm's alarm is set to High volume (see Chapter 2 for how to change the alarm's volume in Prefs).

The section "Menus, Options, and Preferences" later in this chapter tells you how you can make more changes to the Palm's alarm.

The Palm's alarm is not terribly loud, and it only goes off for three sets of beeps. If you don't tap OK, it goes off again every five minutes until you do, which can be irritating. Even set on High, it's quiet enough that if I'd been using it as my morning alarm clock, I never would have finished this book. Unless you're bringing it to church or something, it's unlikely to embarrass you too badly when it goes off. If you set it face up on a hard surface, like a table, it seems to amplify it a bit. The alarm on the Palm V seems to be louder than the others.

Repeating events

The editorial meeting I set the alarm for happens every week. Birthdays and anniversaries happen every year. Date Book calls such recurring activities *repeating* events. To set an event to repeat, tap anywhere on the event's time line in day view (to put the cursor there), tap Details, and tap Repeat. You should see a screen like **Figure 4.17**.

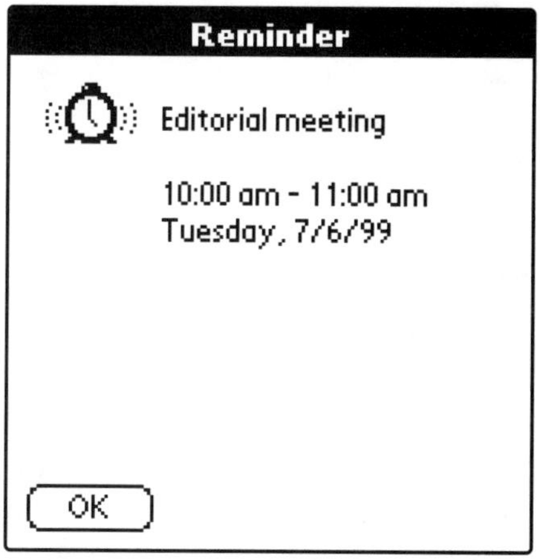

Figure 4.16 The Palm reminds me that the meeting is close at hand.

Figure 4.17 Setting up my weekly meeting in Date Book.

You can make your event repeat every day, week, month, or year by tapping your choice at the top of the screen. If you decide the event shouldn't repeat after all, tap None. If you know that at some point in the future the event will stop repeating, you can choose an ending date by tapping the End on drop-down arrow. I know there will be no end to those editorial meetings, so I leave that option as No End Date.

If you have an event such as a conference or business trip that lasts several days, you can make it a daily repeating event with an end date.

After you make something a repeating event, Date Book adds the event automatically to every week, month, or year. It also adds a little multiple-document icon at the end of its time line (see **Figure 4.18**). That icon is your clue that the event is a repeating event.

```
┌─────────────────────────────────┐
│ Jul 6, 99   ◀│S│M│T│W│T│F│S│▶  │
├─────────────────────────────────┤
│ 8:00                            │
│ 9:00 Status report due          │
│10:00 Editorial meeting      ☺▣  │
│11:00                            │
│12:00 Lunch with Cliff - burritos│
│ 1:00                            │
│ 2:00 Phone conf with Marjorie, Amy,│
│      Andrew, and Owen           │
│ 3:00                            │
│ 8:00 Neil Young concert         │
│11:00                            │
│ ▪ ⠿ (New) (Details) (Go to)     │
└─────────────────────────────────┘
```

Figure 4.18 You can tell by looking in the day view that the meeting has an alarm and is a repeating event.

Attaching notes

You can also attach notes to your Date Book events and tap on them at any time to read them. In day view, tap to put the cursor on the time line of the event you want to attach a note to. Tap Details, tap Note, and write your note (**Figure 4.19**).

If the event is a repeating event, you're first asked whether to attach the note to every event or just the current one.

Now, when you tap Done and go back to day view, you'll see a little folded-over Note icon on the event's time line (**Figure 4.20**). Tap that to bring up the note at any time. To delete it, tap the note and then tap Delete.

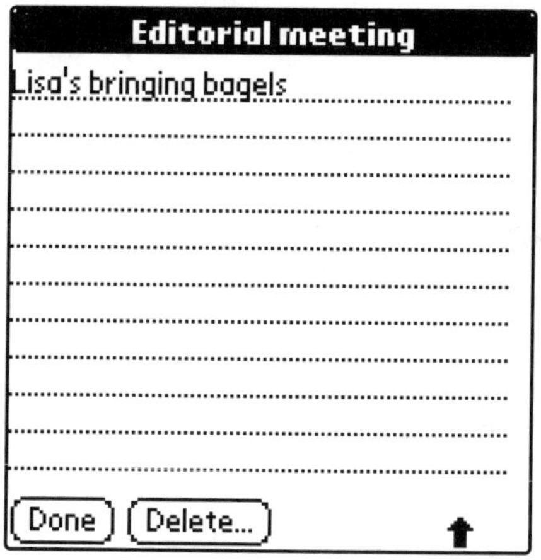

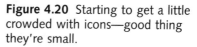

Figure 4.19 Write your very important note.

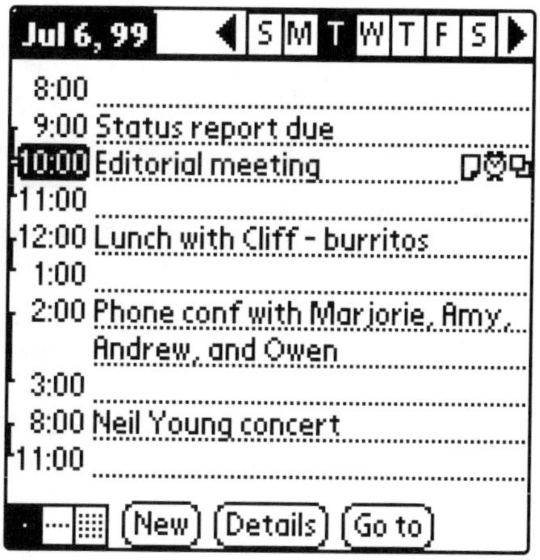

Figure 4.20 Starting to get a little crowded with icons—good thing they're small.

Private events

You can make almost anything private in your Palm, including Date Book records. Marking something private in Date Book (or Address Book, To Do List, or Memo Pad) means that it does not appear onscreen if you also have chosen Hide All Records in the Palm's Security program. To view private records that are hidden, you can set the Palm up so that you need to know the password (or not, I'll explain).

One can imagine many scenarios that would lend themselves to hiding appointments in Date Book. You may have lots of appointments with people whom your competition would love to know about. Maybe you're looking for another job or conducting a secret affair. Or perhaps you're meeting your intelligence case officer who "doesn't exist."

Or, more innocently, suppose I love burritos but am very publicly trying to lose weight. I don't want anyone to know that

Cliff and I are stuffing ourselves with generous slabs of *chorizo y papas* at lunch. I'd want to be darned sure to remember that lunch, but I'd need to hide my lunch plans from anyone who might happen to glance at or snoop through my Palm.

First, tap the event's time line in day view, as usual. Then Tap Details and put a check mark in the Private box (**Figure 4.21**).

Tap OK. The Palm suddenly tells you that you have to do one more thing before your trick will work (**Figure 4.22**). And in fact, when you tap OK, you go back to the day view and the scandalous item is still there.

Figure 4.21 Tap Private to hide stuff from prying eyes.

Figure 4.22 You can run, but you haven't hidden yet.

 Tap the Applications icon, find the Security icon, and tap it. In the Security program, tap Hide, and another Security dialog box will pop up (**Figure 4.23**).

Figure 4.23 To be successfully sneaky, tap Hide and then tap Hide again.

You return to the Security program, and the Hide box is in black, meaning it's selected. Now if you return to Date Book, you won't see any incriminating calorie-related information (**Figure 4.24**). And that's probably good enough burrito security. To crack it, someone would have to get hold of your Palm, go into the Security program, and tap Show Records.

But some things require more security than Mexican food. In those cases, you'll want to set a password. When you use a password, nobody except you can see your data, because you have to enter the password to view hidden records. You'll learn more about passwords and the Palm's Security program in Chapter 8.

Jul 6, 99	◀ S M T W T F S ▶
8:00	
9:00	Status report due
10:00	Editorial meeting
11:00	
12:00	
1:00	
2:00	Phone conf with Marjorie, Amy, Andrew, and Owen
3:00	
8:00	Neil Young concert
11:00	

(New) (Details) (Go to)

Figure 4.24 Lunch? No, I'm skipping lunch today, as usual.

Passwords may protect sensitive data in your Palm from prying eyes, but they can't stop people from viewing the same data on your regular computer. When you HotSync, your hidden records are transferred along with everything else to your computer. And from there it's easy enough to view them in any Word processor. You need to use your computer's security features, which may include more passwords, to protect data on it.

Deleting an event

To delete an event, tap Details and tap Delete (or enter the Graffiti command /D). Date Book asks you whether you'd like to save a copy of it on your PC during the next HotSync. If you do, put a check mark next to Save archive copy on PC.

Another way to delete a record is to drag through it to select all the text it contains and then enter the Graffiti stroke for Backspace (a horizontal line from right to left).

Menus, Options, and Preferences

As you have no doubt noticed, that Details button does a lot of the heavy lifting in Date Book. But really it's just another way of accessing some of Date Book's menus. In day view, Date Book has three menus under the Menu icon: Record, Edit, and Options.

There's no point in going through how to do things you've already learned to do. Instead, let's stick to the stuff that wasn't available under the Details button.

Edit menu

The Edit menu contains commands you're used to using on your regular computer: Undo (/∪), Cut (/✕), Copy (/ℂ), Paste (/℘), and Select All (/𝕊). It also offers alternative ways of accessing the Keyboard (/ᐊ) and Graffiti Help (/𝔾), which you learned about in Chapter 3.

Purging events

After you use Date Book for a while, you'll realize that all those old events are just building up in your Palm, taking up valuable memory space. Every once in a while, you should *purge* your old Date Book events to clear some more room in your Palm. Purging is the same as deleting, except it's easier to purge a bunch of events at one time.

Tap the Menu icon, tap Record, and then tap Purge or write the Graffiti command /ℰ (think "erase"). A screen like **Figure 4.25** asks you two make two decisions: how old an event must be to qualify for purging, and whether you want to save copies of Date Book records on your computer during your next HotSync.

```
Jul 6, 99   ◀ S M T W T F S ▶
  8:00 ....................................
  9:00 Status report due
 10:00 Editorial meeting         ▯▧▣
 11:00
        ┌──────────────────────────┐
        │      Purge            ⓘ   │
        │                          │
        │ (?)  Delete events older │
        │      than: ▼ 1 week      │
        │                          │
        │ ☐ Save archive copy on PC│
        │                          │
        │ ( OK )  ( Cancel )       │
        └──────────────────────────┘
```

Figure 4.25 Choices for purging your old events.

If you elect to save copies on your computer, when you purge the events aren't actually deleted from your Palm until the next time you HotSync.

Beaming events

You can send an event to another Palm device through your Palm's infrared (IR) port. You simply put the cursor in the event's time line, tap Record menu, and then tap Beam Event (or write the Graffiti command /ß). If another Palm is within range (closer than 30 inches or so and pointed at yours), the event magically shows up in that Palm's Date Book. Beaming is covered in Chapter 2 and other appropriate places in this book.

Options menu

The Options menu lets you make changes in Date Book's appearance, and it also contains a command that lets you automatically add phone numbers from Address Book when you write someone's name in an event's time line.

Font: Tap Menu, Options, Font (or write /⌐) to see your choices for how text looks on screen. Tap one to select it. **Figure 4.26** shows how the different choices look.

Preferences: Tap Menu, Options, Preferences to see the Preferences screen (or write /R). See **Figure 4.27**. Here you can change Date Book's day to start and end at whatever times you like. If you work at night, or are an early riser, or start your day later, why not customize Date Book to suit your needs? Just tap Start Time and End Time to make your changes.

If you put a check mark next to Alarm Preset, Date Book sets an alarm for every new event. To me, that would be overkill. I'd be hearing alarms all day long.

> ### Date Book's competition
>
> As nice as Date Book is, it may not offer all the features you need in a calendar application. If you find it wanting, you should check out other add-on calendar programs, such as DATEBK3. More details in Chapter 11.

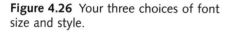

Figure 4.26 Your three choices of font size and style.

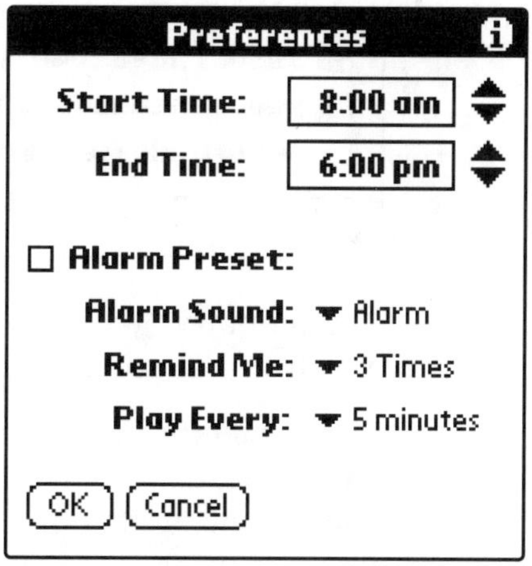

Figure 4.27 Here's where you set Date Book preferences.

*Speaking of alarms, you don't have to settle for the Palm's default alarm sound. Tap Alarm Sound to sample all seven alarms in your Palm (see **Figure 4.28**) and pick the one you want Date Book to use in alerting you.*

By default, Date Book plays the alarm and displays the onscreen reminder three times (it's like setting your clock radio's snooze button to go off three times before giving up)—once every five minutes. You can increase or decrease both settings by tapping Remind Me and Play Every.

Alarm
Alert
Bird
Concerto
Phone
Sci-fi
Wake up

Figure 4.28 Choosing among Date Book's bleeps, warbles, and nerd calls.

Display Options: Tap Menu, Options, Display Options (or write / Ч) to call up the screen shown in **Figure 4.29**. In day view, you can choose to view the time bars or not (those little brackets beside the times—you can see them in Figure 4.26). If you see scroll bars and wish you could get rid of the empty time slots so that you could see all your events at the same time, tap Compress Day View.

Display Options ❶

Day View:
☑ **Show Time Bars**
☑ **Compress Day View**

Month View:
☑ **Show Timed Events**
☐ **Show Untimed Events**
☐ **Show Daily Repeating Evts**

(OK) (Cancel)

Figure 4.29 Date Book's display options for day view and month view.

The month view options let you pick which kinds of events are shown in month view.

Phone Lookup: This is a terrific feature available in Date Book, To Do List, and Memo Pad. Phone Lookup lets you write someone's name, write one Graffiti command, and boom, the Palm fills in that person's full name and phone number from Address Book.

If you haven't added any names and phone numbers into Address Book yet, don't worry. You will in the next chapter.

To use Phone Lookup, enter the last name of a person whom you know has an entry in Address Book and leave the cursor somewhere in the name (**Figure 4.30**). Then write ╱└ in the Graffiti area. Licketysplit, the Palm fills in the phone number for you (**Figure 4.31**).

You may notice the letter W, H, or E beside the phone number. W stands for work, *H stands for* home, *and E tells you it's an email address.*

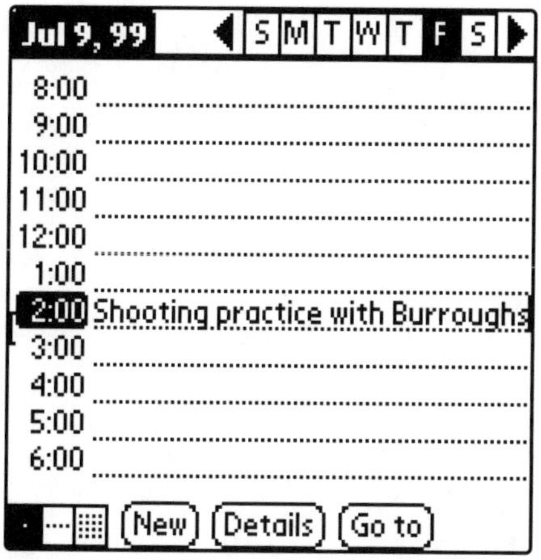

Jul 9, 99 ◀ S M T W T F S ▶	Jul 9, 99 ◀ S M T W T F S ▶
8:00	8:00
9:00	9:00
10:00	10:00
11:00	11:00
12:00	12:00
1:00	1:00
2:00 Shooting practice with Burroughs	**2:00** Shooting practice with William S. Burroughs 555-4675 W
3:00	3:00
4:00	4:00
5:00	5:00
6:00	
· ┈▦ (New) (Details) (Go to)	· ┈▦ (New) (Details) (Go to)

Figure 4.30 If you supply the last name...

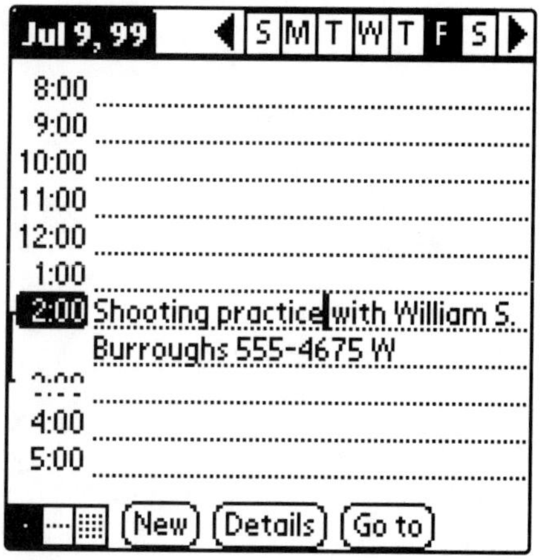

Figure 4.31 ...doing a Phone Lookup makes Palm fills in the rest .

Address Book

As email is the *killer app* of the Internet, in my opinion Address Book is the killer app of the Palm built-in programs. In other words, it's probably the most popular, universal, useful, and elegant use of the technology.

Once you start using Address Book to keep track of contact information for everyone you know, everyone you work with, everyone you email, call, fax, Fedex, and so on, I think you'll agree. It's pretty much the culmination of one of the goals of information technology: critical information easily at your fingertips at all times. Palm hit a home run with Address Book.

Beyond the fact that it's very simple and intuitive to use, there's not a whole heck of a lot to be said about it. You take one glance at the Address Book screen and you think, "Oh yes, now *this* is what I need." It has ready-made fields for everything you can think of, including name, title, company, five phone numbers, email address, physical mail address, plus four fields you can customize any way you please.

On your "real" computer, you may already use a contact manager like Act! or Outlook or any of dozens of others. If so, you can probably save yourself hours of typing by importing the data you have already painstakingly entered there into your Palm Address Book. You may also be able to HotSync directly with those applications, bypassing the Palm Desktop entirely with a software scheme called a conduit. See Chapters 9 and 10 for more.

Address Book is the second button on your Palm, the one with a telephone on it. Press that button, and you'll see Address Book's list view, a screen like **Figure 5.1**, where you can see last and first names at a glance, along with one piece of information (usually the person's work phone number). Tap one of those entries, and the address view shows a lot more information about that person.

Just like all the built-in programs, Address Book also has an icon in the Applications screen.

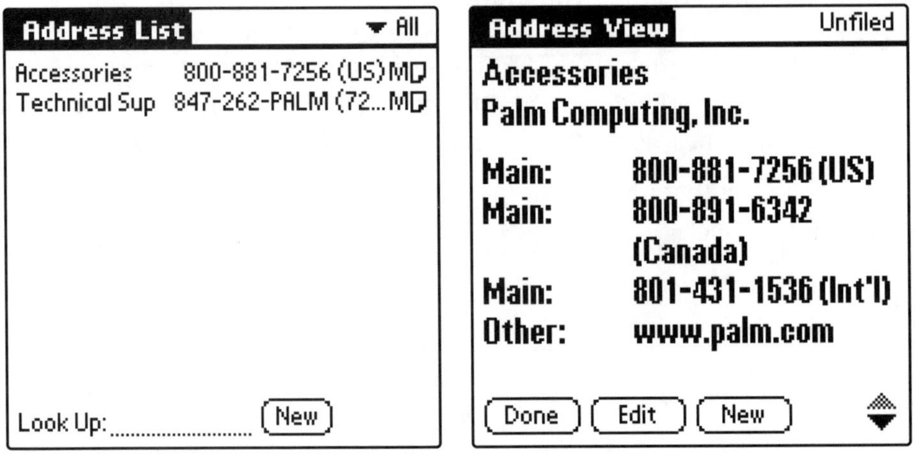

Address List	▼ All
Accessories	800-881-7256 (US) M🗋
Technical Sup	847-262-PALM (72... M🗋

Look Up: .... (New)

Address View　　　　　　Unfiled

Accessories
Palm Computing, Inc.

Main:　　800-881-7256 (US)
Main:　　800-891-6342
　　　　　(Canada)
Main:　　801-431-1536 (Int'l)
Other:　　www.palm.com

(Done) (Edit) (New)　◆

Figure 5.1 Here's what the built-in Palm Computing entries look like in list view... ...and if you tap one of them, here's what it looks like in address view.

Creating Your Business Card

The first entry you add may as well be your own, so I will use mine as an example. When you finish entering your own information, you can designate your entry as your *business card*. (I'll show you how to do that in a minute.) Your business card is just like any other entry in Address Book except it achieves a special status: automatic beaming. Once you have your business card in your Palm, it's a snap to beam it to other Palms.

So, the first entry you'll create will be yours. To create a new entry, in the list view, tap New. The edit screen appears (**Figure 5.2**).

Figure 5.2 You can see what you have to do in the edit view—enter your information using Graffiti.

Fill out your information. Because this is the public version of your information, and since you'll be beaming it to others, you probably want to use your business contact info, and leave personal information such as your home address out of it. (You can put that stuff somewhere else, in another entry that you can even mark as Private.) When filling out your entry, include everything somebody might need in order to contact you (see **Figure 5.3**). Note that it all doesn't fit on the screen at the same time. You have to scroll to get to the rest of it.

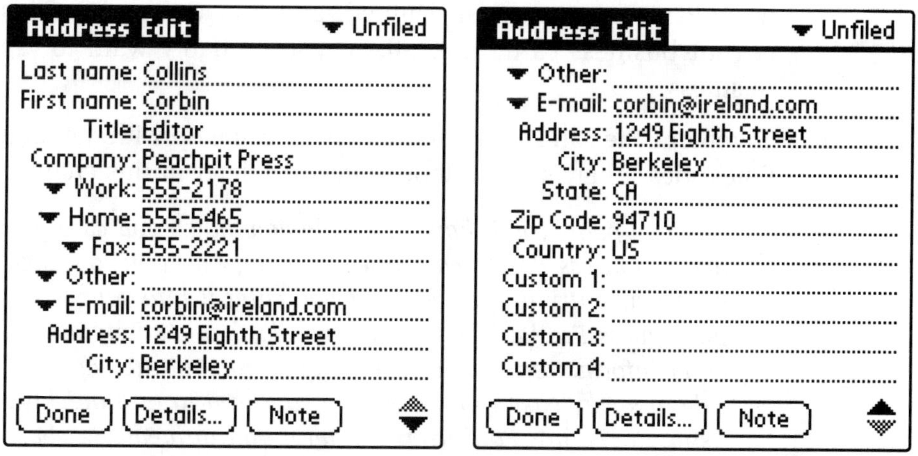

Figure 5.3 Here's opening screen of my business card...

...and the rest of it when I tap the scroll bar.

Address Entry Details ℹ️

Show in List: ▼ Work

Category: ▼ Unfiled

Private: ☐

(OK) (Cancel) (Delete...) (Note)

Figure 5.4 Here's where you can make some changes to how and where your business card will appear in Address Book.

Address entry details

When you've entered all your contact information, you can refine it a bit further if you like. Tap the Details button at the bottom of the screen. An Address Entry Details dialog box like the one shown in **Figure 5.4** appears.

Show in List: Tap the drop-down arrow beside Show in List. Tap to choose which piece of information you want to appear in the list view (the list view was shown in Figure 5.1). Your choices are Work, Home, Fax, Other, and E-mail. Tap one to select it.

This is your chance to perhaps have some small effect on how people contact you. When they start up their Address Books, which open to the list view by default, whatever you select to show in the list view will be what they see beside your name. (Of course, all your info pops up when they tap your entry, and they can always change the list view item to whichever they want.) If you're the type who prefers to receive email instead of a phone call, tap E-mail. Otherwise, I suggest choosing Work, so that your work number appears beside your name.

Category: Tap Category's drop-down arrow to select which category your entry will be filed under. Your choices are Business, Personal, QuickList, Unfiled, and Edit Categories. This is your business card, after all, so you probably want to tap Business.

To rename the category names that Palm came up with, tap Edit Categories. There's more about categories later in this chapter.

At some point you'll have to decide how much you care about Address Book's categories. It is a good habit to assign each new entry to a category as you enter it into your Palm, but I guess I'm lazy because I never do that. As long as you enter information such as company name and the person's title, it's very easy to find anyone you need to find quickly using the Palm's Find icon. If I am a bad influence, so be it—all 194 of my Address Book entries are Unfiled, and it doesn't take longer than a few seconds to find anyone.

Private: Tap a check mark into the Private check box to mark your entry as private—but not on your business card, that would defeat your purpose. Marking an entry as Private means that it will not show up in your Address Book—it's still there but invisible—if you have chosen to Hide Records in the Palm's Security program. You can also assign a password to your entry. See Chapter 8 for more on using the Palm's Security program and marking records Private (Chapter 4 also discusses private records in the context of Date Book, and the process works the same for Address Book).

Delete: This is simple enough. Tap Delete to delete your entry from your Palm. More on deleting later in this chapter.

Note: Tap Note to attach a Note to your entry (see **Figure 5.5**).

Attaching Notes to your business card is a good idea. You might describe a bit more about your job, what you do, which kinds of projects you work on, and so on. Focus on including anything that you think others might want to know about you, or things that that someone who just met you might logically search for once they get back to their office or want to contact you three weeks later. "What was that guy's name?" they might wonder. "I can't remember who she worked for, but she said she was working on a Web commerce project." If you attach notes, you increase the ability of others to find you by searching for extra info with the Palm's Find function.

Collins, Corbin
Likes sushi, African food, kebabs
Cat named Fez
True love named Tracy
Pisces
Moving to Ireland
(Done) (Delete...)

Figure 5.5 Notes are good places to add miscellaneous stuff about you in your business card.

Putting your significant other's name in a Note can help protect against unwelcome advances.

Tap Done when you finish your Note, and tap Done again if you are finished editing your business card. You're popped back into list view. You'll notice a little Note icon at the end of your entry if you attached a Note. And when you tap the entry again, you'll find the note has been appended to the end of your entry in address view.

Designating your entry as your business card

Tap the Menu icon, tap Record, and tap Select Business Card. A dialog box asks you to confirm that you want this entry to be your business card. You do. Tap Yes. Now, at the top of your entry in the address view you'll see the business card icon that tells you yes indeed, this is your business card (**Figure 5.6**).

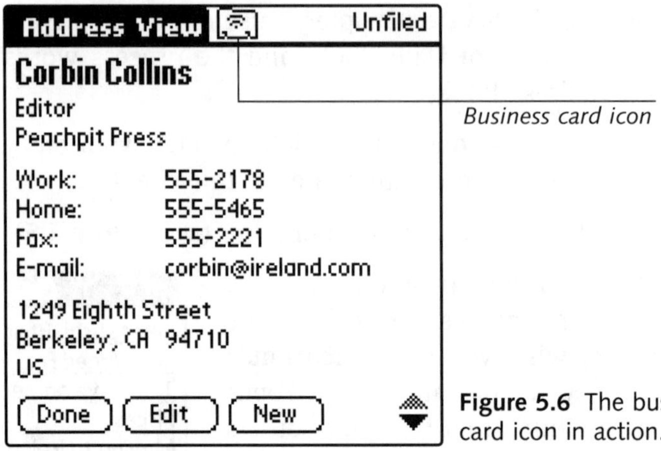

Business card icon

Figure 5.6 The business card icon in action.

Beaming your business card to other Palms

It could hardly be easier to beam your business card to other Palm users. You simply point your Palm at theirs, head to head, so to speak, and less than 30 inches apart (the closer the better), press down on the Address Book button on the face of your Palm and hold it down for a second or two. Your Palm starts searching for another Palm to receive your card (**Figure 5.7**).

Figure 5.7 Don't worry—if another Palm is within reach, yours will find it.

When your Palm finds the other one, it takes another second or two to actually send it. Then you're done. The other person has to tap Yes to receive it, and that's that. Your entry goes straight into their Palm's Address Book.

Managing Your Entries

You probably have dozens or hundreds of contacts. And if the prospect of writing them all out in your Palm's Graffiti area seems boring and tedious, I couldn't agree more. Fortunately, you have a few alternatives:

- **Import contacts from another program:** This is the easiest way. As I mentioned at the beginning of this chapter, if you use a contact managing program on your regular computer you may be able to import them into the Palm Desktop program and then HotSync them into your Palm. Or you could try a conduit program, which lets you HotSync directly from your normal contact manager.

- **Type them into Palm Desktop on your regular computer:** If you've been using a physical address book or can't import contact information from another program, you should definitely enter the bulk of your Address Book entries using Palm Desktop's Address Book. Graffiti is great in that it works at all, but it can't hold a candle to typing (assuming you can type at least 20 words per minute). You'll learn more about Palm Desktop in Chapters 9 and 10.

- **Type them into your Palm with the GoType keyboard:** For $79.99, you can buy a nifty little keyboard that accepts your Palm like the cradle does. It's smaller and not nearly as rugged as your regular keyboard, but it does work and it's still faster than Graffiti.

- **Use Graffiti:** Once you have typed or imported the bulk of your addresses into your Palm, use Graffiti to enter new ones as they come up.

Keep your little black book
After you've entered everything from your address book into your Palm, don't toss it out! Just put it away somewhere, because you never know what will happen. You could have to hard-reset your Palm and lose all its data. True, you should be able to HotSync and restore it from Palm Desktop, but every hard drive will die one day—and usually at the very worst possible moment.

Categories

I already admitted I don't use categories as I should. You may want to use categories if you have hundreds and hundreds of entries, or if you like to draw a sharp line between business and personal information, or maybe you just like categories. If so, you can create your own.

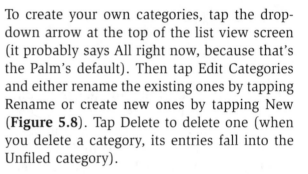

Figure 5.8 If you're going to use categories, create ones that make sense to you.

To create your own categories, tap the drop-down arrow at the top of the list view screen (it probably says All right now, because that's the Palm's default). Then tap Edit Categories and either rename the existing ones by tapping Rename or create new ones by tapping New (**Figure 5.8**). Tap Delete to delete one (when you delete a category, its entries fall into the Unfiled category).

Don't be afraid to make whatever categories you like, to break the rules. The whole point of the Palm is to be useful to you and your particular style of organizing information. You can always tap to select the All category again to bring everyone into a big, happy family again.

 You can merge two categories by renaming one to the other one's name.

Beaming categories: You can easily beam a category to another Palm. In list view, tap the Menu icon, Record, and Beam Category. Whichever category was onscreen at the time will be beamed. If All was selected, all of your addresses will be beamed to the other Palm.

Navigation

Once you enter many addresses, the list view begins filling up (**Figure 5.9**). Pretty soon, you'll be scrolling through your names.

 Don't forget the scroll button on the face of your Palm. It's usually faster to scroll with that than with the little tappable onscreen scroll arrows.

Address List ▼ All

Accessories	800-881-7256 (US)	MⱰ
Antoinette, Marie	756-0445	H
Bolivar, Simon	447-9083	H
Caesar, Julius	jc@rome.gov	O
Cleopatra	494-3092	W
de Sade, Marquis	mrpain@paris.fr	E
Hannibal	hb@carthage.mil	E
Khan, Genghis	gk@mongols.mil	E
Sitting Bull	872-0312	W
Socrates	509-2775	H
Technical Sup	847-262-PALM (72...	MⱰ

Look Up:|................ (New) ▲▼

Figure 5.9 Scroll arrows appear once you start filling up Address Book.

Find: As always, the Palm's Find program will find any text you want, including names, bits of a half-remembered email address, the person's dog's name if you attached a note with that in it—anything. That's why it's good to attach notes to entries.

Find searches your whole Palm every time, but it always searches the application that is open first. So, if you have Address Book open and you search for "nephew," Find will bring back whatever has "nephew" in it (**Figure 5.10**). Then you simply tap on the item you want in Find's list, and you are taken straight to it (**Figure 5.11**).

Find

Matches for "nephew"

———————— Addresses ————————
Caesar, Julius   jc@rome.gov O
———————— Datebook ————————
———————— Mail Messages ————————
———————— Memos ————————
———————— To Do Items ————————

(Cancel)

Figure 5.10 I knew I put something in here about someone's nephew.

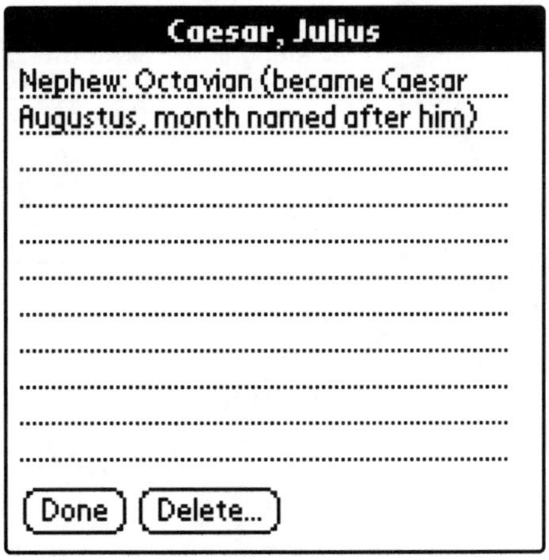

Caesar, Julius

Nephew: Octavian (became Caesar
Augustus, month named after him)

(Done) (Delete...)

Figure 5.11 And now I know what it was.

Perhaps the fastest way to jump straight to where you want to be is to write the Graffiti stroke for the first letter of the person's last name. Address Book leaps right to that part of the list. Write the second letter of the name and Address Book leaps to names that start with those two letters. And so on. By writing the first couple of letters of someone's last name, you can easily find that person's entry.

Menus and Options

Address Book has many of the usual menus of the built-in Palm programs. You've already learned what's under the Record menu (beaming stuff).

Edit menu

The Edit menu contains exactly what you'd expect it to: the typical editing commands that you are used to (see **Figure 5.12**). No surprises there.

Record	Edit	Options

Accessories	Undo	✓U
Antoinette,	Cut	✓X
Bolivar, Sim	Copy	✓C
Caesar, Juli	Paste	✓P
Cleopatra	Select All	✓S
de Sade, Mc	Keyboard	✓K
Hannibal	Graffiti Help	✓G
Khan, Gengnis	gk@mongois.mil E
Sitting Bull	872-0312 W
Socrates	509-2775 H
Technical Sup	847-262-PALM (72... MD

Look Up:.......................... (New)

Figure 5.12 Address Book's commands should be familiar.

Options menu

Address Book's display preferences and such are found under the Options menu. Tap the Menu icon and then tap Options.

Font: You have the same three font choices you had in Date Book: small, bold, and large.

If you can read it okay, I recommend choosing the small font, because more things can fit on the screen at once.

Preferences: See **Figure 5.13**. Address Book's slim selection of preferences include the option to open Address Book to whichever category was open last time you were in Address Book. Put a check mark beside Remember last category if you want that.

Figure 5.13 Choose how to sort your addresses in the Preferences dialog box.

The other choice is to list your entries alphabetically by last name, first name or by company, last name. Pick whichever suits your needs best.

Rename Custom fields: Remember those four fields that you can customize to whatever you like? Here's where you do that. **Figure 5.14** shows some suggestions. In Family, I note the existence of spouses, children, and pets. Computer tells me about the person's computer system. Birthday is a good place to keep that info (Date Book is another good place). And Interests is a good spot to jot down what the person does when not at work.

Rename Custom Fields

Create your own field names by editing the text on the lines below:

Family
Computer
Birthday
Interests

(OK) (Cancel)

Figure 5.14 I customized these fields to reflect my own needs.

The Computer field I created is particularly helpful to me. A good chunk of my day is spent emailing files back and forth with people whose machines run every flavor of operating system—Windows, Macintosh, Linux, and others—plus every kind of email program and every persnickety version of Microsoft Word. Knowing in advance what kind of system a person has saves me many headaches and much time. Your own needs for custom fields are probably different. Try to think of what drives you nuts about working with different people and create fields for those things.

To Do List

To Do List, not surprisingly, is where you keep track of everything you have to do. You can categorize your *tasks* or *items*, rank them according to priority, assign them due dates, and check them off when they're done and then delete (purge) them. You can choose different preferences for how To Do List displays your tasks.

At first, I wasn't sure of the differences between Date Book and To Do List, or why they are two separate programs. After all, before I bought my Palm, I wrote down stuff I needed to do on my calendar. But since I've been using them, it's starting to make more sense. I end up using To Do List at least as often as Date Book. It turns out that I write down a lot more things in To Do List, and I wouldn't want to clutter up my appointment calendar with stuff like "Pick up Drāno" or "Do laundry."

I think of Date Book as the framework for stuff that is going to happen to me no matter what: meetings, conferences, trips, appointments, lunch and dinner dates. To Do List is more of a catch-all receptacle to write down every task that I will eventually have to do. And unlike Address Book, I use categories in To Do List to keep my work and personal tasks separate.

Entering Tasks

To Do List is the second-to-right button on your Palm. Press it or tap the To Do List icon in the Applications screen. Each time you press the To Do List button, it cycles through and displays the different categories. **Figure 6.1** shows the opening screen on a new Palm, almost free of To Do items.

By now, you are familiar with the basic routine of the built-in programs. To enter a new task, tap New and type its description. Because I like to keep my personal and business items separate, I'll tap the drop-down arrow at the top and select the Personal category. I happen to be moving to Galway, Ireland next month, and there's a lot I need to do before that can happen (see **Figure 6.2**).

To Do List	▼ All
☐ 1 Don't forget to register! .... 🗋	

(New) (Details...) (Show...)

Figure 6.1 Wouldn't it be nice if the only thing you had to do was register your Palm?

To Do List	▼ Personal
☐ 1 Ask bank if they'll forward statements to Ireland	
☐ 1 Take Fez to Marla and Eddie's for a trial week	
☐ 1 Get a credit report to bring	
☑ 1 Buy plane tickets	
☑ 1 Rent a car	
☐ 1 Call Galway realtors	
☑ 1 Get letter from health ins co.	
☐ 1 Have sidewalk sale	
☐ 1 Forward mail	

(New) (Details...) (Show...)

Figure 6.2 Now, that's more like it—lots of things to do.

Completing tasks

You'll notice that some of the items in **Figure 6.2** have check marks next to them. I put those check marks there when I completed those tasks. I could have deleted them, but it's nice to see progress being made, so I'll leave them for now and purge them later. To complete a task, tap the box next to it to put a check mark in it.

Like Date Book, To Do List lets you purge records, which is a way to delete them en masse when they are no longer useful. In Date Book, you purge based on how old the events are. In To Do List, you purge the tasks that have check marks in them.

Priorities

Another thing you'll notice in **Figure 6.2** is that every task is assigned the numeral 1. That number represents the task's priority. If you just add the tasks and don't reassign priority, To Do List automatically makes every task priority 1.

Figure 6.3 Reassign priorities by tapping the number itself and picking from the list.

Changing priorities: To change a task's priority, tap the priority number and select a new priority from the popup list (see **Figure 6.3**).

There are four tasks in my list that can wait a few weeks, so I reassign them to priority 2. You can see in **Figure 6.4** that To Do List shoves priority 2 tasks to the bottom of the list.

Figure 6.4 Some things can be put off longer than others, and lower priority items go the back of the line.

To Do Preferences

Tap Show at the bottom of the screen to get to To Do List's Preferences screen, shown in **Figure 6.5**.

Figure 6.5 The Preferences screen is where you can change To Do List's display.

Sorting

Tap on the Sort by drop-down arrow to see the four different ways in which To Do List can sort items (**Figure 6.6**). The default is that items are first sorted by priority, and then by due date.

| Priority, Due Date |
| Due Date, Priority |
| Category, Priority |
| Category, Due Date |

Figure 6.6 Your sorting choices.

What to show onscreen

It's up to you to decide what you want To Do List to show you.

Show Completed Items: Keep this checked if you want the satisfaction of seeing completed tasks onscreen. If you remove the check mark here, from then on when you tap an item's box in To Do List, it disappears. It's still in there somewhere, but it's invisible.

Show Only Due Items: Tap this, and To Do List only displays items that are due. (You'll learn about setting due dates in the next section.)

Record Completion Date: If you check this, and you also check Show Due Dates, To Do List automatically displays the date when you check off a task in the due date column (see **Figure 6.7**).

Recording the completion date is a great way to keep track of when you complete tasks.

To Do List   ▼ Personal

☑ 1	Buy plane tickets	7/11
☑ 1	Rent a car	7/11
☑ 1	Get letter from health ins. co.	7/11
☐ 1	Ask bank if they'll forward statements to Ireland	—
☐ 1	Get a credit report to bring	—
☐ 1	Call Galway realtors	—
☐ 1	Take Fez to Marla and	—

(New) (Details...) (Show...)

Due date column

Figure 6.7 Now, not only can I see which tasks I completed, I can see when I completed them.

Show Priorities: You can turn off showing priorities by tapping in the box to get rid of the check mark. To Do List still assigns priorities to your items, but it keeps that information invisible.

Show Categories: Tap this, and to the right of the due date column the name of each item's category appears.

Show Categories is helpful only if you are showing more than one category at a time, that is, if you have selected All in the drop-down category list at the top right corner of the screen.

Item Details

Like Date Book and Address Book, To Do List makes extensive use of the Details button at the bottom of the screen. In Details, you can assign categories, due dates, and priorities, attach Notes, and mark items Private. After you enter an item in To Do List, tap Details to get to the Details screen. **Figure 6.8** shows To Do List's Details screen.

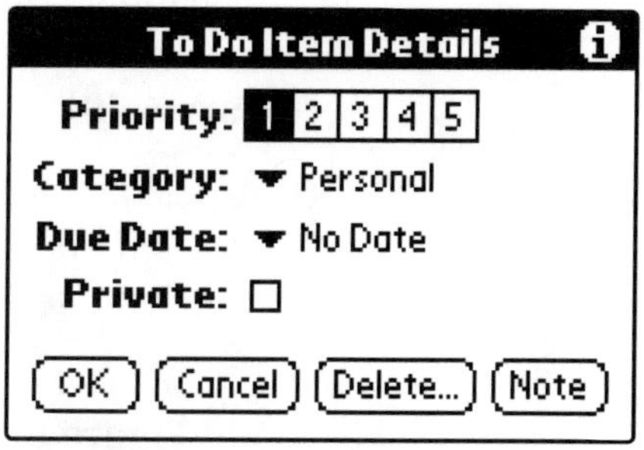

To Do Item Details   ⓘ

Priority: 1 2 3 4 5
Category: ▼ Personal
Due Date: ▼ No Date
Private: ☐

(OK) (Cancel) (Delete...) (Note)

Figure 6.8 Details is where most of the item-changing action is in To Do List.

Due dates

By default, To Do List assigns no due date for items. If an item needs to be completed by a certain date, you can set a due date for it. To set a due date, tap somewhere in the task's description to put the cursor there, tap Details, and tap the drop-down arrow beside Due Date.

Due Date

◀ **1999** ▶

| Jan | Feb | Mar | Apr | May | Jun |
| Jul | Aug | Sep | Oct | Nov | Dec |

S	M	T	W	T	F	S
				1	2	3
4	5	6	7	8	9	10
11	12	13	(14)	15	16	17
18	19	20	21	22	23	24
25	26	27	28	29	30	31

(Cancel) (Today)

Figure 6.9 Pick a due date, any due date.

Your choices are: Today, Tomorrow, One week later, No Date, and Choose Date. If you tap Choose Date, you'll see a screen like **Figure 6.9**, where you can select any date you like from the Due Date calendar. Tap the date you want. The due date will appear in the due date column item's Details screen from now on, and if you checked the check box next to Show Due Dates in the Show screen, the due date appears in its own column in To Do List's main screen.

There is no alarm in To Do List. If the due date comes and goes and you haven't checked off the item, the only warning you get is a little exclamation mark (!), which appears in the due date column (but only if you have chosen Show Due Dates in the Show screen). There are third-party add-on programs that replace To Do List which do allow you to set a reminder alarm—see Chapter 11 for more.

Category

Tap the drop-down arrow beside Category to pick which category the item will be filed under. The defaults are Business, Personal, Unfiled, and Edit Categories. Tap Edit Categories to add new categories or rename or delete existing ones (see **Figure 6.10**).

You can have up to 15 categories, and category names can only be up to 15 characters long. To merge two categories, rename one to another's name. Items in deleted categories don't go away; they merely move to the Unfiled category.

In **Figure 6.10**, you can see that I added a few new categories. You don't have to accept Business or Personal as categories, either—they are merely suggestions by Palm. Create and use whatever categories make sense to you. To see everything you have to do in all categories at one time, choose All from the category drop-down arrow.

Figure 6.10 The Edit Categories screen is where you make changes to your To Do List categories.

Keep in mind that the idea isn't to pile up lots of tasks in a complicated assortment of categories, but to get things done without letting anything slip through the cracks. If the uncompleted portion of my To Do List starts scrolling, for example, I take it as a sign that I've spent too much time fiddling with To Do List and not enough time actually completing the tasks I should be doing.

Marking items Private

Tapping the Private box makes the item private, but as with Date Book and Address Book, you have to choose to hide private records in the Palm's Security program. You can also require that a password be entered to view private records. Chapter 4 talks in more detail about Private records (as applied to Date Book) and the process works the same in To Do List. See Chapter 8 for more on the Security program.

Menus

To Do List menus work just like the menus in Date Book and Address Book, so I won't repeat here what you already learned in Chapters 4 and 5.

Purging

Like Date Book, To Do List accumulates old records unless you delete, or purge, them. In To Do List, you should periodically purge all items that have been accomplished (that is, all the ones with your check marks). To purge these old tasks, tap the Menu icon, tap Record, and then tap Purge. The Purge screen appears (see **Figure 6.11**)

Figure 6.11 Tap OK to send your old, completed tasks to oblivion.

If you want to save a copy of those old tasks for posterity, put a check mark in the box marked Save archive copy on PC. Then, during your next HotSync session, a list of the completed items is saved on your computer and deleted from your Palm.

Phone lookup, beaming, and attaching notes

Phone lookup, beaming, and attaching notes to items all work the same in To Do List as they do in Date Book—see Chapter 4 for a refresher.

Memo Pad 7

When you need to write a memo, take notes, capture a brainstorm, make lists, or just jot down random thoughts, Memo Pad is there for you. It's a bare-bones kind of electronic scratch pad, a good place to simply record stuff into your Palm for later use, perhaps elsewhere. In fact, there's not much to Memo Pad— of the main built-in applications, it's the least full-featured.

Making good use of Memo Pad on your Palm naturally requires a fair amount of Graffiti skill (which you learned about in Chapter 3). Memo Pad is also a great place to practice writing longer pieces. The more you use Graffiti, the faster you get, and the more natural it will seem.

Because writing in Graffiti is not nearly as fast as typing, if you need to create a document longer than a paragraph or two, you're better off typing it into the Memo Pad equivalent in the Palm Desktop software. Then you can HotSync it to your Palm (see Chapters 9 and 10 for more on HotSyncing and the Palm Desktop).

Memo Pad Basics

Press the Memo Pad button to start Memo Pad (it's the far-thest right button along the bottom of your Palm) or tap the Applications icon and then tap the Memo Pad icon. You should see a screen like **Figure 7.1**, which is the Memo List view. As you can see, Palm Computing has already put a few memos in your Palm.

```
┌──────────────────────────────┐
│ Memo List            ▼ All   │
│                              │
│  1. Handheld Basics          │
│  2. Three Ways to Enter Text │
│  3. Download Free Applications│
│  4. Power Tips               │
│                              │
│                              │
│                              │
│                              │
│                              │
│                              │
│ ┌──────┐                     │
│ │ New  │                     │
│ └──────┘                     │
└──────────────────────────────┘
```

Figure 7.1 Memo Pad was the natural place for Palm Computing to put in some notes to you.

The Palm memos are recommended reading. They contain lots of good tips on everything from Palm basics to installing add-on applications.

Replacing Memo Pad

For serious Palm users, Memo Pad is a glaring candidate for replace-ment. Numerous freeware and shareware add-on programs called *doc readers* exist that take document creation and text reading far beyond Memo Pad's minimalism. These doc readers turn your Palm into an amazing electronic book, for one thing, where you read *etexts*, which are available in abundance on the Web. You can even reprogram the Memo Pad button to launch a Doc reader instead of Memo Pad. Doc readers usually offer advanced features such as more full-featured find and replace, better editing tools, advanced scrolling options, multiple views, bookmarks, and enhanced beaming. Three popular Doc readers are AportisDoc, TealDoc, and SmartDoc. There are also document con-verters which can convert your Microsoft Word documents into Palm documents. You can find out more about popular doc readers and other text-related software in Chapter 11.

The Memo List view shows you all the memos that are in your Palm, in the order they were created. To change their order, press the stylus down on one and drag it up or down to where you want it to go. Memo Pad automatically moves it and renumbers every memo to reflect the new order.

To read a memo, tap once on its description. Tap on the first Palm memo, and its contents appear in a new screen, called the Memo view (see **Figure 7.2**).

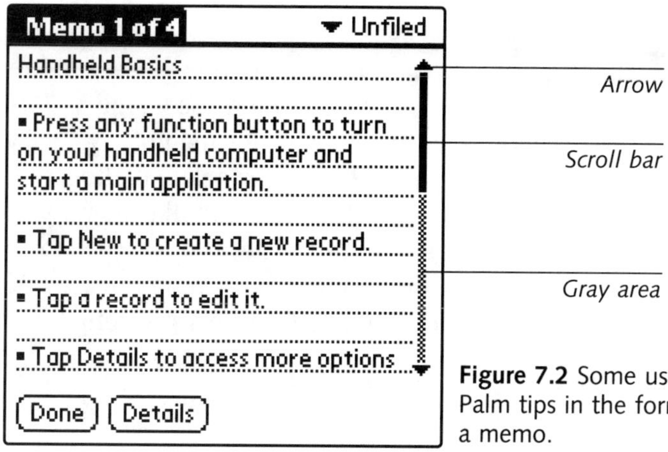

Arrow

Scroll bar

Gray area

Figure 7.2 Some useful Palm tips in the form of a memo.

Scrolling

Note the scroll bar along the right side of **Figure 7.2**. As I've mentioned elsewhere, scroll bars on the Palm work just like they do on your computer. Tap an arrow to scroll up or down one line at a time. Tap the gray area to scroll up or down one screenful. You can also press the stylus down on the black part of the scroll bar and drag it up or down as far as you want.

Figure 7.3 The two handy Go to commands move you instantly to the beginning or end of a memo.

To move to the top or bottom of the memo instantly, tap the Menu icon, tap Options, and choose one of the Go to choices (see **Figure 7.3**).

Don't forget the scroll rocker button at the bottom of your Palm, which scrolls one screenful at a time every time to press it up or down. With long documents, it is usually easier and faster to press that button with your thumb than it is to tap that skinny scroll bar with the stylus.

Memo Details

Tap the Details button to pop up the rather spare Memo Details screen (see **Figure 7.4**), where you can change the memo's category, make the memo Private, or delete it altogether. These functions should be familiar by now, so I won't repeat myself—they work just the way they do in the other built-in programs, which you learned about in Chapters 4 through 6.

Figure 7.4 Not many Details are available for memos.

You can delete a memo quickly by writing /⅁ in the Graffiti area.

Creating a New Memo

Tap the New button at the bottom of the screen or write Ⅳ in the Graffiti area. A new, blank memo is created that looks a lot like **Figure 7.5**. Memo Pad categorizes your memo as Unfiled by default. Later, you can put your memo in any category you want by tapping the Category drop-down arrow in the Details screen (shown in **Figure 7.4**).

To begin your memo, just start writing it using Graffiti. Use whatever shorthand way of writing notes or memos that you normally use (see **Figure 7.6**). Unless the memo needs to be read on a Palm by someone else, your goal is to get down the information in a quick and efficient manner as possible. You can always HotSync it into Palm Desktop and expand or edit it later on your computer, using the lightning-fast luxury of your keyboard (you never suspect how much you could love a keyboard until you get a Palm device).

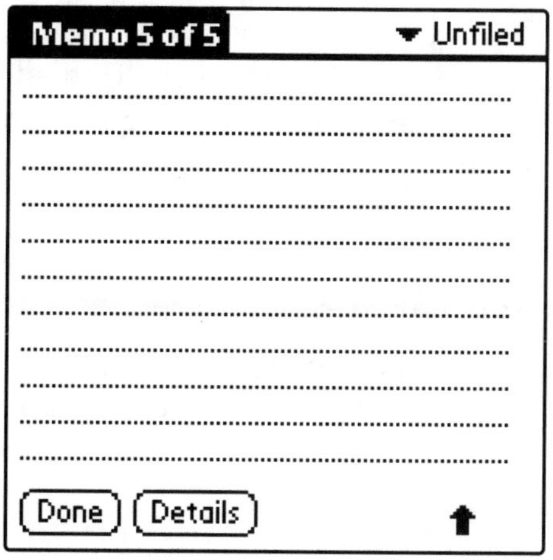

Memo 5 of 5	▼ Unfiled
....	
....	
....	
....	
....	
....	
....	
....	
....	
(Done) (Details)	⬆

Figure 7.5 This blank, lined piece of electronic paper is ready for you to start writing.

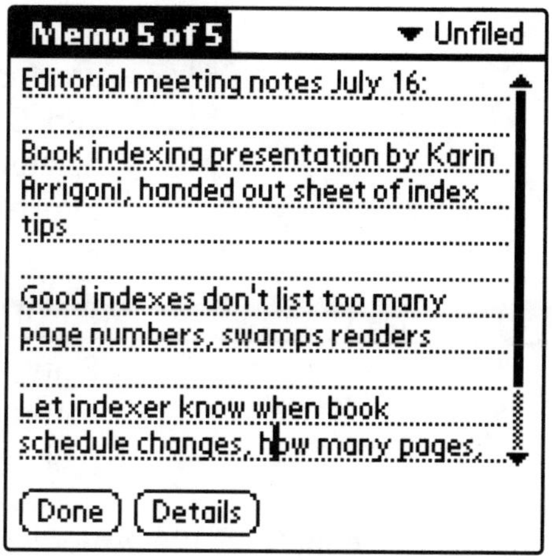

Memo 5 of 5	▼ Unfiled
Editorial meeting notes July 16:	▲
Book indexing presentation by Karin Arrigoni, handed out sheet of index tips	
Good indexes don't list too many page numbers, swamps readers	
Let indexer know when book schedule changes, how many pages,	▼
(Done) (Details)	

Figure 7.6 Use Memo Pad in whatever way is useful to you.

One good thing about taking notes on your Palm is that you never have to worry about not being able to decipher your own handwriting later—that all happens up front, as the Palm deciphers your Graffiti.

Just as there are replacement programs for Memo Pad, there are replacement programs for Graffiti, some of which let you use the whole screen as the writing area. These programs are often easier to use and have even more accurate recognition systems than Graffiti does. See Chapter 11 for more on Graffiti replacements.

As with everything else in the Palm, you don't have to save your document—it's just there in memory as soon as you write it. The next time you open up Memo Pad, your memo will be there in the list with the others. Memo Pad uses the first line as the "title" that appears in the Memo List view.

Edit Categories... ⓘ

Business
Meeting notes
Personal

(OK) (New) (Rename) (Delete)

Figure 7.7 I created a new category for my memo.

Categories

Your new memo is created as Unfiled, but you can place it in a different category if you like. Tap Details, tap the Category drop-down arrow, and select your category. Your choices are (as usual) Business, Personal, Unfiled, and Edit Categories. Tap Edit Categories to delete, rename, or create new categories (see **Figure 7.7**).

Memo Pad Menus

Being the least complicated of the main built-in programs, Memo Pad offers slim menu pickings.

Menu List view menus

In the Menu List view (the one where you see a list of all your memos), tap the Menu icon to reveal two meager menus: Record and Options.

Record: As you see, the Record menu contains a single command: Beam Category (see **Figure 7.8**). Tap Beam Category to beam all the memos in the current category to another Palm device.

Beaming categories is a good way of distributing notes among a team of Palm users.

Options: Tap the Options menu to see the available choices (see **Figure 7.9**).

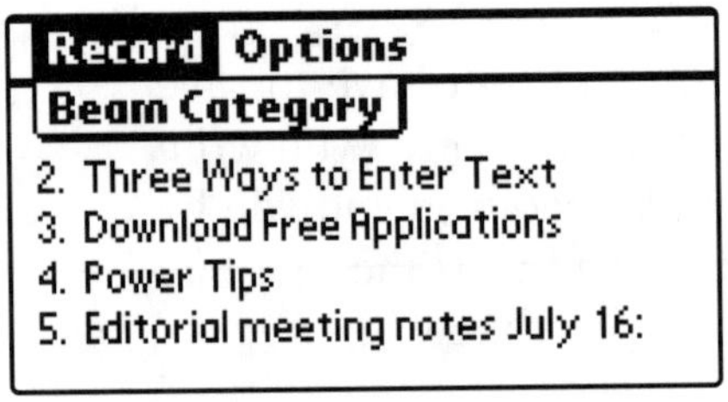

Record	**Options**
Beam Category	
2. Three Ways to Enter Text	
3. Download Free Applications	
4. Power Tips	
5. Editorial meeting notes July 16:	

Figure 7.8 The Memo List view's menus are not much to look at.

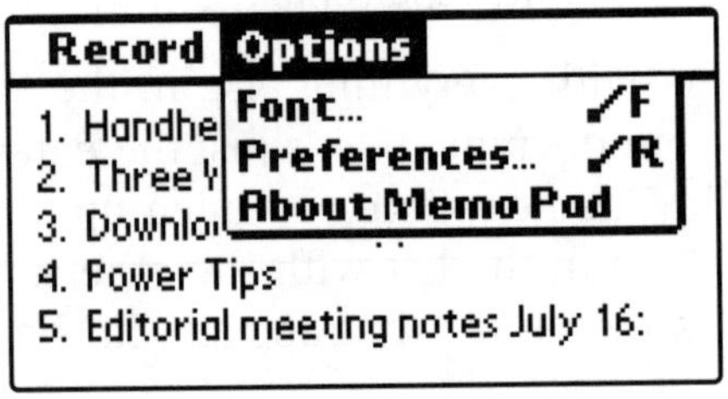

Record	**Options**	
1. Handhe	**Font...**	✓F
2. Three \	**Preferences...**	✓R
3. Downlo	**About Memo Pad**	
4. Power Tips		
5. Editorial meeting notes July 16:		

Figure 7.9 Font and Preferences are all the Options you have.

Tap Font to see the three fonts available for Memo Pad—they are the same three fonts you've seen in the other programs: small, bold, and large. Tap whichever font you'd like Memo Pad to use. The screen shots in this chapter were taken using the small font, which I like because it allows more text to fit on each screen (less scrolling for me). But some folks prefer larger type for easier reading. Suit yourself. **Figure 7.10** shows what the editorial meeting notes (shown back in **Figure 7.6**) look like in bold and large fonts.

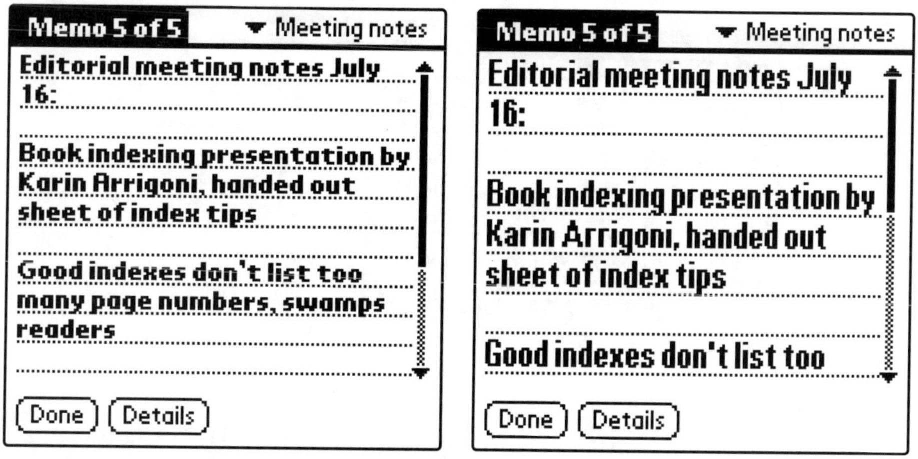

Figure 7.10 Here are bold font (left) and large font (right) versions of my meeting notes.

Tap Preferences to open up Memo Pad's Preferences screen (see **Figure 7.11**), which offers two choices of sorting your memos: manual and alphabetic. Manual sorting is the default setting in Memo Pad and the one that allows you to drag memos up and down the list using the stylus. Alphabetic sorts all your memos alphabetically.

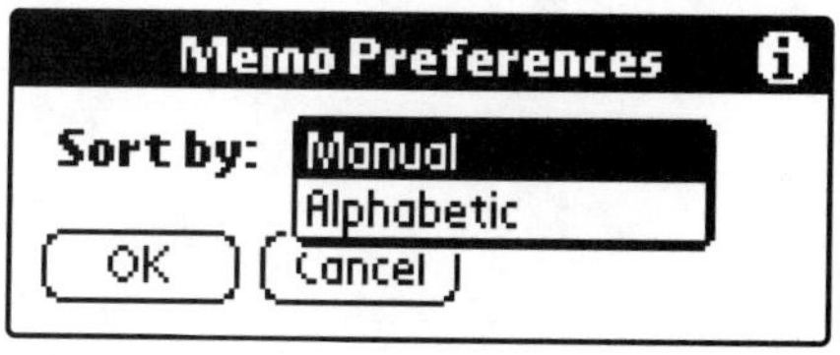

Figure 7.11 Manual and alphabetic are your sorting options in Memo Pad.

Memo view menus

You have more menus to choose from while you are actually reading or writing a memo. Open up a memo to the Memo view by tapping its description and then tap the Menu icon to reveal Memo view's three menus: Record, Edit, and Options.

Record: Tap Record to create a new memo (or write N), delete the memo (D), or beam the memo to another Palm device (B).

Edit: The Edit menu offers the same old editing functions available in the other built-in applications (see **Figure 7.12**).

Figure 7.12 The familiar Edit menu commands.

Options: The Options menu offers commands to change the font (or write ⌐), to go to the top or bottom of the page, and to do a Phone Lookup (or you can write L). As you know from previous chapters, Phone Lookup inserts the full name and phone number if you invoke it while the cursor is resting on the last name of a person in your Address Book.

Expense, Security, and Calculator

8

Compared to the main programs you learned about in the previous chapters, these three, which round out Palm's suite of built-in programs, are relatively minor-league, lacking many of the features of the four main ones. (Security isn't even really a program per se but a series of settings that affect other programs.) Still, they're mighty handy tools for any businessperson. Expense is nearly as full-featured as the main programs. And Calculator is just what its name implies.

Mail is a major built-in program which enables you to HotSync to retrieve your email from your computer. HotSyncing is covered in Chapters 9 and 10, and Mail is covered in Chapter 13.

If you have a Palm VII, you have *several* more built-in programs. Using these special Palm VII programs (called Palm Query Applications or PQAs) requires you to activate the Palm.Net service. You learn how to activate the service and use those programs in Chapter 15.

Expense

The Palm's Expense program is a fine way to track business expenses, especially while you're on the road. When you return, you HotSync with your computer, and Expense dumps your expense information into a handy Excel spreadsheet, which you can print and hand in to request reimbursement. If you don't have Excel, you're out of luck—unless you have a Mac (see the end of Chapter 10 for the getting Expense data into your Mac).

Expense basics

To start Expense, tap the Expense icon in home base. You will see a blank Expense screen with three buttons at the bottom (see **Figure 8.1**).

Tap the New button to add a new expense. Expense pops up a line with three pieces of information, two of which—expense type and dollar amount—you have to fill in (**Figure 8.2**). Today's date is added for you automatically (tap the date to call up a calendar, where you can change it).

The cursor is ready for you to type in the amount of your expense, so go ahead and do that. Use Graffiti on the number side, and use a period (two taps) for the decimal point.

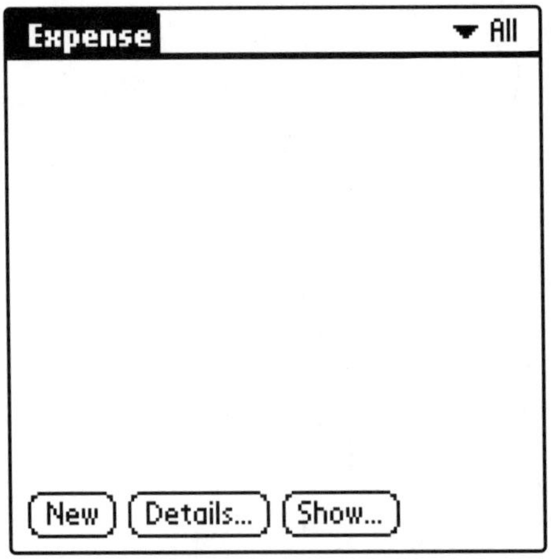

Figure 8.1 The Expense screen doesn't show much of anything until you start adding expenses.

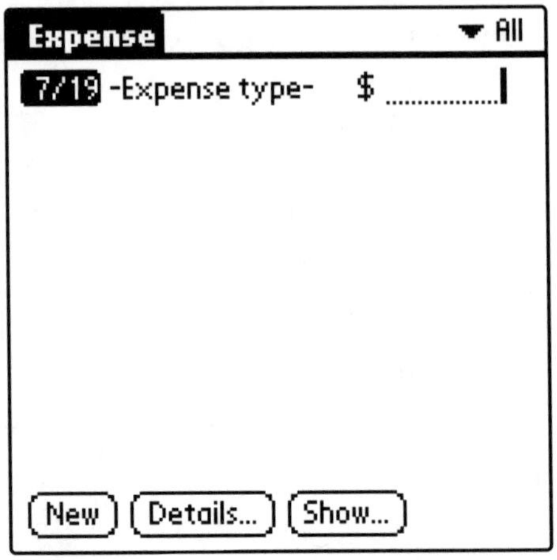

Figure 8.2 Expense needs you to fill in the amount and the Expense type.

My Palm is set up to record the expense in United States dollars because I told my Palm when I set it up that's where I live. But you can easily change the currency if you are traveling elsewhere. You'll learn how in a minute.

Next tap—Expense type—to call up the list of expense types. In all, you have 28 types of expenses to choose from. **Figure 8.3** shows all of them.

Airfare		Incidentals ↑	Mileage ↑
Breakfast		Laundry	Other
Bus		Limo	Parking
Business Meals		Lodging	Postage
Car Rental		Lunch	Snack
Dinner		Mileage	Subway
Entertainment		Other	Supplies
Fax		Parking	Taxi
Gas		Postage	Telephone
Gifts		Snack	Tips
Hotel		Subway	Tolls
Incidentals ↓		Supplies ↓	Train

Figure 8.3 Whoa, you have lots of choices when selecting the Expense type.

Twenty-eight choices may sound like a lot, but life on the road is complicated, and you'll probably learn to love the "Incidentals," "Other," and "Supplies" types. As with any of the four main programs, you can attach Notes to Expense items that provide quick explanations to these catchall categories if you need to.

See? It's very easy and quite convenient (dare I say fun?) to use the Palm to track your expenses. You just keep entering items as you spend money. As always, you don't have to save anything, because everything is tucked away in memory.

Filling in the details

Once you have entered a day's worth of bare-bones Expense items (see **Figure 8.4**), back in your hotel room (or wherever you have some time) you may want to look through the list and fill in some of the details, while they are still fairly fresh in your mind.

Tap on an item, and the cursor should start bouncing on the item's amount. Then tap the Details button. You should see the Receipt Details screen, which looks like **Figure 8.5.**

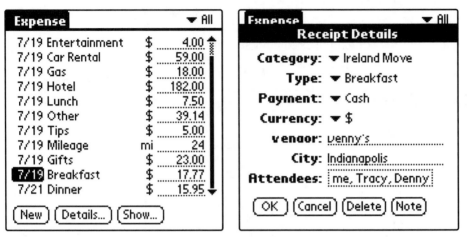

Figure 8.4 Money is obviously burning a hole in my pocket.

Figure 8.5 I'll probably forget most of this stuff soon, so it's good to fill it in while I remember.

Category: Tap the drop-down arrow to change the item's category (by default it's created as Unfiled). To create a new category, tap Edit Categories. I created the Ireland Move category to track our expenses as Tracy and I make our journey. Category names can be up to 15 characters long, so be pithy. It's a good idea to create a category for each trip or project for which you need to track expenses. The Palm folks must spend a lot of time in New York and Paris because they used them to give you examples of categories.

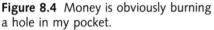

Type: Tap the arrow if you don't like the type you first selected.

Payment: Tap the arrow to choose your payment (**Figure 8.6** shows your choices).

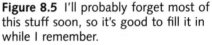

Figure 8.6 The Palm knows you want to pay in cash, plastic, check, or that it was a prepaid item.

Currency: If you're traveling through many countries, you'll be tapping on this a lot. But notice that only U.S. dollars, British pounds, and German marks are available when you tap the arrow. Those are fine nations, but if you're in a different one you'll want to tap Edit currencies and add more currencies in the Select Currencies screen. You can have up to five currencies available at any one time to choose from (**Figure 8.7**).

One good reason to install the Palm OS 3.3 upgrade is because you have to if you want that cute little Euro symbol to appear in your Palm—the regular Palm OS (3.0 through 3.2) didn't include the new monetary symbol for the European Union in its currencies. (In the meantime, you may want to create a custom currency for the Euro—see the nearby sidebar "What if I'm in Cameroon?" for more on custom currencies.)

3.3

Select Currencies

Select the currencies that display in currency list.

Currency 1: ▼ United States
Currency 2: ▼ Ireland
Currency 3: ▼ Netherlands
Currency 4: ▼ United Kingdom
Currency 5: ▼ Germany

(OK) (Cancel)

Figure 8.7 Now that's more useful to me.

Vendor: Enter the name of the establishment in the Vendor line.

City: You should have no problem with this one. Tip: It's probably on your receipt.

Attendees: This is a good place to record the names of people you met with, ate with, bought Silly String with, and so on.

Deleting and attaching Notes: To delete an expense item, tap Delete in Details, or tap the Menu icon, the Record menu and then Delete, or write the Graffiti command ╱Ď. To attach a Note to an item, tap Note, just like you're used to in the other programs, and then write your note in the space provided.

What if I'm in Cameroon?

Expense knows about the currencies of 24 countries, which means it's missing a whole lot of them. If you're traveling in Yaounde, Cameroon, for example, you'll have to teach your Palm about the Cameroon franc. To do that, tap the Menu icon, tap Options, and tap Custom Currencies. Tap the Country 1 box and then enter the name of the country and whatever you'd like its symbol to be. With a name like Cameroon franc, I might enter CFR as the symbol.

Don't feel you have to fill in all this stuff if it's not necessary. If your boss doesn't care whether you ate in Tipton or Kokomo, don't put a city in there. The Palm is fun, to be sure, but the idea should be to save time, not to waste it.

Expense options and preferences

Put the cursor on an item and tap the Show button to bring up the Show Options screen (**Figure 8.8**). Here you can change the way Expense sorts items (by date or type), select miles or kilometers for your mileage, and decide whether to show the currency symbol onscreen or not.

Mileage is the one Expense type that doesn't have a currency attached to it. Instead, it simply tots up the amount of miles you drive.

Tap OK to close the Show Options screen. Then tap the Menu icon, tap the Options menu, and tap Preferences to make the Preferences screen appear (**Figure 8.9**).

Default currency: You select your default currency here by tapping the drop-down arrow and selecting it from the list that pops up. Default currency just means that Expense will use that currency if you never change the currency type for an item.

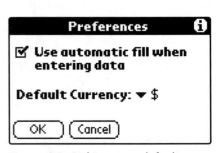

Figure 8.8 Expense's Show Options are rather meager.

Figure 8.9 Picking your default currency and getting your automatic fill.

Automatic fill: This is a pretty neat feature, and there's no reason to ever turn it off, so leave that check box checked. Automatic fill lets you use Graffiti to enter just the first letter or two of an item type (or city or vendor), and then Expense fills in the rest. For example, to enter a new item, you don't even have to tap New—if you write an "o" in the Graffiti area, Expense figures that you're adding a new "Other" item and creates it for you. It also detects cities and vendors—provided you've already entered them at least once—and automatically fills those in if you write the first letter.

> *If there is more than one choice that starts with "b," for example, automatic fill chooses the first one and then waits for you to write the next letter to refine the type. If you write "B" in the Graffiti area, automatic fill creates a "Breakfast" item. But if you then write a "U," it knows you actually wanted to enter a "Bus" item.*

Exporting your expense report to Excel

This is jumping the gun a bit, but because you're on the verge of learning about HotSync and the Palm Desktop in the next two chapters, I'll give you a preview. It's very easy—almost eerily so (to do this, be sure you have Microsoft Excel on your PC). Mac users see Chapter 10 for your Expense counterpart (it's on the MacPac 2 CD-ROM).

Take your trip or finish your project and record your expenses in your Palm, just like you've been learning about. When you get back, simply place your Palm in its cradle and press the HotSync button. The Palm and your computer talk to each other and update each other's files. In this case, your Palm is telling your computer about your expenses. After the HotSync is finished (it usually takes a minute or so), launch the Palm Desktop program and click on the Expense button. Believe it or not, Microsoft Excel starts right up, and before you know it you are staring at your completely filled out, nicely formatted expense report, ready for printing.

Purging

Like Date Book and To Do List, which deal with events that go away with time, Expense offers a Purge function. When you have finished a project, or returned from your trip, and turned in your status report and no longer need to keep those items in your Palm, you should purge them to retrieve the memory space they are taking up.

Purging happens to categories, which is another reason why it's a good idea to make a category for each trip or project. To purge items, write the Graffiti command / P. Or tap the Menu icon, tap the Record menu, and tap Purge. The Purge Categories screen appears. Tap the category you want to purge and tap Purge. A dialog box pops up to see if you're sure you want to purge—if you're sure, tap Yes.

Security

You already learned a bit about the Palm's Security program in the Date Book chapter, Chapter 4. To recap, Security allows you to do three things. Using Security, you can:

- Choose to hide records and require a password to show the records again.

- Choose to hide records until you (or someone) chooses to show the records again without having to know the password.

- Make it so nobody can see anything in your Palm unless they know your password.

Hiding stuff with passwords

To hide your private records in Date Book, Address Book, To Do list, and Memo Pad, first make sure that you marked certain records as private in those programs. See the appropriate chapter for how to do that.

Go into the Security program by tapping the Security icon in home base. You'll see the Security screen, which looks like **Figure 8.10**. The first thing you need to do is come up with a password that you will remember but which nobody else can guess.

Creating a password: Tap the box beside Password that says –Unassigned–. The Password screen appears and ask you to write your password (see **Figure 8.11**).

Figure 8.10 This is all the interface there is to the Security program.

Figure 8.11 A serviceable and not very guessable password—perfect, as long as I can remember that the Frankish ruler Charlemagne was crowned in the year 800.

Write your password with Graffiti. *Be sure you wrote what you intended to write.* Double-check it because as you know, Graffiti is not perfect (or rather, you're not perfect, you're only human). Tap OK.

Password tips

Your password can be up to 31 characters long. It can be made up of letters or numbers or even punctuation—or any combination thereof. You can use uppercase and lowercase letters, but the Palm doesn't notice a difference when you reenter it. The longer and more unusual a password is, the harder it becomes for someone else to guess it or enter it by chance—but the harder it may be for you to remember it. Your password should be at least five characters long, and preferably more. Avoid obvious passwords like your pet's name, significant other's name, birthday, and so on. Or use those, but add numbers or punctuation to them to make them nearly impossible to guess.

A verification screen asks you to enter your password again, to explicitly make you write it twice—here is where you may discover that what you wrote the first time isn't what you meant to write (**Figure 8.12**). If Graffiti misses the "g" in Charlemagne, for example, and you tap OK, you'll be informed in no uncertain terms that you screwed up (**Figure 8.13**).

Figure 8.12 I write the password really fast...

Figure 8.13...and Security lets me know I got it wrong.

Once you get your password successfully into your Palm, tap OK, and you are brought back to the Security screen, where you can see at a glance that your password has been assigned (**Figure 8.14**).

Figure 8.14 The Assigned box tells me that I'd better know the password.

Changing a password: You can change your password at any time, and you should from time to time. In Security, tap Assigned, enter your password, and then enter your new password.

If you can see that your password is assigned, tap the Hide box beside Private Records. Now go back to any program that has private records by pressing its button at the bottom of your

Palm. Let's take Address Book as an example. Suppose you've hidden your lover's or your bookie's entry but you've forgotten his or her ZIP code and need it. Address Book opens but the mystery person's name doesn't appear because you've hidden it. No one would have a clue that the person existed. The record is successfully hidden, which means all your hidden records are hidden.

But you need the ZIP code. To get it, tap Show Records in Security. A password dialog box appears that asks you to enter the password. Do so and tap Show. If you are successful, you'll see the person now in Address Book (**Figure 8.15**), and you can tap to get to the ZIP code.

Address List	▼ All
Accessories	800-881-7256 (US) M☐
Antoinette, Marie	756-0445 H
Bolivar, Simon	447-9083 H
Caesar, Julius	jc@rome.gov○☐
Cleopatra	494-3092 W
Collins, Corbin	555-2178 W☐
de Sade, Marquis	mrpain@paris.fr E
Hannibal	hb@carthage.mil E
Khan, Genghis	gk@mongols.mil E
Lovah, Ille Licit	
Sitting Bull	872-0312 W
Look Up:	(New) ▲ ▼

Figure 8.15 The hidden record is revealed.

To hide your records again, you have to remember to tap the Hide box in Security.

Hiding stuff without a password

You can tap Security's Hide box and hide records without assigning a password. Why would you do that? Well, it would provide a small measure of security for your hidden records without your having to mess with the danger of using passwords. Unless a snoop knows a fair bit about the Palm, they wouldn't even know about hidden records, nor would they have reason to suspect that to show hidden records they'd have to tap Show in the Security program.

Deleting a password: To use Hide without requiring a password, you first have to delete the password you just assigned. In Security, tap Assigned, enter your password, and then tap the Delete button. You can see now that your Palm's password is unassigned.

With the password unassigned, if you tap the Hide box, your records are still hidden, but anyone could show them by tapping Show.

If you forget your password

Be very careful with passwords. If you don't feel you need to use them, don't, because if you use hidden records and you forget your password, it's fairly bad (but not as bad as locking up your Palm and forgetting your password—see the next section). You can tell the Palm sheepishly that you forgot the password, and the Palm will forgive you—but first it will punish you by deleting all your Private records.

Yes, that is mean, but it is that way so that someone who finds your Palm and taps Forgotten Password can never see any stuff you made Private. You can restore your Private records at your next HotSync—but only those records that were there at your last HotSync will be restored. So, HotSync early and often (see the next chapter for more on HotSync).

If you forget your password, tap Forgotten Password. You will see the scary screen in **Figure 8.16**. Read it carefully. If it makes you too nervous or you think there is a possibility that you will remember it, tap No. You can always come back here. But if you know you'll never be able to remember your password, tap Yes.

You will come back to the Security screen and notice that the Password is now unassigned. At your next HotSync, all the Private records that existed when you last HotSynced will be restored, and you'll be able to view them. But any Private records entered since your last HotSync are gone forever.

Delete Password

⚠ **Deleting a forgotten password will remove all records marked Private. Previously synchronized private records will be restored at the next HotSync operation. Do you wish to proceed?**

[Yes] [No]

Figure 8.16 The Palm reads you its riot act.

Locking up your Palm

Palm calls it "locking the device" and that's just what it does. A locked Palm won't let anyone past the password screen unless they know the password. What if you lose your Palm at the airport, in a taxi, or leave it on a sushi counter? You will wish that you'd locked it, of course, so that no one can use it or, perhaps more importantly, see any of your data.

To lock your Palm, first make sure you have assigned a password (the Palm won't let you lock it unless have). Then, in the Security program, tap Turn Off & Lock Device. The System Lockout screen appears (**Figure 8.17**). Tap Off & Lock.

Your Palm's screen goes blank. When you turn it on again, another System Lockout screen appears, which shows the Owner information you entered in Chapter 2 and asks for the password. So, not only will someone who finds your locked Palm be unable to use it, they will see your contact information, which will prompt them to call you or send it to you. Hopefully.

Forgotten password on a locked Palm: If you turn off your Palm and lock it and then forget your password, you have only one course of action, and it is an ugly one: You have to do a hard reset (see the end of Chapter 2 for how). After a hard reset, your Palm will start up normally, but it will have erased everything you ever entered into it—not just your Private records, *everything*—and returned it to the state it was in the day it left the factory.

However, all is not lost, thanks to Hot-Sync. You can still recover the data you had in the built-in programs by performing a HotSync. When you HotSync, your computer refills your Palm with everything that was on it during your last Hot-Sync. If you had data in your add-on programs, you may not be able to restore that data unless you've been using Backup Buddy (see Chapter 11 for more on Backup Buddy).

Figure 8.17 You do remember your password, don't you?

Calculator

The Palm's Calculator program is a real no-brainer, with no frills, no thrills. You already know how to use it, most likely—just like you would any simple calculator (**Figure 8.18**). But there are a few things about Calculator worth mentioning.

Figure 8.18 Yep, it's a calculator all right.

Unless your fingers are the size of my high school shop teacher's, you can probably use Calculator without the stylus. You can also use Graffiti to enter numbers, but only masochists would do that.

Using calculations in other programs

You can use whatever numbers appear in the Calculator's screen in your other Palm programs using the Copy and Paste commands. For example, you might divide up your share of a bill for a business dinner using Calculator and then copy that number into the Expense item. And you can paste numbers from other programs (again, probably Expense) into Calculator, crunch some numbers, and then paste the result somewhere else. Calculator's menus are in the usual place, under the Menu icon.

The M and C buttons

You may have seen the M buttons (M+, MR, and MC) on calculators but not really understood what they do.

M + : This button adds the currently displayed number to a subtotal stored in the Palm's memory. Think of M + as your back pocket. You can calculate some numbers, tap M + to put the result in your back pocket, and then tap C to clear the decks for another calculation. When you tap M + again, you add whatever number is onscreen to the number in your back pocket.

MR: MR stands for Memory Recall. Tap this button to see what's in your back pocket.

MC: MC stands for Memory Clear. It clears whatever was in your back pocket and resets it to 0.

CE: CE stands for Clear Entry. If make a boo-boo while typing, tap CE to clear the number and start over where you were in the calculation before you entered the wrong number.

C: Clear resets the display to 0.

part three

Connecting with Your Computer

Aside from the brilliance of the Palm device itself, the simplicity and elegance of its HotSync and Palm Desktop programs are a couple of reasons the Palm is so much more popular than other handheld computers. It's just incredibly easy to synchronize the data in your Palm with that in your computer's in a HotSync session. The Palm Desktop duplicates the four main programs you've been using on your Palm—it's like having another Palm on your desktop or laptop. It doesn't matter if you made some changes in your Palm or in Palm Desktop, because HotSync brings them up to date with each other across the board.

The Windows and Macintosh versions of the HotSync and Palm Desktop differ so significantly that I thought it best to address them into two separate chapters. They do pretty much the same things, just differently. If you use a Windows machine, read Chapter 9 to learn about HotSyncing and the Palm Desktop; if you use a Mac, read Chapter 10. We'll all meet up again in Chapter 11, where you learn to install Palm add-on programs regardless of which kind of computer you have, and get some hints on which programs are worth installing.

Windows HotSync and Palm Desktop

HotSyncing is what happens when you place your Palm in its cradle and it has a conversation with your PC. They ask each other "Do you have anything new?" and if one of them does, it transfers the information to the other one, so that they are both synchronized. The transfer usually consists of data records from the main built-in programs—such as contact info in Address Book or tasks in To Do List. HotSyncing is also the way you add new Palm programs you've purchased or downloaded from the Internet (Chapter 11 has more on installing add-on programs and reviews many of them).

The Palm Windows software is free and is located on the CD-ROM that shipped with your Palm. The Palm Desktop and HotSync Manager are the two Windows applications you have to install in order to HotSync your PC and your Palm.

HotSync Basics

There are two main kinds of HotSync: Local and Modem.

Local HotSync

When you perform a Local HotSync, you're HotSyncing your Palm and PC directly using the cradle, and that's what you'll learn to do in this chapter. If you're like most Palm users, this probably the only kind you'll ever need to do, so if I just say "HotSync," I mean a Local HotSync.

Modem HotSync

A Modem HotSync means you HotSync by dialing from a modem connected to your Palm over the phone lines to a modem connected to your PC. (See Chapter 12 for more on using modems with your Palm.) The modem attached to your Palm can be either the Palm modem accessory or a computer modem you can hook up to your Palm using a special adapter available for purchase from 3Com or other vendors.

Modem HotSyncs can come in handy if you're traveling and need to HotSync with your computer at home or the office. It involves hooking up a modem to your Palm and then dialing in to your computer, whose modem is set up to answer your Palm's call.

I suspect that not many people actually use Modem HotSyncs very often, because with so many steps the complications outweigh the benefits—besides, you can always HotSync when you get back home or to the office. Modem HotSyncs are fraught with complications and possibilities for errors, and are really beyond the scope of this little book. Your Palm's Handbook *contains some instructions on performing a Modem HotSync. I do discuss the basics of Modem HotSyncing in Chapter 12, which also covers using modems to connect your Palm to the Internet.*

Regardless of the type of HotSyncing you do, the first time you HotSync your Palm and your computer, you have to do so by a Local HotSync because there is some more setup that cannot be completed over a phone line.

HotSyncing after a hard reset

If for some reason you've had to resort to a hard reset, erasing all the data on your Palm, you can refill it with the data that has been HotSynced previously. HotSyncing after a hard reset can restore your Palm to the state it was in the last time you HotSynced, before you did the hard reset. To do this, you put your Palm in its cradle and HotSync as you normally do, except you set up HotSync to make your computer's files overwrite your Palm's (you'll learn how to do that in this chapter). Your computer then restores all your addresses, To Do items, Date Book entries, and memos to your Palm.

> **Other kinds of HotSyncs**
>
> Actually, there are other ways to HotSync your Palm to your computer, two of which are called Network and Remote Access HotSyncs. These are for people who need to HotSync over their corporate network or via the network's remote access software. In a Network HotSync, you can connect your Palm's cradle to any computer on the network and HotSync with your computer. Your network server must be running TCP/IP software, and your computer must be turned on and running HotSync Manager. A Remote Access HotSync lets you dial in with your Palm from home and HotSync with your computer at work. You'll need to ask your network administrator for details on setting up Network and Remote Access HotSyncs.

Cradles

The Palm III, IIIx, IIIe, and VII all use the same kind of cradle. In other words, if you upgrade from a Palm III to a Palm VII, you can use either Palm in the same cradle to HotSync. A new cradle comes with every new Palm, so you probably won't ever have to ever test this. Same goes for modems and other accessories too—if they work for a Palm III, IIIe, or IIIx, they'll work for a Palm VII.

The Palm V cradle is another story. Because the Palm V has a different design, its cradle has a different design, and that means you can't use it with any other kind of Palm, nor can you use another model of cradle with the Palm V. Same with modems. This is the downside of that sleekness and coolness you love about your Palm V—its accessories are not compatible with the rest of the Palm family.

Preparing to HotSync

Make sure your computer is off and connect the cradle to the serial port in the back of your computer. If you don't have a free 9-pin serial port in the back of your computer, you will have to use the adapter that came with your Palm to attach it to a free 25-pin serial port. The "Getting Started" pamphlet that came with your Palm has very clear instructions for doing this.

When the cradle is connected, turn on the computer. Leave your Palm aside for now—you'll be told when to place it in the cradle.

 Palm V cradles also have an AC adapter. You already learned how to connect your AC adapter in Chapter 1 in order to charge the Palm V battery.

Installing the software

Put the Windows CD-ROM into your CD-ROM drive. The Setup program should start up by itself. If it doesn't, in My Computer or Windows Explorer, navigate to your CD-ROM drive and double-click the Setup file.

When the Setup program appears, click Install (**Figure 9.1**). The Quick Tour is a multimedia presentation showing what you can do with a Palm—if you're this far in the book, you don't need this tour. Help Notes contains good additional information, but you can read that later straight from the CD-ROM (they are text files in the Helpnote folder).

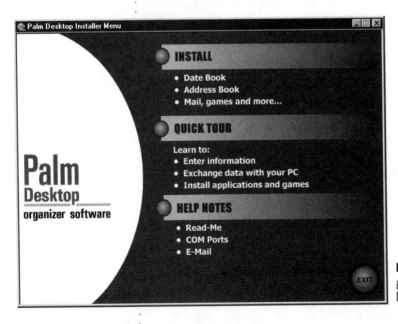

Figure 9.1 Click Install to go straight to the installation setup program.

Follow the instructions onscreen. I recommend that you select Typical rather than Custom installation and leave the Destination folder as C:\Palm. When prompted, put your Palm in its cradle. Click OK to make the Setup software automatically detect your cradle.

If Setup can't find your cradle, you may have to manually choose a COM port from two or more choices. Try COM 1 first.

If you have Microsoft Outlook on your computer, Setup will detect it and ask you whether you want to use Outlook or Palm Desktop as your Personal Information Manager (PIM). If you use Outlook regularly and like it, you may want to select Outlook and have Setup install only the conduit software that will let you use Outlook as your Palm's PIM. For space reasons, this book assumes you want to use Palm Desktop as your PIM.

The Palm IIIe doesn't include the Outlook conduit software. Palm IIIe users have to use Palm Desktop as their PIM.

If you have a Palm VII, Setup shows you a screen where you can elect to install additional query applications (**Figure 9.2**). Query applications are the special Palm VII programs that you can use to connect wirelessly to various information services. Click some boxes to put check marks next to any that you may be interested in and click Next. Only install what you think you'll use, because they do take up space on your Palm VII (obviously, if you're not a Bank of America customer, that one won't do you much good). While you're here, you may as well install some now and give them a test drive. You can always install or delete any of them later, after you're finished

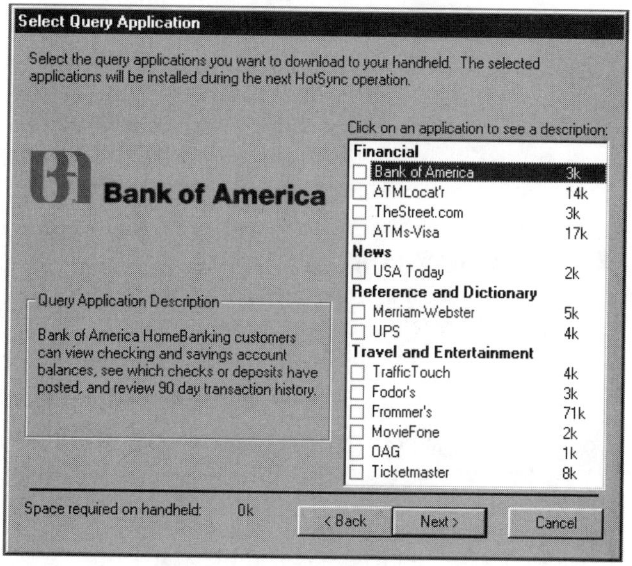

Figure 9.2 Select any additional Palm VII programs you'd like to install and try out.

with Setup. Palm VII Setup also offers you some information on the difference between the Palm programs iMessenger and Mail, which you can view if you want.

Click Finish. You are sent back to the Windows Desktop, where you will see two new icons: HotSync Manager and Palm Desktop.

 The HotSync Manager will always appear from now on in your Windows Start bar at the far right, along the bottom of your screen. When you see the HotSync Manager, you know you are ready to HotSync at any time, as long as your cradle is connected and the Palm is in it. By default, HotSync Manager is installed in such a way that it always starts up whenever you start your computer.

The other icon shows up as a new shortcut called Palm Desktop, the program that gives you Windows versions of the Palm's main programs and stores their data on your PC. You'll learn how to use Palm Desktop later in this chapter.

Your first HotSync

You are now ready to HotSync your Palm and your PC. Make sure the Palm is in its cradle and that you see the HotSync icon in the bottom right-hand corner of your computer screen. Your Palm doesn't even have to be turned on, because starting the HotSync will turn it on.

Press the HotSync button on the cradle. It's hard to miss, since there's only one button.

Cradleless HotSyncing

If you travel a lot and don't feel like bringing that bulky cradle everywhere you go, you can buy a HotSync cable from Palm or other vendor. It does the same thing as a cradle, but it's just a cable that attaches to your Palm's serial port and connects to your laptop or desktop computer. The cable doesn't have a HotSync button, so to start the HotSync using the cable you have to tap the HotSync icon and then tap Local HotSync.

You'll hear bright little chirping notes, and on your Palm you'll see the HotSync screen (**Figure 9.3**).

Then, on your computer, you'll see a Users screen, where you have to select a user (**Figure 9.4**). What you enter here will become the way your computer identifies your Palm device.

Each Palm that HotSyncs with your computer must have a unique user name, or things can get discombobulated. So if another Palm ever HotSyncs with your computer, it must use a different name.

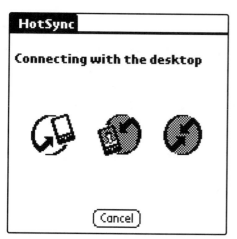

Figure 9.3 Your Palm is connecting to your computer.

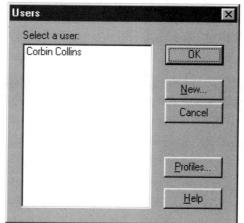

Figure 9.4 Choose or enter your Palm's user name.

On your computer, select or enter the unique user name that you will use only for this Palm. A screen will appear on your Palm, asking you to reset it by tapping Reset. When you tap the Reset button, your Palm restarts.

You have successfully set up Local HotSyncing for your Palm and computer. The data in your Palm has been transferred and synchronized with the new Windows program, Palm Desktop.

If you had trouble or if the HotSync didn't work, run the installation again and choose a different COM port.

HotSync Manager

Move the mouse pointer over the HotSync Manager icon at the bottom right-hand corner of your computer screen and click the right mouse button (if you only have one mouse button, press Ctrl as you click). A list of choices pops up, as shown in **Figure 9.5**.

Figure 9.5
HotSync Manager has a rather minimal interface—this is all there is to it.

As you can see, HotSync is currently set up for Local HotSyncing. You should leave this setting alone—unless you've read Chapter 12 and have set up your Palm modem and want to perform a Modem HotSync, or you have your network's system administrator by your side and want to set up a Network HotSync.

Setup

Click Setup in the list of choices. The Setup dialog box appears (**Figure 9.6**). It has four tabs and is open to the General tab. Here is where you can change when HotSync Manager runs. If you want HotSync Manager to run only when you are running Palm Desktop, click the "Available only when Palm Desktop is running" radio button. If you want to have to start HotSync Manager yourself every time, click the "Manual" radio button. Unless HotSync Manager seems to be causing problems in the way your computer runs, there's no need to change this setting. If it's always running, then you're always ready to HotSync your Palm.

You can ignore the Modem and Network tabs (unless your network's system administrator asks you to do something with them). Click the Local tab (**Figure 9.7**). If you're having trouble getting HotSync to work, try a different port by clicking the drop-down arrow next to Serial Port and selecting a different COM port. If everything is working fine, leave everything as it is.

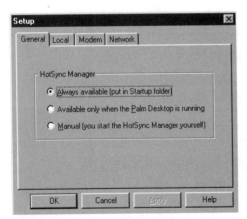

Figure 9.6 The General tab of the Setup dialog box lets you make changes in HotSync Manager's operation.

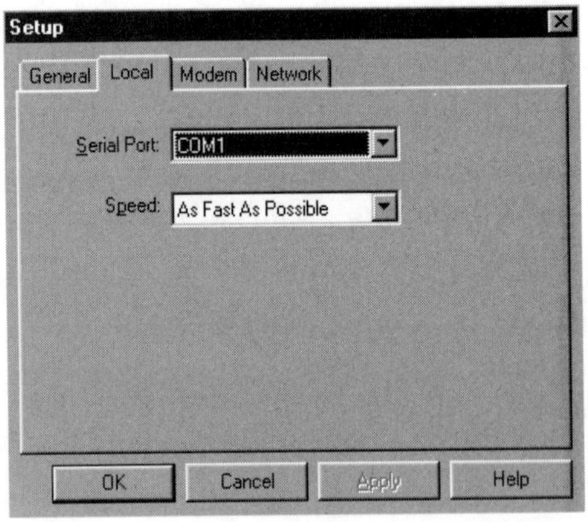

Figure 9.7 The Local tab lets you change your port settings.

Conduits: changing HotSync actions

Each Palm program requires a conduit in order to synchronize its data with your PC. A conduit is a piece of software that handles the HotSync details for that program. The main Palm programs all have their own conduits, and there are conduits for other aspects of HotSyncing, such as your Palm System preferences, and for other programs, such as Mail. A conduit can perform three actions:

- Have your PC and your Palm bring each other up to date. If anything changes on either machine since the last Hot-Sync, both machines will now reflect the changes.

- Have the information in your PC overwrite the information in your Palm. Whatever was on your Palm will be deleted and replaced by what was on your PC.

- Have the information in your Palm overwrite the information in your PC. Whatever was on your PC will be deleted and replaced by what was on your Palm.

Click Custom in the HotSync Manager popup list to see the Custom dialog box (**Figure 9.8**). This screen lists what each conduit is set up to do.

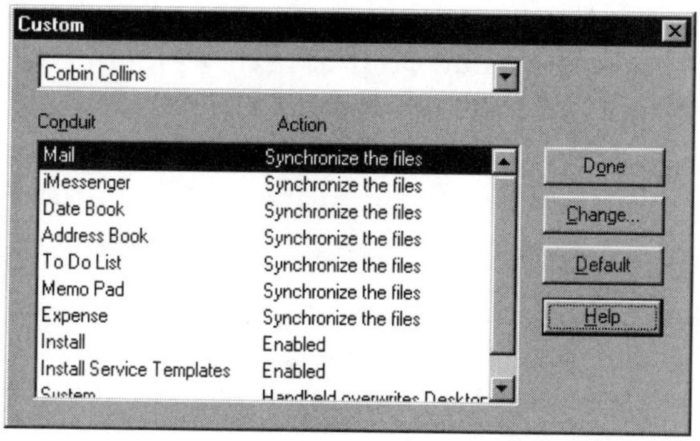

Figure 9.8 The Custom tab is where you can see which direction HotSync will flow between your Palm and your computer for each of your conduits.

Most of the time, just leave these actions alone. However, there are times when you want your PC's data to overwrite whatever is in your Palm, or vice versa. Or you may want nothing to happen for a particular application when you HotSync. To change the action of a conduit, double-click it. The Change HotSync Action dialog box appears (**Figure 9.9**). Click on the appropriate radio button to change the action. Clicking the "Set as default" box makes that action the default action for the conduit from now on—leave it unchecked if what you are doing is a one-time action. When you're all set, click OK.

After a hard reset, you want the information in your PC to overwrite the information in your Palm, and here's where you specify that by clicking the "Desktop overwrite hand-held" radio button. That's how you restore information to a blank Palm.

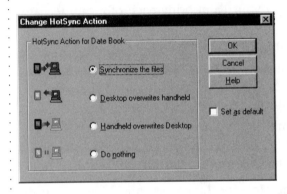

Figure 9.9 Change the action for a conduit in the Change HotSync Action dialog box.

File Link

The File Link feature lets you automatically pull information out of a periodically updated file on your network. For example, your company may post a new staff list every month with all the new people's phone extensions, email addresses, and so on. If you want to use File Link to import data into Palm Desktop and your Palm, you'll have to set it up with your system administrator.

Conveniently, all of these HotSync options are also available in Palm Desktop under the HotSync menu.

Palm Desktop

You've been hearing about Palm Desktop for several pages now. To start it, double-click the Palm Desktop icon (shown in **Figure 9.10**).

Figure 9.10 The Palm Desktop icon is located on the Windows Desktop.

Palm Desktop launches (**Figure 9.11**). Note the buttons that correspond to the main programs on your Palm: Date Book, Address Book, To Do List, Memo Pad, and Expense. The first four of these buttons launch the different Palm Desktop modules that synchronize data with the corresponding programs on your Palm.(Expense is covered in Chapter 8, and Install in Chapter 11.) If you added data in your Palm before the Hot-Sync you performed a few pages ago, that data will be there in the Palm Desktop, too. And if you now add data to Palm Desktop's modules, during your next HotSync, the data is sent to your Palm.

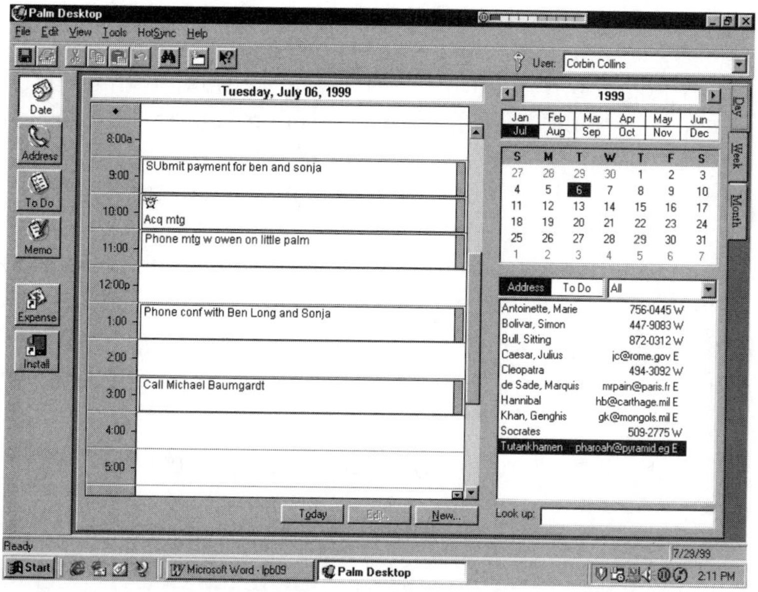

Figure 9.11 The Palm Desktop, with its buttons for each of the main, built-in Palm programs, puts your Palm's data on your PC.

The Palm Desktop is a large, full-fledged Windows application. Covering all the features and nuances of it could fill a book of its own, and this wouldn't be *The Little Palm Book* anymore. So instead, I'll try to give you some tips on doing the most useful things in each module.

Like the Palm's Date Book program, Palm Desktop opens to today's Daily view in the Date Book module. Your PC's screen is much bigger than your Palm's, and Palm Desktop doesn't waste it. As you can see in **Figure 9.11**, it also shows you this month's calendar and has a window at the bottom with your Address Book entries and alternatively, if you click To Do, your To Do List items.

Click on any day in that calendar to jump to that day.

Palm Desktop tips

- Use Palm Desktop to do any kind of mass entering of information into your Palm. Assuming you're at least a barely competent typist, it's much, much faster to type a large amount of stuff into Palm Desktop and then Hot-Sync it to your Palm than to plod along entering it directly with Graffiti (no offense to Graffiti, but facts are facts). For example, if you need to enter all the contact information from your little black book or Rolodex into your Palm, *definitely* do that in Palm Desktop Address Book module.

- Click the Find button on the toolbar to find any text in Palm Desktop. It works just like the Find icon on your Palm.

- Click Print to print out anything in Palm Desktop. You will usually be offered a few formatting options to choose from.

- Access the HotSync options by clicking the HotSync menu.

- The familiar Edit tools are in the Edit menu, ready to copy, cut, paste, and delete data.

Date Book

3Com obviously thinks Date Book is pretty important, since it comes up right off the bat, so let's start with that one.

You can make Palm Desktop start up with any of the four main modules, not just Date Book. Click Tools > Options and select the one you want to see when Palm Desktop starts up.

Views

Note the tabs along the right side: Day, Week, and Month. The Day view tab is selected by default. Click on the Week view tab, and the whole screen changes into one big week (**Figure 9.12**).

To fit everything into the time slots, the Date Book module clips off the end of the descriptions of some events. To view the rest of the text, double-click the gray bar beside the event—more on that in a minute.

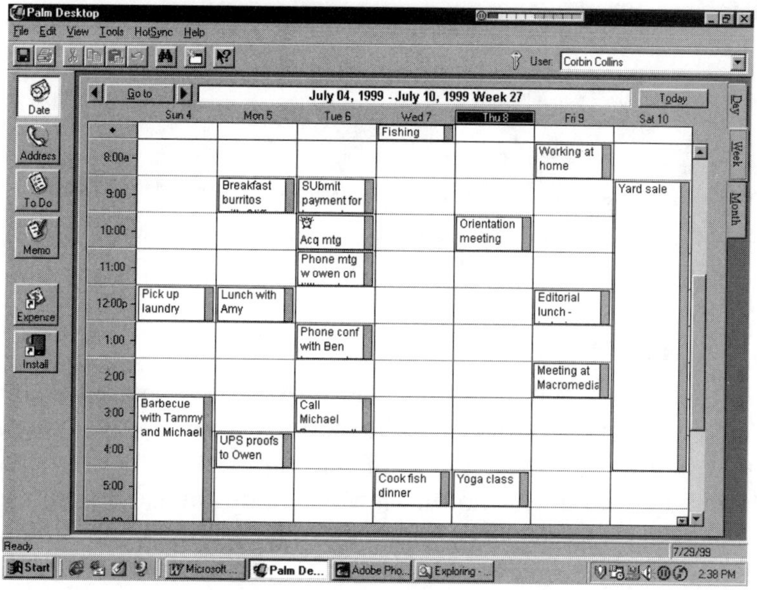

Figure 9.12 Your week at a glance is available when you click the Week view tab.

Click the Month view tab to turn your screen into a giant monthly calendar (**Figure 9.13**). Double-click on any day to bring that day into the Day view.

In Day view, above the mini-address list, you'll see a drop-down box labeled All. That's your category list. Click it to select a category (Business, Personal, and so on). Select Edit Categories to edit, delete, or create Date Book categories.

To show or hide Private records, click the View menu and put a check beside either "Show Private Records" or "Hide Private Records."

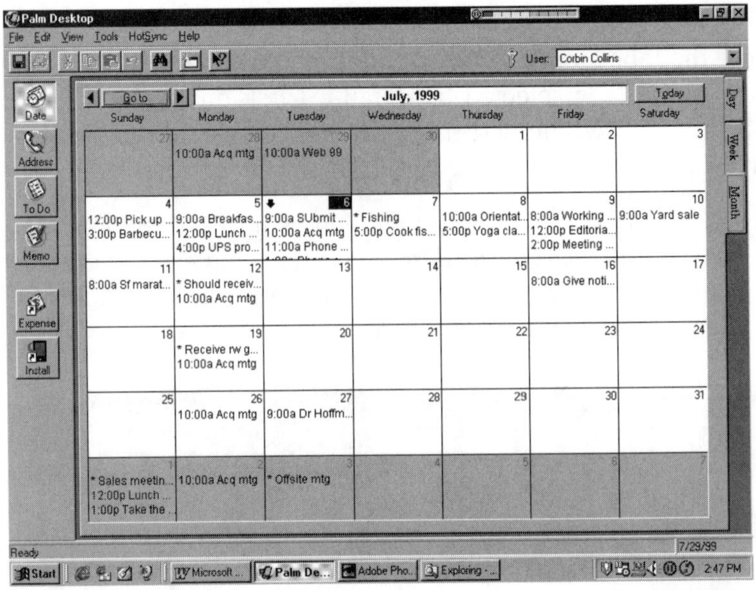

Figure 9.13 The month view lets you read actual events rather than just see gray bars, as it does on your Palm.

Figure 9.14 The arrows and Go To button make it easy to skip around the Date Book module.

Navigation

In the Week and Month views, arrows at the top of the screen surround a Go To button (**Figure 9.14**). Click on the arrows to skip ahead one week in Week view, one month in Month view. Click on the Go To button itself to select a week or month, depending on which view you're in.

Less usefully, in Day view, arrows at the top of the screen around the year (1999) haul you backward or forward one year from that day. Then again, Day view also has that sub-calendar where you can easily jump to the month and day you want.

Also in Week and Month views, there is a Today button at the top right that will always send you back to today in Day view. In Day view, the Today button is at the bottom of the screen and sends you back to today, no matter which day you were viewing.

Creating an event

Creating an event in Palm Desktop works almost exactly the same as on your Palm. Go to Day view and click New. The Edit Event dialog box appears (**Figure 9.15**). In this box, you can enter a description of the event, start and end times (click the little clock to select the times), and the date of the event (click the calendar to browse dates). You can also attach a Note, make it a repeating event, set an alarm, or make the event Private—just like you do in Date Book in your Palm (see Chapter 4).

Figure 9.15 You can create new events right in Palm Desktop. After you Hot-Sync, the events will show up in your Palm.

If you right-click on an existing event, you can choose to delete, attach a Note, set an alarm, or edit the event.

Address Book

Click on the Address Book button in Palm Desktop to launch the Address Book module. The Palm Desktop screen changes to show the Address Book entries (**Figure 9.16**). One entry is selected, and its details are shown in a pane on the right-hand side of the screen. Address Book opens to show entries in all categories by default. Click the drop-down arrow labeled All to show only a particular category, or to edit, create, or delete categories.

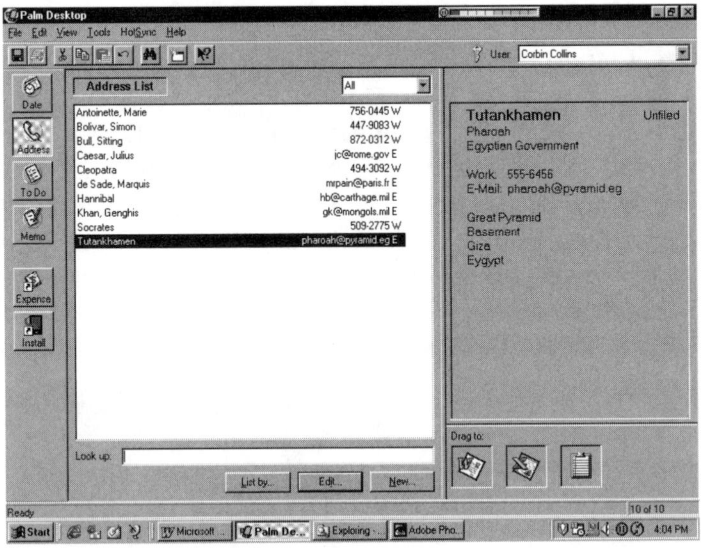

Figure 9.16 The Windows version of the familiar Address Book appears when you click the Address Book button.

Click on a different entry to see its details appear in the right-hand pane.

Adding and editing entries

To edit an entry, click the Edit button at the bottom of the screen. The Edit Address dialog box pops up, where you can make any kind of changes or additions to it as you like (**Figure 9.17**). Click the Address tab to enter or change postal address information, and click on the Note tab to create a Note.

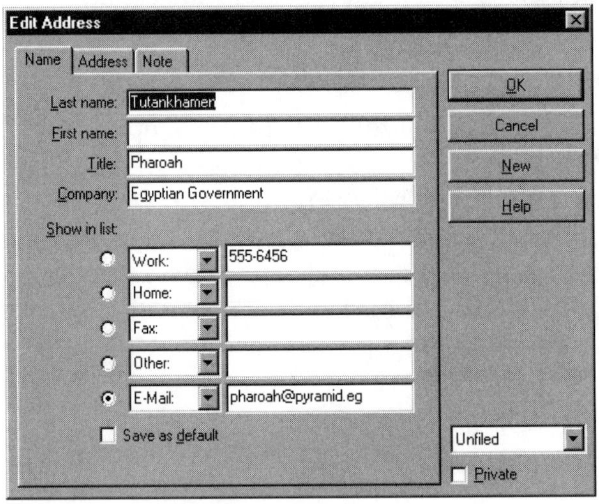

Figure 9.17 Edit your Address Book entries here—it's much easier than doing it on your Palm with Graffiti.

To create a new entry, click the New button in Address List. The same Edit Address dialog box pops up, except this time it's blank.

Address Book tips

- In the Edit Address dialog box, click on a radio button under "Show in List" to make that information appear in the Address List on your PC and your Palm. In **Figure 9.17**, the radio button next to "E-Mail" is selected, and that's why pharoah@pyramid.eg. is shown in the Address List instead of a phone number.

- Click the Private box to mark the item Private. Private entries are transferred between your PC and Palm just like other entries. To show or hide Private records, click the View menu and choose either "Show Private Records" or "Hide Private Records."

- You can change how entries are sorted by clicking the List by button in Address List. Your choices are to sort by last name, first name (Collins, Corbin) or by company, last name (Peachpit Press, Collins).

- Select an entry in Address List and then click Edit > Dial. Palm Desktop awakens the Windows Phone Dialer, and if your computer is connected to a phone line, it calls the phone number shown in the list! Phone Dialer must already be set up, and your computer must be connected to a modem on the same line as your phone.

Dragging addresses into Word, Excel or the Clipboard

If you have Microsoft Word or Excel, you can drag Address Book entries over to the icons at the bottom right-hand section of your screen (**Figure 9.18**), the appropriate program will launch and display the address in ways that you can customize. (The third icon will deposit the address into the Windows Clipboard, and from there you can paste it into any application.) This is a handy way to save time that you would otherwise spend typing out or copying and pasting addresses into letters, mailing labels, and envelopes. Just click on an address in Address List, drag the item across the screen, and drop it onto one of the icons.

Figure 9.18 You can drag Address Book entries onto the Word, Excel, and Clipboard icons.

If you drop an address onto the Microsoft Word icon, Word starts up and a Word macro asks you how you want the address to be formatted. Similar deal with Excel. If you drag it onto the Clipboard icon, it may look as if nothing happens, but rest assured, your address is in the Windows Clipboard, ready to paste into another application.

To Do List

Like the Palm program, Palm Desktop's To Do List is pretty simple. Click the To Do button to launch the module (**Figure 9.19**). Your tasks are listed in the left-hand side of the screen, and the details of a selected task are shown on the right (click on a task to select it). At the top of the To Do List is the category drop-down list, where you choose which of your To Do categories will appear in the list.

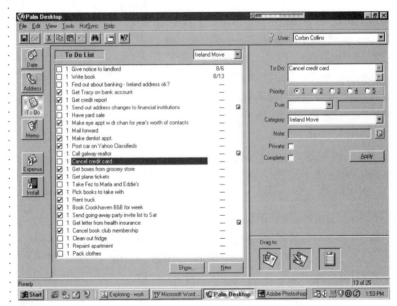

Figure 9.19 The To Do List module in Palm Desktop.

Editing and creating To Do items

The detail pane on the right-hand side of the screen is where you edit tasks. Click on a task to bring its info into the detail pane. You can change your task's description, priority, due date, and category. You can also attach Notes, mark items complete, and mark items private. Click apply to make your changes appear in the To Do List.

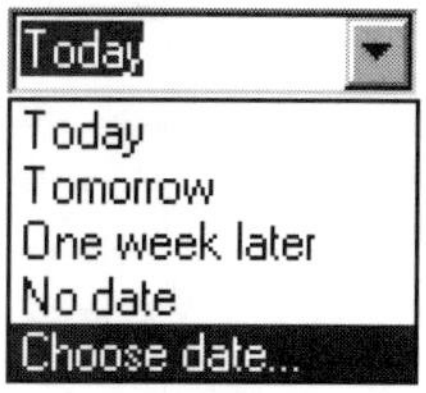

Change the due date by clicking on the Due drop-down arrow. A little list pops up offering a few choices (**Figure 9.20**). You can also click directly on a task's due date column in To Do List to bring up the same choices.

Note icons in To Do List indicate the presence of a Note. A Note's contents appear in the right-hand side of the screen when its To Do item is selected. To edit a Note, click on a task's Note icon, as you do in the Palm, and the Note Editor appears (**Figure 9.21**). To add a new Note to a selected task, click on the Note icon in the task's detail pane.

Right-click an item and click Delete to delete it.

Changing what To Do List displays

Click the Show button at the bottom of the To Do List screen to make the Show Options dialog box appear (**Figure 9.22**). This dialog box offers exactly the same options as the To Do preferences do in your Palm.

Figure 9.20 Pick a new due date or create one by tapping the Due drop-down arrow.

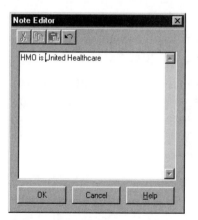

Figure 9.21 Edit Notes in the Note Editor.

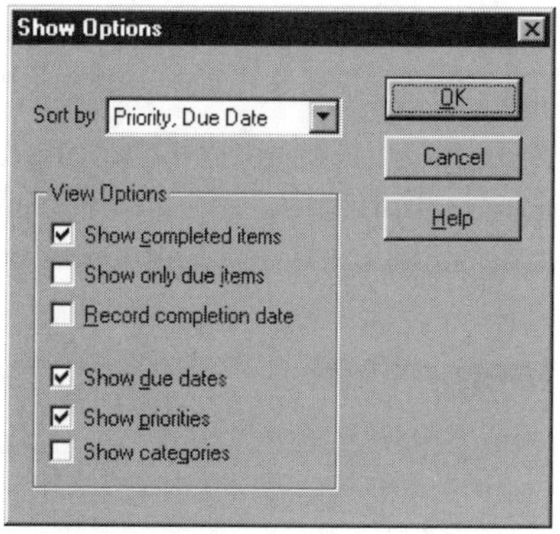

Figure 9.22 Show Options lets you change what To Do List shows onscreen.

Dragging tasks into Word, Excel, and the Clipboard

As with Address Book (see earlier in this chapter), To Do List lets you open items in Microsoft Word or Excel by dragging them onto to icons in the bottom right-hand side of the To Do List screen. Drag one or more To Do List items to the Word icon to start the process. Microsoft Word will launch (if it is installed in your computer), and a pre-built Word macro will pop up a dialog box offering you three choices of formatting (see **Figure 9.23**):

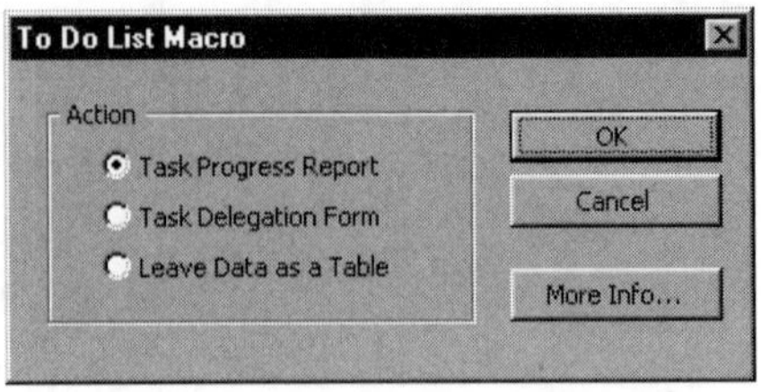

Figure 9.23 The To Do List Word macro automatically sets up your To Do items in a Word document in one of three ways.

- Task Progress Report: Formats your To Do items as a memo you can submit to your boss.

- Task Delegation Form: Formats your To Do items as an assignment with check boxes that you can hand to someone else, such as someone who reports to you.

- Leave Data as Table: Simply creates a Word table filled with your To Do List items, which you can format however you want.

Dragging items to the Excel icon launches Excel and opens your data in a simple spreadsheet (**Figure 9.24**).

Dragging items to the Clipboard icon puts them into the Windows Clipboard, and from there you can paste them into any program that can accept pasted text.

Memo Pad

Memo Pad is even simpler than To Do List. As you've seen on your Palm, Memo Pad doesn't even qualify as a word processor—it is a very basic text editor. On the Palm Desktop, it almost surely becomes the most stripped-down text editor on your computer (it's even less sophisticated than Windows Notepad). Memo Pad can only open or create files that are around

800 words or less (a paltry 4K). Still, if you think of Palm Desktop's Memo Pad strictly as a fast way to enter text into your Palm, it does come in handy.

1	2	3	4	5	6	7
To Do List						
Item Description	Due Date	Priority	Completed	Note	Category	
Give notice to landlord	7/30/99	1	No		Ireland Move	
Write book	8/13/99	1	No		Ireland Move	
Find out about banking - Ireland address ok?		1	No		Ireland Move	
Get Tracy on bank account		1	Yes		Ireland Move	
Get credit report		1	Yes		Ireland Move	
Send out address changes to financial institutions		1	No	Banks, credit card, stocks	Ireland Move	
Have yard sale		1	No		Ireland Move	
Make eye appt w dr chan for year's worth of contacts		1	Yes		Ireland Move	
Mail forward		1	No		Ireland Move	
Make dentist appt.		1	Yes		Ireland Move	
Post car on Yahoo Classifieds		1	Yes		Ireland Move	
Call galway realtor		1	No	realtor@galway.net	Ireland Move	
Cancel credit card		1	No		Ireland Move	
Get boxes from grocery store		1	Yes		Ireland Move	
Get plane tickets		1	Yes		Ireland Move	
Take Fez to Marla and Eddie's		1	No		Ireland Move	
Pick books to take with		1	Yes		Ireland Move	
Rent truck		1	Yes		Ireland Move	
Book Crookhaven B&B for week		1	Yes		Ireland Move	
Send going-away party invite list to Sat		1	Yes		Ireland Move	
Get letter from health insurance		1	No	United Healthcare	Ireland Move	

Figure 9.24 The Excel version of your To Do List stuff.

Memo Pad basics

Click the Memo Pad button in Palm Desktop to make Memo Pad appear (**Figure 9.25**). You can see that your memos are listed in the left-hand window, and the selected memo's contents are displayed in a window on the right.

> *Click the List by button at the bottom of the screen to change the order in which Memo Pad sorts the memos. By default, your memos are shown onscreen in the order you have them on your Palm. Your other choice is alphabetically by title.*

Click the Category drop-down arrow in the right-hand window to change the current memo's category. The available categories that drop-down are, of course, the same Memo Pad categories you had on your Palm at the last HotSync. To create new categories or rename the old ones, choose Edit Categories.

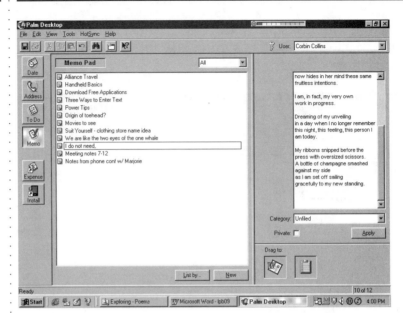

Figure 9.25 Click on an item on the left to reveal its contents on the right.

Click the Private box to mark a memo Private. Click the Apply button to make changes in the right-hand window appear in the list on the left.

Creating and editing memos

Obviously, if you have a lot of text to enter, it's faster to type it into Palm Desktop's Memo Pad than use Graffiti to enter it into your Palm. Click the New button to create a new memo. A blank line appears in the left-hand window, and a cursor starts bobbing in the blankness on the right. Just start typing to begin the memo.

Memo Pad automatically uses the memo's first line as the title—to change the title, add the new title on its own line at the beginning of the memo.

If your memo grows beyond the 4K limit, Memo Pad automatically breaks it into two memos. For the title of the second one, it uses the original title and tacks on a (2) on the end.

To edit a memo, just click on it in the left-hand screen and edit it in the one on the right.

Importing files from Word and other applications

A common question Palm users have is, How do I get my Word documents on my Palm? Luckily, Palm Desktop makes that pretty easy, because it imports text (.TXT) files and lets you save them as Memo Pad files, which you can HotSync to your Palm.

First, open the document(s) in Microsoft Word (or any other program that can save documents as text files) and save as a text file by choosing File > Save As and selecting Text Only from the "Save as type" drop-down list box (**Figure 9.26**). You'll lose all formatting, of course, such as font size, type styles (bold, italic, underline, etc.).

> *Because Windows gets some of its information about file types from a filename's extension, it's a good idea to add the filename extension .txt to the end of the filename in the Filename box. That habit has the added virtue of keeping your ".TXT" files easily distinguishable from your ".DOC" (Microsoft Word) files.*

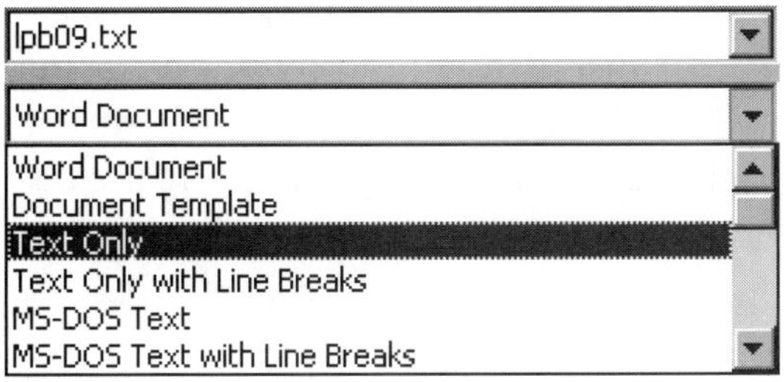

lpb09.txt

Word Document

Word Document
Document Template
Text Only
Text Only with Line Breaks
MS-DOS Text
MS-DOS Text with Line Breaks

Figure 9.26
Save your Word documents as "Text Only."

Then in Palm Desktop, click File > Import to open the Import dialog box and navigate to the folder where your text documents are. Click on the "Files of type" drop-down list box and select "Text (.txt)." That makes the Import dialog box display all your text files. Select the one you want to import and double-click it. The Specify Import Fields dialog box appears (**Figure 9.27**).

Unless you care about the category or making the memo private right off the bat, uncheck the Category and Private boxes but leave a check box next to Memo. Click OK. Your text file is now a Memo Pad file and shows up in the left-hand window, with its contents on the right. To get it into your Palm, do a HotSync.

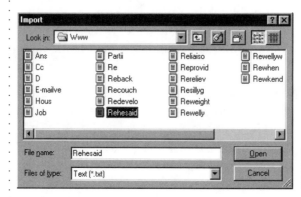

Figure 9.27
Importing a text file into Memo Pad.

What about that Expense button?

I cover creating an expense report from your Palm's Expense data in Chapter 8.

Dragging memos into Word and the Clipboard

Nothing fancy happens when you drag a memo onto the Word icon. Word launches, and the memo appears as a plainly formatted Word document that you can edit, format, and save where you like.

The only other major feature of Palm Desktop is the Install button, which is how you install new add-on software into Palm Desktop and then HotSync it into your Palm. Turn to Chapter 11 to learn about finding, installing, and using the best Palm add-on software.

Mac 10 HotSync and Palm Desktop

A HotSync is the process in which your Palm sits in its cradle and has a conversation with your Mac. They ask each other, "Do you have anything new?" and if one of them does, it transfers the information to the other one. The data transferred usually consists of records from the main built-in programs, such as appointments in Date Book or meeting notes in Memo Pad. HotSyncing is also how you install new add-on Palm programs that you purchase or download from the Internet (you'll learn more about installing add-on programs in Chapter 11).

Remember, the Palm software for the Windows platform is free and comes on a CD-ROM shipped with every Palm. Mac users have to purchase the MacPac 2 software separately (see Chapter 1 for an inventory of what comes with each platform and information on how Mac users can purchase the MacPac 2 software).

If you have an earlier version of the MacPac software, you can download a free upgrade to the MacPac 2 software from the Palm Web site at www.palm.com.

HotSync Basics

There are two primary types of HotSync: Local and Modem.

Local HotSync

A Local HotSync means you HotSync directly with the cradle to your Mac. This chapter shows you how to perform a local HotSync, which, if you're a typical Palm user, is probably the only kind of HotSync you'll ever need to do. In this book, if I just say "HotSync" I mean a Local HotSync.

The first time you HotSync, you must do a Local HotSync because there is some final setup that cannot be done over a modem.

Modem HotSync

A Modem HotSync means you HotSync by dialing from a modem connected to your Palm to a modem connected to your Mac. The modem attached to your Palm can be either the Palm modem accessory or a computer modem you can hook up to your Palm using a special adapter available for purchase from 3Com or other vendors (see the Accessory Catalog that came with your Palm).

A modem HotSync can come in handy if you're traveling and need to HotSync with your Mac back at home or the office. It involves hooking up a modem to your Palm (see Chapter 11), having a modem in your Mac, and having the Mac connected to a phone line in such a way that only the computer will answer the call you place through your Palm. I suspect that not many people actually use modem HotSyncing very often. Modem HotSyncs are fraught with complications and possibilities for errors, and are really beyond the

Other kinds of HotSyncs

Actually, there are other ways to HotSync your Palm to a computer, two of which are called Network and a Remote Access HotSyncs. These are for people who need to HotSync over their corporate network or via the network's remote access software. In a Network HotSync, you can connect your Palm's cradle to any computer on the network and HotSync with your computer. Your network server must be running Palm Desktop and TCP/IP software. A Remote Access HotSync lets you dial in with your Palm from home and HotSync with your computer at work. You'll need to ask your network administrator for details on setting up Network and Remote Access HotSyncs.

scope of this little book. Your Palm's *Handbook* contains some instructions on performing a Modem HotSync. I do discuss the basics of Modem HotSyncing in Chapter 12, which also covers using modems to connect your Palm to the Internet.

HotSyncing after a hard reset

If you had to hard reset your Palm—which means that all its data was erased—you can refill it with the data that is stored on your computer. HotSyncing after a hard reset can restore your Palm to the state it was in the last time you HotSynced before you did the hard reset. Put your Palm in its cradle and HotSync like you normally do, except you set up HotSync to make your Mac's files overwrite your Palm's (you'll learn how to do that in this chapter). Your computer then restores all your addresses, To Do items, Date Book entries, and memos that were deleted from your Palm during the hard reset.

Cradles

The Palm III, IIIx, IIIe, and VII all use the same kind of cradle. That is, if you have a Palm III and then buy a Palm VII, for example, you can use either Palm in either cradle to Hot-Sync. A new cradle comes with every new Palm, so you probably won't have to ever test this. This cross-compatibility goes for modems and other accessories too.

If you have Palm V, your cradle has a different design because your Palm has a different design, and you can't use your Palm V's cradle with any other kind of Palm. Same with modems. This is the only drawback to that sleekness and coolness you love about your Palm V—its accessories are not compatible with the rest of the Palm family.

Getting Ready to HotSync

To HotSync with your Mac, first you have to set up the Hot-Sync software. Your MacPac 2 software package came with a Macintosh adapter that you connect to the end of the cradle's cord. This adapter enables your Palm's cradle to plug into either your Mac's Modem port or Printer port. Pick one of these ports, and remember which one you picked because the Installer will ask you about it at some point in the installation.

Installing the MacPac 2 software

Make sure your Mac is turned off. Then connect the Macintosh adapter, which is attached to your cradle's cord, to either the Modem Port or Printer port in the back of your Mac. The "Getting Started" pamphlet that came with the MacPac 2 software shows you how to do this.

When the cradle is connected, turn on your Mac. Leave your Palm aside for now—you'll be told when to place it in the cradle.

 Palm V cradles are a little more complicated because they also have an AC adapter. You already learned how to connect your AC adapter in Chapter 1 in order to charge the Palm V battery.

Put the MacPac 2 CD-ROM into your CD-ROM drive. After a few seconds, the Palm MacPac v2 CD-ROM icon will appear on your desktop. Double-click the icon to open the MacPac window, which contains the four items shown in **Figure 10.1**.

The iMac and infrared HotSyncing

If you have one of the original iMacs that does not have any serial ports at all but does have an infrared (IR) port, you cannot HotSync the normal way (with the cradle). But all is not lost. Check out the Read Me First! file on the MacPac 2 CD-ROM for more information. It may be possible to HotSync your Palm and your iMac through the Palm's IR port, but you'll have to jump through configuration hoops to do it. Infrared HotSyncing is supposed to be easier with the the next Palm OS upgrade. The Palm Web site at www.palm.com also has more late-breaking information on the serialless iMac issue and infrared HotSyncing in general.

I recommend at least skimming through Read Me First! which is a SimpleText file that contains useful information about Palm software installation for the Macintosh. You should especially read this if you are upgrading from an older version of the MacPac software.

Double-click the Palm MacPac v2 Installer. The Read Me file appears again in a dialog box, in case you didn't read it before. Read it if you haven't done so and click Continue. Click Agree when you come to the End User License Agreement. Select Easy Install in the next window and click the Install button.

You will be asked where to install the software. If the default location of a new folder called Palm on your hard drive is okay with you, click Install. If you want to put the software someplace else, navigate there, select or create a folder, and click Install. You're probably better off letting the Installer create a fresh, new Palm folder. While the software installs, you are shown a series of tips and advertisements for 3Com.

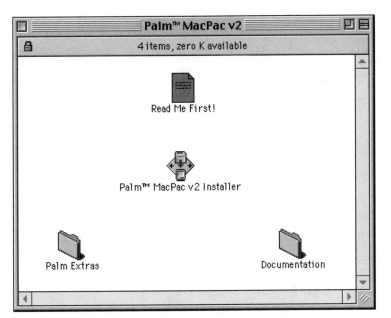

Figure 10.1 Inside the MacPac 2 CD-ROM window.

Finally, you'll see a screen that asks for two things: a User Name and which port you plugged the cradle into—either the Modem or the Printer port. Select the port you chose when you attached the cradle and click on it now.

> *What you enter as your User Name is important. The User Name becomes the way your Mac identifies your Palm device. If you only have one Palm, this is not such a big deal. Each Palm that HotSyncs with your Mac must have a unique user name, or things can get discombobulated. So if another Palm ever HotSyncs with your computer, it must use a different User Name.*

Enter the User Name which you will use for only this Palm. Click Save & Restart. Your Mac will restart. After it does, you'll see a new Palm window open on your Desktop (**Figure 10.2**). You have successfully installed the Palm MacPac 2 software.

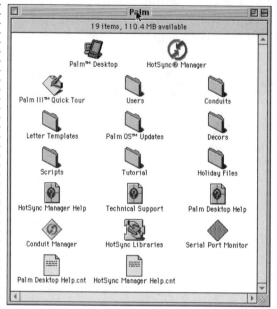

Figure 10.2 Here's what's inside the Palm folder, where all the Palm action happens on your Mac.

HotSyncing for the first time

Place your Palm in its cradle and press the HotSync button (the only button on the cradle). HotSync screens appear simultaneously on your Palm and on your Mac. The one on your Mac is shown in **Figure 10.3.**

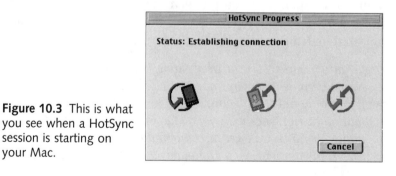

Figure 10.3 This is what you see when a HotSync session is starting on your Mac.

Soon, a dialog box appears and asks you to select your User Name. The one you entered during Setup is already entered as your choice. Leave it there and click OK. The HotSync process continues as the data on your Palm and Mac flows back and forth, synchronizing with each other. When it's finished, the HotSync window disappears. A screen appears on your Palm, asking you to reset it by tapping Reset. When you tap the Reset button, your Palm restarts.

You have successfully set up Local HotSyncing for your Palm and computer. The data in your Palm has been transferred and synchronized with the program Palm Desktop.

If the HotSync didn't work, try connecting the cradle to the other port. Remember to choose that port when prompted during the installation.

HotSync Manager

The HotSync Manager is where you control different aspects of the HotSync process on your Mac. Double-click the HotSync Manager icon in the Palm window to start it up. HotSync Manager launches and opens the HotSync Software Setup screen. The program has two tabs, the HotSync Controls tab and the Serial Port Settings tab. **Figure 10.4** shows the HotSync Controls tab.

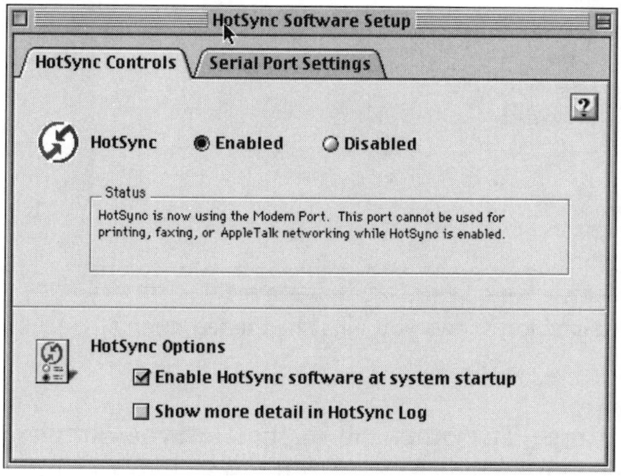

Figure 10.4 The HotSync Controls tab of the HotSync Software Setup screen.

HotSync Controls: Click the radio buttons to make HotSync Enabled or Disabled on the chosen serial port. By default, Hot-Sync is enabled, but if you need to use that serial port for something else, you can disable it here.

There are two HotSync options available in the lower half of the dialog box. By default, "Enable HotSync software at system startup" is checked so that every time your start your Mac, you are ready to HotSync automatically. Check "Show more detail in HotSync log" if you want the HotSync log to show a more detailed description of what transpired during your last HotSync. The log is a file that HotSync manager creates every time you HotSync. An example of a log appears in **Figure 10.5**. To show the log, in HotSync Manager click the HotSync menu and then click Log.

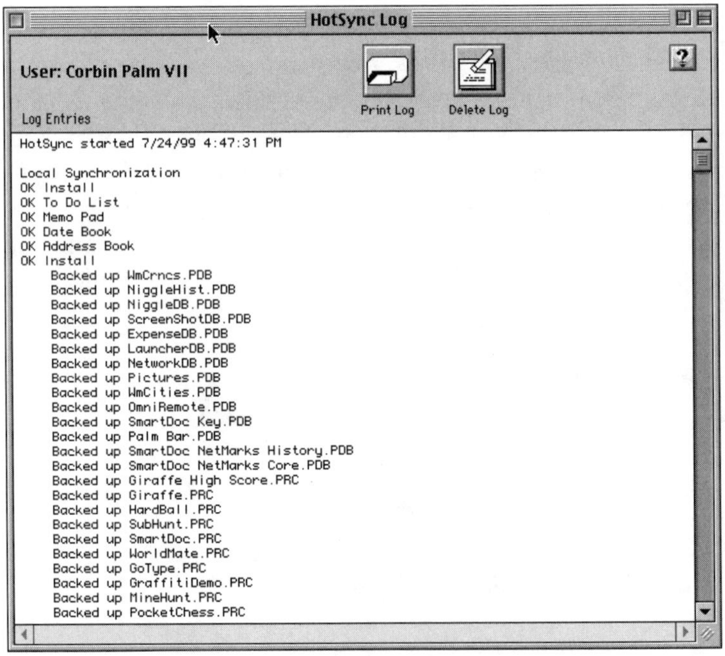

Figure 10.5 A HotSync log shows you what happened during your last HotSync.

Serial Port Settings: The other tab in the HotSync Software Setup screen lets you make changes to the serial port settings (see **Figure 10.6**). You probably don't need to mess with these.

The speed settings should already be optimized to transfer data as fast as possible and to use the serial port you selected.

> *You will need to click the Modem Setup radio button if you plan to try a modem HotSync, as that makes your Mac "listen" for a call from your Palm's modem over a phone line.*

The PalmOS 3.3 upgrade includes performance enhancements that can cut your HotSync time in half.

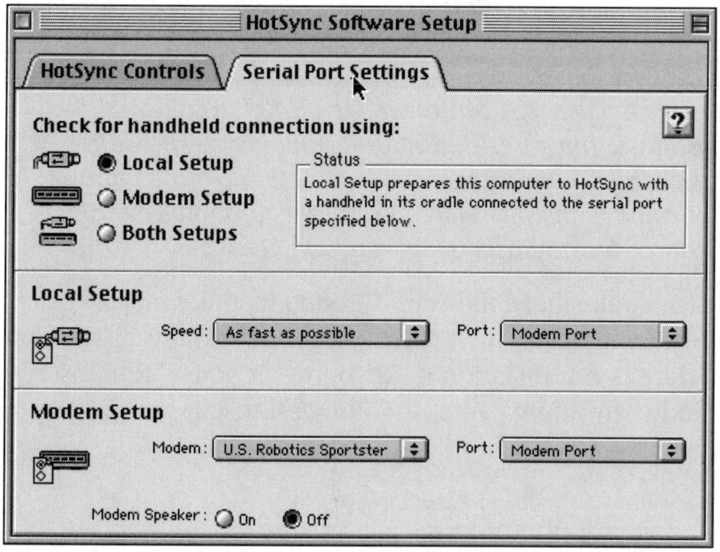

3.3

HotSync Software Setup

/ **HotSync Controls** \ / **Serial Port Settings** \

Check for handheld connection using: [?]

○ ● **Local Setup**
□ ○ **Modem Setup**
□ ○ **Both Setups**

─ Status ─
Local Setup prepares this computer to HotSync with a handheld in its cradle connected to the serial port specified below.

Local Setup

Speed: [As fast as possible ▼]   Port: [Modem Port ▼]

Modem Setup

Modem: [U.S. Robotics Sportster ▼]   Port: [Modem Port ▼]

Modem Speaker: ○ On   ● Off

Figure 10.6 Here's where you can make changes to HotSync serial port settings.

> *The only other thing you normally need to concern yourself with in HotSync Manager is the Install command in the HotSync menu. You'll learn to install add-on software using the Install command in Chapter 11.*

Palm Desktop

If you're wondering where these Palm-equivalent programs are on your Mac now, they are in the application called Palm Desktop, and they are called *modules*. To start Palm Desktop, double-click the Palm Desktop icon in the Palm folder (**Figure 10.7**).

Palm™ Desktop

Figure 10.7 The Palm Desktop icon launches the Palm Desktop program.

When you HotSync, the data from your Palm is transferred to Palm Desktop. When you launch Palm Desktop and click the button for one of the modules, you'll see the data from your Palm already entered and formatted in the module. In Palm Desktop you can add, edit, or delete information, print your Palm's data, view data that you deleted from your Palm (but elected to save on your Mac), or import data from other programs on your Mac.

Palm Desktop is a full-fledged Mac application with enough features, possibilities, quirks, nooks, and crannies to fill a small book of its own (it began life as Claris Organizer). For space reasons, I can only give a brief overview of its most basic functions and most commonly used features in this chapter. I encourage you to look through the manual that came with your MacPac software for more coverage of the more obscure aspects of Palm Desktop.

Note that, confusingly, the Palm Desktop modules are not called by the same names as their corresponding programs are in your Palm! Here is a translation guide between your Palm applications and their equivalents in Palm Desktop:

What it's called on your Palm	What it's called in Palm Desktop
Date Book	Calendar
Address Book	Contacts
To Do List	Tasks
Memo Pad	Notes

Palm Desktop launches and opens by default to today's view in the Calendar module, (**Figure 10.8**). Along the top of the screen, the Palm Desktop toolbar contains 14 buttons that help simplify the most common tasks. They are grouped into buttons for the four module groups, plus three more buttons for printing, finding, and deleting items.

Move the mouse pointer over each button and let it rest there briefly to reveal the name of the button.

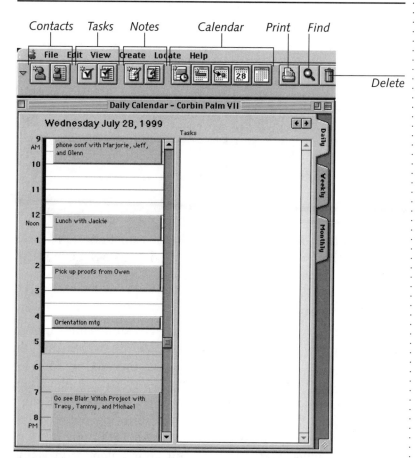

Figure 10.8 Palm Desktop launches the Calendar module by default.

Instant Palm Desktop

In the upper right-hand corner of your Mac's screen, you'll see a little green icon. That's the Instant Palm Desktop icon, and it is always there. Click on it to drop-down a very handy list of frequent commands (**Figure 10.9**).

Switch to Palm Desktop: This launches the Palm Desktop program. This is the easiest way to start Palm Desktop at anytime.

HotSync Manager: This launches the HotSync Manager program.

Find Contact: This brings up a little dialog box where you can type a few letters to quickly find an Address Book entry (called a Contact in Palm Desktop).

Create: This is the easiest way to jump directly to creating a new Appointment, Task, Contact, Note, or Event Banner (untimed event).

Figure 10.9 The Instant Palm Desktop icon allows easy access to many useful commands, available onscreen at all times.

At the bottom of Instant Palm Desktop, your important Tasks for today (if any), Appointments, and Contacts associated with those Tasks are conveniently listed.

Printing

You can print from anywhere in Palm Desktop, and a modular Print dialog box will appear and ask you which module you want to print (**Figure 10.10**). Select the module to print by clicking on its button in the Print dialog box. You have lots of printing options to choose from. The Contacts and Calendar modules offer especially elaborate printing options. For example, you can print your Contacts (Address Book entries) as mailing labels, and you can print your Calendar in Daily, Weekly, or Monthly views. The Automatic Preview shows you what your printout will look like.

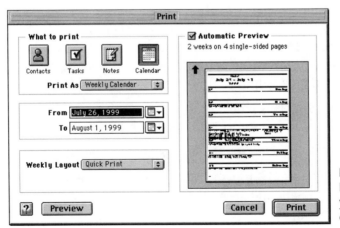

Figure 10.10 The Print dialog box lets you print from any of the four modules.

Calendar

Calendar works very similarly to the way Address Book works on your Palm. Figure 10.8 shows Calendar's version of your Date Book entries for today. I HotSynced, and my Date Book entry for today went into the Calendar module in Palm Desktop. Originally, on my Palm, it looked like **Figure 10.11**.

There is, obviously, a lot more screen real estate in Palm Desktop, so you can see more of your day in one view. If I wanted to add an appointment to today, I could add it in Calendar and then HotSync, and the appointment would show up in my Palm.

Figure 10.11 What my Date Book entry looked like on my Palm.

Adding an appointment

Double-click on the time slot when your appointment begins, or click the Create Appointment button. The Appointment dialog box appears (**Figure 10.12**). Change the text in the various text boxes to make your appointment reflect what you want, and then click OK or press Return.

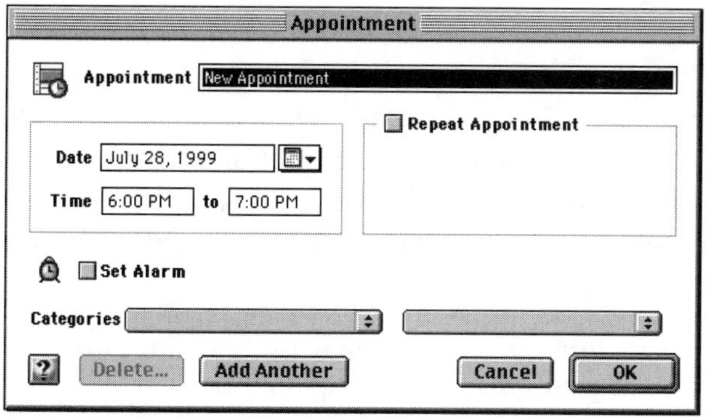

Figure 10.12 The Appointment dialog box lets you add a new appointment in Calendar.

Appointment: The Appointment text box enters "New Appointment" as default text. Just select the text and type in the new name for your appointment.

Date: Click in the Date boxes to change the date of your appointment. If your cursor is in the box, press the plus (+)

and minus (-) sign keys on your keyboard to go to the next or previous day. Press Shift + or Shift - to skip a month at a time. Click the drop-down arrow to call up a little monthly calendar where you can pick any day you want.

Time: Put your cursor in the starting Time and ending Time boxes and press the plus (+) and minus (-) keys on your keyboard to advance or go back one day at a time. Press Shift + or Shift—to move forward or backward one minute at a time.

Repeat Appointment: Put a check mark in the Repeat Appointment check box if your appointment happens regularly (such as every day or every week). Additional options appear that let you fine tune exactly when and how often your repeating appointment happens, and you can even set a date to stop the repeating.

Set Alarm: Put a check mark in the Alarm box to set an alarm for your appointment. After you HotSync the appointment into your Palm, the appointment appears in Date Book, of course, and any alarms you set will go off on your Palm and a reminder screen will appear on your Mac's screen!

Categories: Click the Categories bars to assign a category for your appointment.

The three Calendar views

You've been looking so far at the Daily view of Calendar (see the tabs along the right side). Like the Palm, Calendar has three views, which you can access via the tabs. Click on the Weekly tab to open the Weekly view (**Figure 10.13**). Double-click on an appointment to edit it.

It's easy to reschedule an appointment in Calendar: Just click on it and drag it wherever you want.

The Monthly View pops up a huge calendar showing the whole month (**Figure 10.14**). You can drag appointments around to reschedule them in Monthly view just like in Weekly view.

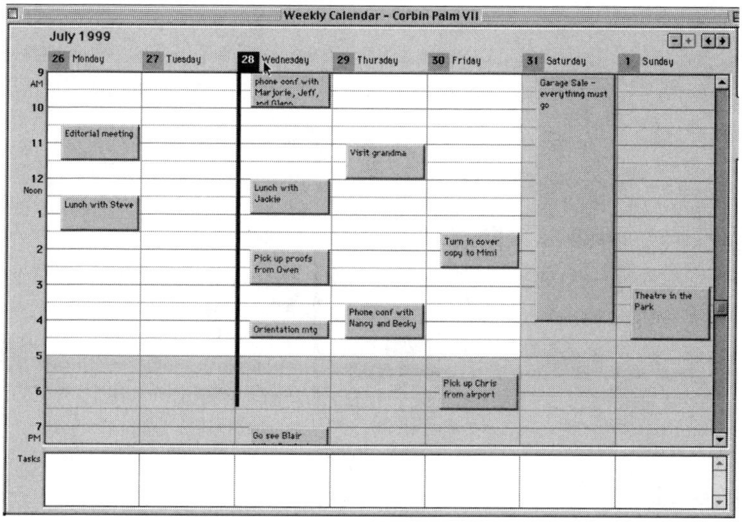

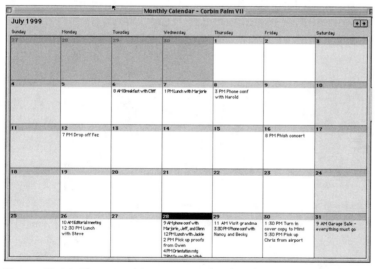

Figure 10.13 Calendar's Weekly view lets you see your whole week.

Figure 10.14 The Monthly view in Calendar shows you the entire month.

Double-click on any day to pop up a different dialog box—this one asks you what you want to create (**Figure 10.15**), a task (To Do List item), an appointment (Date Book event), or an event banner (an untimed event in Date Book, such as a birthday). Click the appropriate button and click OK. You can adjust your item from there in further dialog boxes.

You can call up the big monthly view, where you can add items that will show up in Date Book or To Do List, by clicking the View Calendar button on the Palm Desktop toolbar.

What do you want to create?

Task	Appointment	Event Banner

Cancel   OK

Figure 10.15 You can add a new Date Book or To Do List item by double-clicking a date in Calendar's Monthly view.

Contacts

Palm Desktop's Contacts module correlates to Address Book in your Palm. Click on the View Contacts button in the Palm Desktop toolbar to launch the Contact List (**Figure 10.16**). There are more columns off to the right of the screen, including physical address information, if you scroll. Or you can widen the window by dragging on its bottom right-hand corner.

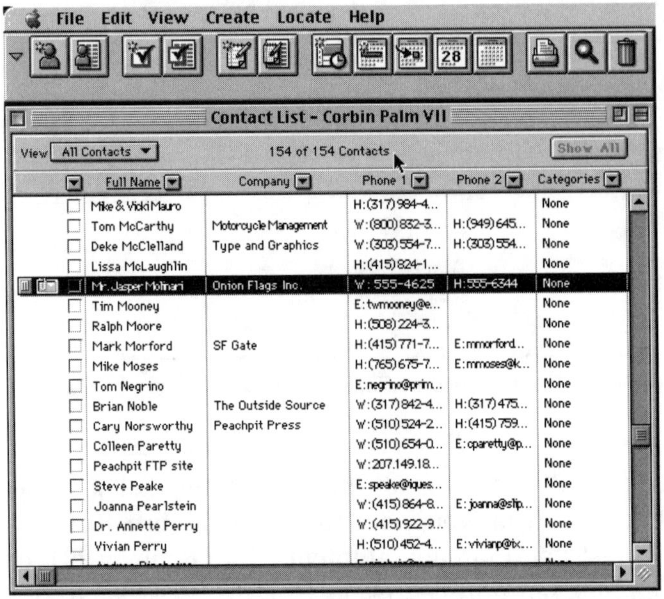

Figure 10.16 Your Address Book entries as seen in Palm Desktop's Contact List.

To edit a Contact's information, double-click anywhere on its row in Contact List. The Contact window appears (**Figure 10.17**), showing five light gray areas where information is grouped.

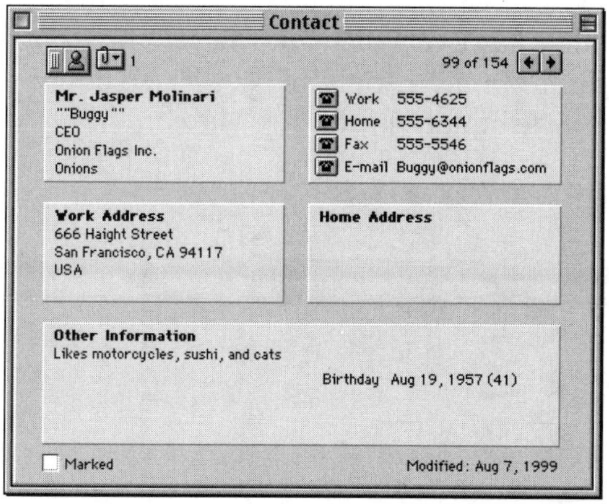

Mr. Jasper Molinari		

Contact

1   99 of 154 ←→

Mr. Jasper Molinari
""Buggy""
CEO
Onion Flags Inc.
Onions

☎ Work 555-4625
☎ Home 555-6344
☎ Fax   555-5546
☎ E-mail Buggy@onionflags.com

Work Address
666 Haight Street
San Francisco, CA 94117
USA

Home Address

Other Information
Likes motorcycles, sushi, and cats

Birthday Aug 19, 1957 (41)

☐ Marked   Modified: Aug 7, 1999

Figure 10.17
Information about a Contact appears in the Contact window.

Note that there are fields for information, such as Nickname, that do not appear in the Palm's Address Book program. Stuff you put in the "Other Information" area winds up in your Palm as a Note attached to the entry.

Editing a Contact entry

Click in one of the light gray areas to edit the information in that area. Another small window pops up, where you can add, change, or delete information as you please (**Figure 10.18**). Click on drop-down arrows to select from predetermined choices. Click on the arrows in the upper right-hand corner to page through your Contacts.

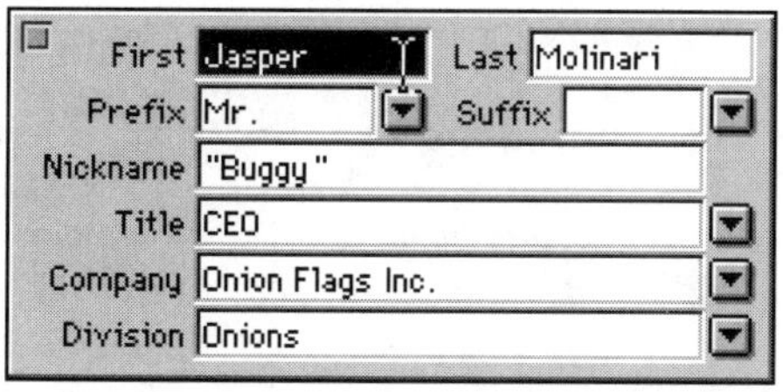

☐ First Jasper   Last Molinari
    Prefix Mr. ▼ Suffix   ▼
 Nickname "Buggy"
    Title CEO   ▼
  Company Onion Flags Inc.   ▼
  Division Onions   ▼

Figure 10.18 Editing in the window that pops up when you click on a light gray area of a Contact.

Note that fields that don't exist in your Palm's Address Book, such as Prefix, Suffix, and Division, don't get HotSynced to your Palm. They stay right there on your Mac, though.

Adding a new Contact

To add a new Contact, click on the Create Contact button in Palm Desktop (the first button). A blank Contact window appears with the first gray area's information box opened, ready for you to enter information to create the new entry (**Figure 10.19**). When you're done, simply close the window by clicking its close box (the square in the top left corner).

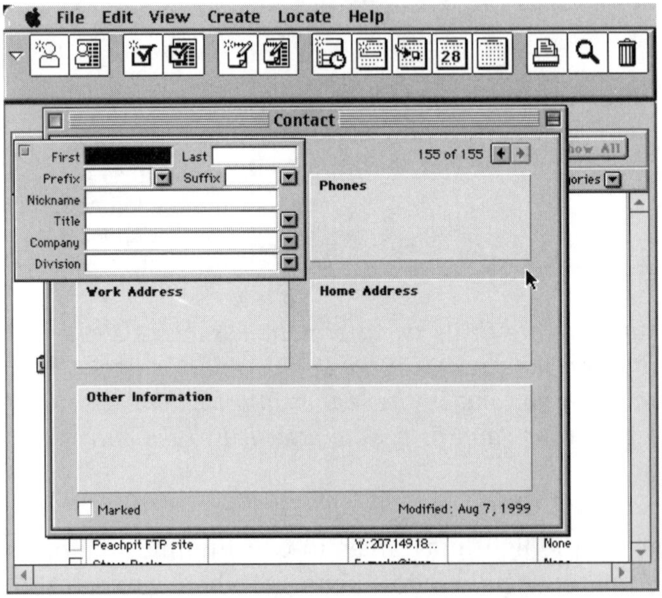

Figure 10.19 A blank slate for your new Contact.

Attaching module items

That little icon that looks like a person in the upper left-hand corner of the Contact window lets you attach the Contact to a Task or Appointment or Note by dragging and dropping (provided you arrange the windows in such a way that you can view both at the same time). If you don't have the windows arranged like that, click the paper clip icon just to the right of it, select Attach To, and select where you want to attach the Contact. If you select File, you can attach any file on your Macintosh, such as a Word document or Excel spreadsheet, to your Contact—from then on, a little attachment icon will appear next to the person's name in the Contact List, and if you click it and select File, your file appears and launches whatever program created that file. Attaching works in all the modules, and it is a handy way to associate documents with Contacts, Appointments, and Tasks. Just note that the attaching doesn't get HotSynced to your Palm.

Sorting Contacts and filters

Click the title for each column in Contact List view (Full name, Company, Phone 1, and so on) to sort the column by that column's contents (**Figure 10.20**). For example, if you click on the column title Company, your Contacts are sorted alphabetically by Company name. By default Contacts are sorted alphabetically by last name.

Contact List – Corbin Palm VII							
View [All Contacts ▼]		156 of 156 Contacts					[Show All]
[▼] Full Name [▼]	Company [▼]	Phone 1 [▼]	Phone 2 [▼]	Categories [▼]	Email [▼]	Birthday [▼]	Primary Address [▼]

Figure 10.20 Column titles offer sorting options.

Beside each column title is a little drop-down arrow. Click it, and you'll see at least three choices: Sort, No Filter, and Custom Filter (**Figure 10.21**). Choices beneath offer automatic filters that let you show only those Contacts. For example, if you clicked on the 3Com-Palm Computing, Inc. choice, only Contacts at 3Com would appear in the Contact List screen.

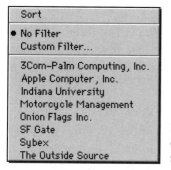

Figure 10.21 The column drop-down arrows offer sorting and filter options.

Sort: Click Sort to sort the column alphabetically—or numerically in the case of the phone number columns—by its contents (just like clicking the column title).

No Filter: The default, No Filter shows all Contacts in the column.

Custom Filter: Click Custom Filter to enter criteria controlling which Contacts appear onscreen. For example, in the Company column, Custom Filter lets you choose among several options (**Figure 10.22**).

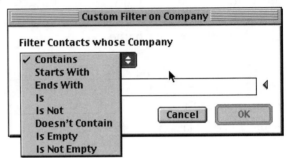

Figure 10.22 Choose the filter you want to use to limit the Contacts that appear in Contact List.

Remember, filters filter out everything but what you choose. So, if you choose the filter "Starts with" and enter the letter S in the text box, only companies that start with the letter S will appear in the Contact List.

Tasks

Palm Desktop's Tasks module works very much the same as To Do List does on your Palm. You can create and edit Tasks, change their priority, and mark them completed when you're done with them.

To view your Task List, click on the View Tasks button (the fourth button) in the Palm Desktop toolbar (if you move the cursor over it and leave it there momentarily, its name is revealed). Your Task List appears onscreen (**Figure 10.23**).

Check marks in the boxes before Tasks descriptions indicate completed Tasks. As in Contacts, click on the Column titles (Task, Priority, and so on) to sort your Tasks by that column's contents, and click on the drop-down arrows to use filtering to limit which Tasks appear onscreen. See the section "Sorting Contacts and filters" earlier in this chapter for an overview of how sorting and filtering works.

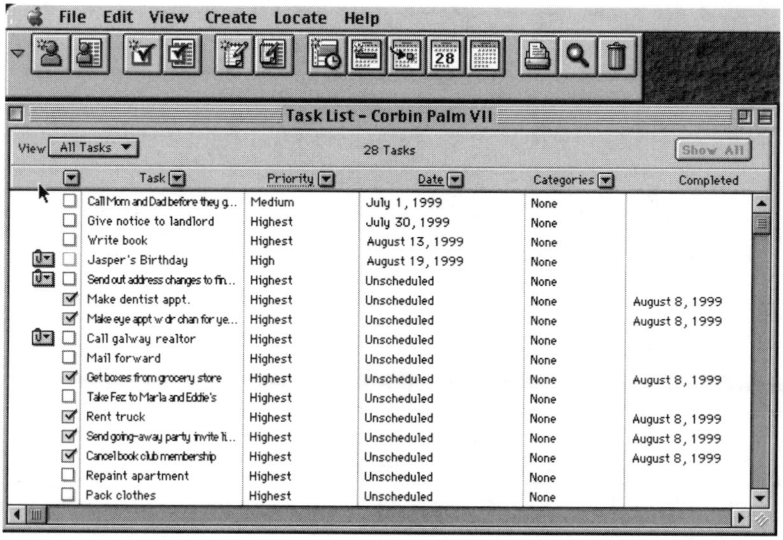

Figure 10.23 Viewing your Tasks in Palm Desktop's Task List.

Creating and editing a new Task

Click on the Create Task button in the Palm Desktop toolbar (it's the fifth button) to call up a new Task window, where you can enter your new Task's information (**Figure 10.24**). The window has several fields.

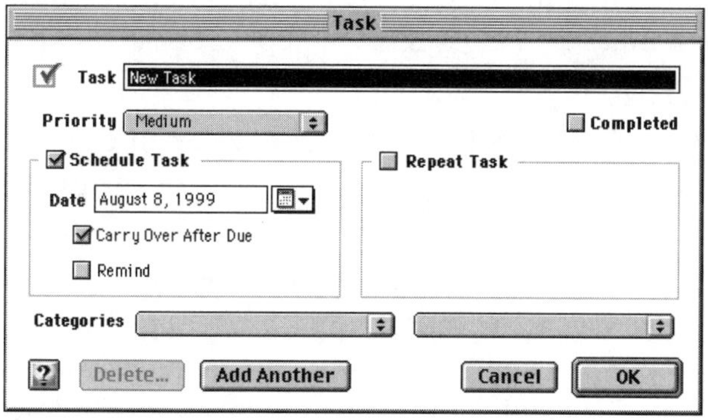

Figure 10.24 Creating a new Task in Palm Desktop.

Task: Type the description of the Task in this text box.

Priority: Click the Priority drop-down list to select a new priority (it's Medium by default).

Schedule Task: The check mark in this box means your Task will have a due date—today, if you do nothing. Uncheck the box to give your Task no due date.

Date: Change the text in the Date box to change the due date or click on the drop-down arrow beside it to pick a new date from a little pop-up calendar (**Figure 10.25**). The arrows pointing right and left flip the calendar forward or back one month.

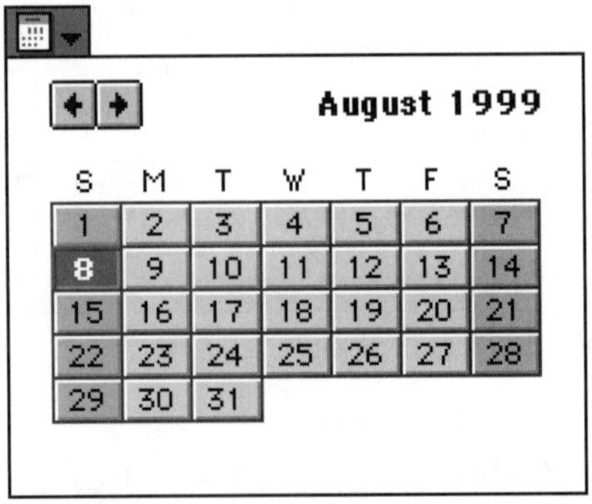

August 1999

S	M	T	W	T	F	S
1	2	3	4	5	6	7
8	9	10	11	12	13	14
15	16	17	18	19	20	21
22	23	24	25	26	27	28
29	30	31				

Figure 10.25
Picking a date for
your new Task.

Carry Over After Due: Put a check mark in this box if you want your uncompleted Tasks to keep "rolling over" into today's Task List.

Remind: Check the Remind box and select the number of days before for your reminder. A message will appear on screen that many days before your Task is due to remind you of it.

Completed: When you complete your Task, you can check it off here—although it's probably easier to check it off in the Task List view, as described earlier in this section.

Repeat Task: If your Task is something you do regularly, such as submitting a weekly status report, put a check mark in this box and select the frequency from the list that appears. If you know the repeating Task will stop repeating on a certain date, select an Until date.

After a HotSync, a repeating Task winds up your Palm as a single To Do List item. Unlike Date Book, To Do List doesn't let you schedule repeating items. But on your Mac it will keep showing up according to how you scheduled it.

Categories: Assign a category to your Task here. Click on the Category bar and select from the existing categories or click Edit Categories to create or rename categories **(Figure 10.26)**. If you select None, your Task will enter your Palm as Unfiled.

> *Note that you can assign a Task to two different categories in Palm Desktop. But the Palm only lets you assign one category to any To Do List item. Therefore, whatever second category you select on Palm Desktop's Tasks module doesn't transfer to your Palm. But it's still there on your Mac.*

Add Another: This button stores your Task and clears all the fields again so you can go right into creating another Task.

When you're done, click OK, and your Task now appears in the Task List with all the others.

Notes

Notes is an odd bird because it corresponds both to the Palm's Memo Pad program and to the Notes that you're used to attaching to items in your Palm—not to mention that it's confusingly named the same as the latter. Click on the View Notes button in the Palm Desktop toolbar (the sixth button from the left). The Note List appears.

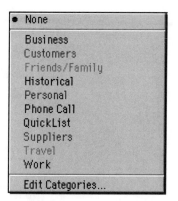

Figure 10.26 Pick a category (or None) from the categories drop-down list.

> *The trick to differentiating Palm Notes from Memo Pad items is the paper clip icon, which you can see positioned to the left of some items in Figure 10.26. The paper clip icon tells you that the item is a Note that is attached to something in your Palm. To see which Palm program contains the item the Note is attached to, look in the item's Title column. Notes attached to Palm Programs have titles that begin with "Handheld Note." Click on the paper clip icon itself to see the name of the item it's attached to (you're offered the chance to detach it here as well). Memo Pad documents have titles that are simply the first line of the documents.*

Creating and editing Notes

Double-click anywhere on a Note's row to view it in the Note window (**Figure 10.27**) or click the Create Note button on the toolbar to show a blank Note window. You can change the title, add a date and time, and pick a category for your Note. In the big white space at the bottom, you enter or read the Note's contents.

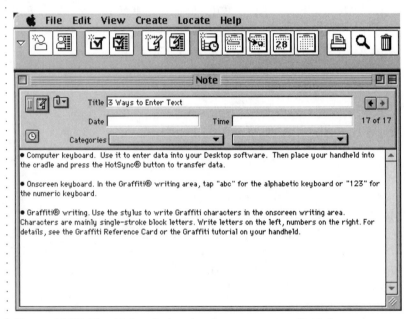

Figure 10.27 The Note window is where you can edit Notes.

Click the paper clip icon to attach the Note to an existing or new item in any module (**Figure 10.28**). If you choose Existing Item, a window pops up with an icon that you click on and drag to the item—which means you must arrange the windows so you can see both at the same time. Choose New Appointment, Task, Contact, Note, or Event Banner to open a window where you can create the item you want the Note attached to. Choose File to attach the Note to any file on your Mac (from then on, when you view the Note you can click the paper click icon to launch the program associated with the file you picked).

If the windows are arranged such that you can see the item to which you want to attach the Note, you can drag the icon beside the paper clip icon to that item (your cursor turns into a little hand to let you know you can drag it)

Attach To ▶	Existing Item...
Detach...	
Date	New Appointment...
	New Task...
Categories	New Contact...
	New Note...
	New Event Banner...
File...	

Figure 10.28 Select what you want to attach the Note to.

Click the little clock icon to enter the current time at the beginning of your Note.

The right and left arrows in the upper right-hand corner of the Note window cycle forward and back through your Notes one Note at a time.

When you're done creating or editing a Note, click the window's close box to close it. It appears in the Note List.

Expense

You'll note that Palm Desktop makes no mention of Expense. However, on your MacPac 2 CD-ROM, there is a separate program called Informed that can take your Palm's Expense data and format it on your Mac so that it's ready to print and submit as an expense report.

Wait until you've already entered your Expense data into your Palm and HotSynced it to your Mac before installing the Informed software.

Double-click on the MacPac CD-ROM icon, open the Palm Extras folder and open the Shana Corporation folder. Double-click on the Informed Palm Expense Installer. The Informed Installer starts (**Figure 10.29**). Slick Install when the Installer screen appears (keep the Basic Install option).

Figure 10.29 Installing the Informed Expense program on your Mac.

After the software is installed, you'll see the Informed folder open. The Informed Filler icon you see is an interesting program in itself—don't forget to check it out later. But for now, double-click the Palm folder to reveal the Expense Creator icon (**Figure 10.30**). Double-click it to start the Expense Creator setup. Enter your information when prompted, and click Accept when the time comes. The Expense Creator dialog box appears (**Figure 10.31**)

Figure 10.30 Double-click the Expense Creator icon to set up Expense Creator.

Click the Setup button and navigate to the Palm:Users:*Yourname* folder on your Mac's hard drive, where *Yourname* is whatever your Palm's username is. When you find that folder, click on it to highlight it and then click the button below the list of folders.

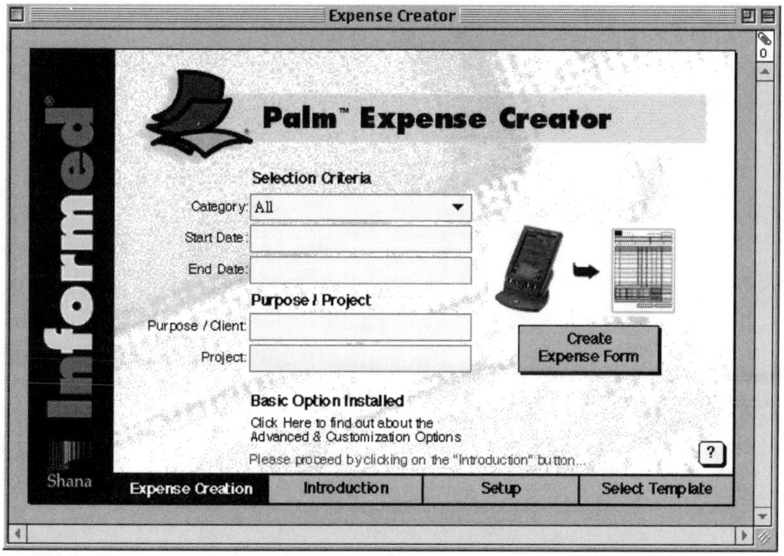

Figure 10.31 Click the Setup button to find your Expense data on your hard drive and set up Expense Creator on your Mac.

Back at the Expense Creator dialog box, you can customize and configure your Expense report by clicking on the various buttons. When you're ready, click on the Expense Creation button, add any information you want to appear in the report, and click Create Expense Form. From there, you can print it and submit it to your company for reimbursement.

Add-On 11 Software

The software that comes built into your Palm is great, but it's not the only game in town. 3Com likes to think of the Palm as not merely a device, but the Palm Computing Platform—an operating system environment where programs run, like on Windows or the Macintosh. Therefore, thousands of other programs have been created by thousands of individual software developers. You'll find these programs on many Web sites, ready to download. Some of them are free, some are shareware (which means if you like it, you pay for it), and some are demoware (which means the software works, mostly, but certain key features will be disabled or missing until you pay).

But using other software means an additional step: You have to install it. Fortunately, it's easy to install software on your Palm. This chapter shows you how to find other software on the Web, how to install it into your Palm, and gives tips on which programs are worth trying out.

Downloading Software from the Web

Dozens of Web sites offer Palm software for download. One of the best is Palm Central, and I'll use it as an example here. See the Appendix for more Web sites you should try. Using your regular computer, connect online and use your Web browser to go to www.palmcentral.com. The Palm Central home page looks like **Figure 11.1**.

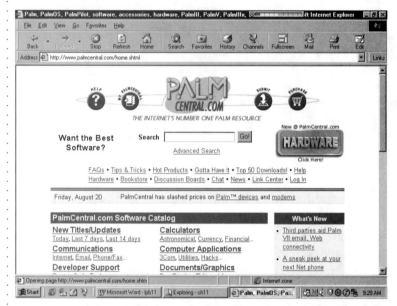

Figure 11.1 PalmCentral: Learn it, love it, bookmark it.

You can browse Palm Central all you like, looking through the categories in the Software Catalog. Or you can search for something you've heard of. Let's say you love chess and have heard from someone or read somewhere that PocketChess is the best Palm chess program. Enter **PocketChess** in the Palm Central home page Search box and click Search. In a few seconds, the Web site returns another page listing PocketChess under the category Board Games (**Figure 11.2**).

The listing tells you that the latest version of PocketChess is 1.1, that it's shareware, that Palm Central has logged 12,809 downloads of it (it would seem to be pretty popular), and this version is from July 12, 1999. To get more information about it, click on the link (the name of the software—in this case Pocket-Chess v1.1). You'll see a screen like **Figure 11.3**, which tells you a lot more about the program.

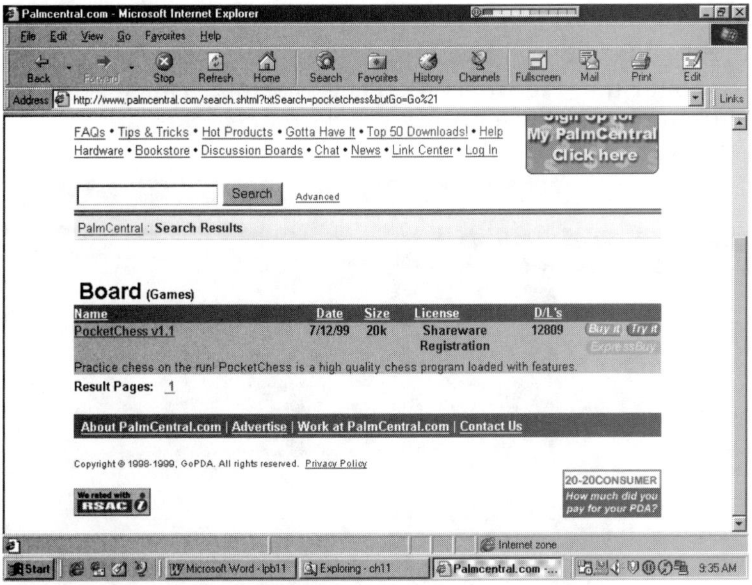

Figure 11.2 PalmCentral's search engine found PocketChess.

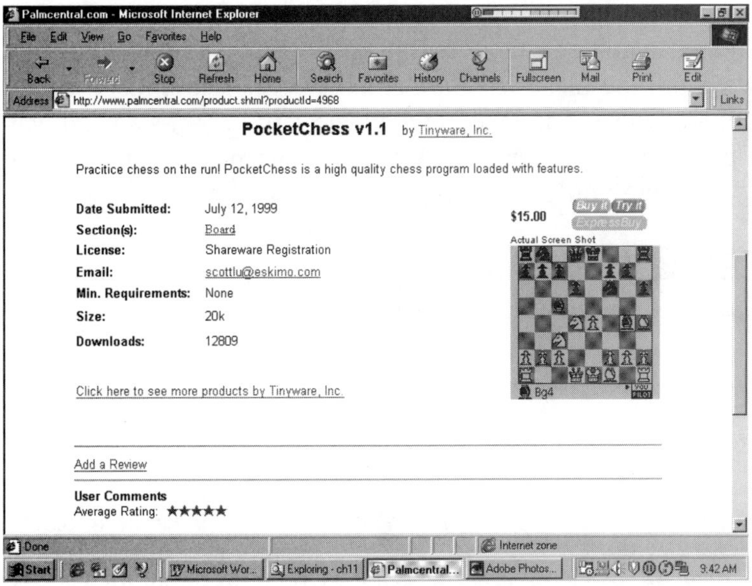

Figure 11.3 More info on PocketChess for your reading pleasure.

If you want to try PocketChess before you pay for it, click the Try it button. If you're sure you want to just pay for it and get it over with all at once, click the Buy it button. It's smart, I think, to try software before buying it—that's why it's shareware. So click Try it. A dialog box will appear that suggests you save the file to your hard disk, and that's exactly what you should do (**Figure 11.4**). (The Macintosh dialog box is slightly different but does essentially the same thing.)

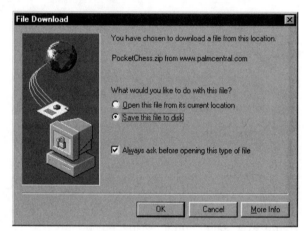

Figure 11.4 When you click the link, you save the file from the Web to your computer's hard drive.

Click OK. Another dialog box appears, asking you where on your disk you want to save the file (**Figure 11.5**). On my hard drive, I created a folder called Temp, and when I download stuff I always put the files there. You should create folder just for your downloaded stuff and call it whatever you like—it's a good way to keep track of your downloaded programs. Navigate to the folder where you want to put the file and click Save.

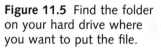

Figure 11.5 Find the folder on your hard drive where you want to put the file.

It won't take long to download—Palm files are tiny compared to the files you're used to dealing with on your computer. When it's done downloading, disconnect (if you're using a modem) and go find the folder where you downloaded the file using Windows Explorer or by opening your Mac's hard drive icon.

Installing a Downloaded Palm Program

Palm files that you download from the Web may be in different formats. In the case of PocketChess, it was a Zip file, which means you need WinZip or another program (such as Stuffit for Mac users) that can unzip Zip files.

If you don't have Winzip (Windows) or Stuffit (Mac), get back on the Web, go to www.shareware.com, download the WinZip installer (Windows users) or a Mac Unzip program installer (Mac-heads), install it by double-clicking it, and then come back to this point.

Unzip or unstuff the file (if necessary—most Palm program files you'll find on the Web aren't zipped at all, in fact). When you get down to a file that has the extension .PRC (which stands for Palm resource) or .PDB (Palm database), you have found the Palm program file.

Drag the .PRC or .PDB file into your Palm: Add-On folder (Windows) or into your Palm: User: [User name]: Files to Install folder (Macintosh). This is a special folder. Any software you want to install into your Palm should be placed in this folder. From here, the process is a little different depending on whether you have a Windows machine or a Mac (actually, the process is nearly done on the Mac at this point).

For more detailed information on HotSync and the Palm Desktop program, see Chapter 9 (Windows users) or Chapter 10 (for Mac folks).

Installing a program in Windows Palm Desktop

The fastest way to install Palm programs (.PRC and .PDB files) is to simply double-click them in Windows Explorer or My Computer. That launches the Install tool. Or you can do it the long way, as follows:

Launch Palm Desktop by double-clicking the Palm Desktop icon or clicking Start > Programs > Palm Desktop > Palm Desktop. Palm Desktop opens (**Figure 11.6**).

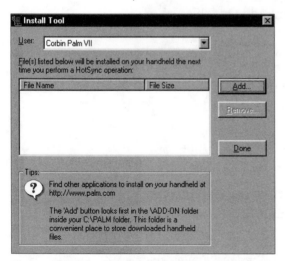

Figure 11.6 Your old buddy Palm Desktop should be familiar to you by now—if not, see Chapter 9.

Figure 11.7 The Install tool appears when you double-click a Palm file or click the Install button in Palm Desktop.

Click the Install button to start the Install tool (**Figure 11.7**). Click Add. A dialog box opens to the Palm: Add-On folder and shows you all your Palm files—you can also navigate to find any .PRC or .PDB file anywhere on your computer (**Figure 11.8**). Find the PocketChess .PRC file and double-click on it to enter it into the Install tool dialog box (**Figure 11.9**).

Click Done. A little dialog box will pop up to tell you that the next time you HotSync, the program will be installed on your Palm (**Figure 11.10**). Go ahead and HotSync, and sure enough, when it's finished the new program's icon will appear in your

Applications screen on your Palm. Tap the icon to launch the program (see later in this chapter for more on PocketChess).

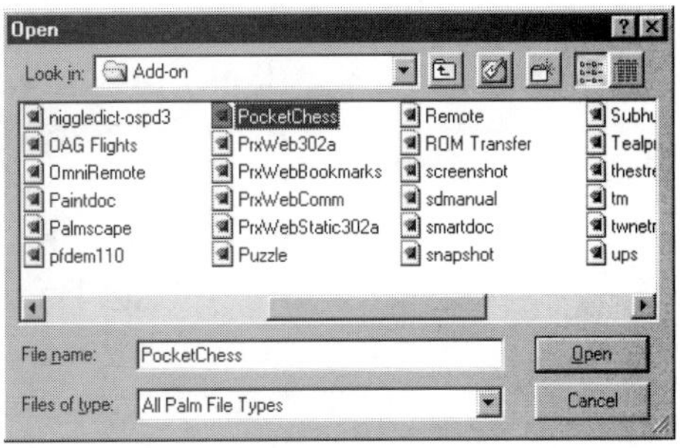

Installing a program in Mac Palm Desktop

It's extremely simple to install Palm files from your Mac to your Palm. Just drag the Palm file you want to install into the folder on your hard drive called Palm: User: [Username]: Files to Install. The next time you HotSync your Palm and your Mac, any Palm program files you put in that folder will be installed on your Palm.

Figure 11.8 The files in your Add-on (Windows) or Files to Install (Mac) folder are shown in this dialog box.

Some Cool Palm Add-On Programs

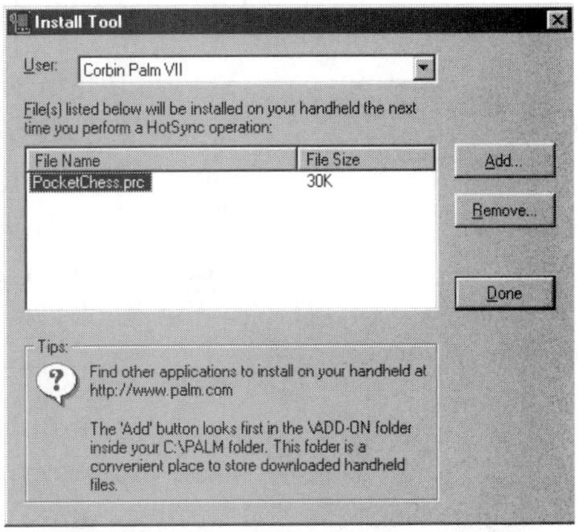

Thousands of add-on programs are available for your Palm, and more are coming down the pike everyday. It would take forever to try to describe them all (because they appear faster than they could be found and described).

Fortunately, the Palm-related Web sites are there to satisfy the need for information on them. Almost all the programs described in this section can be found at PalmGear (www.palmgear.com) and Palm Central (www.palm-central.com), and many can also be downloaded from EuroCool (www.eurocool.com).

Figure 11.9 Double-click the Palm file you want to be installed during the next HotSync.

See the Appendix for more Palm Web sites. Those sites are where you want to begin your Palm software quest. This book can do little more than point the way toward a few of the choicer pieces of Palm software. And that's what this section is about.

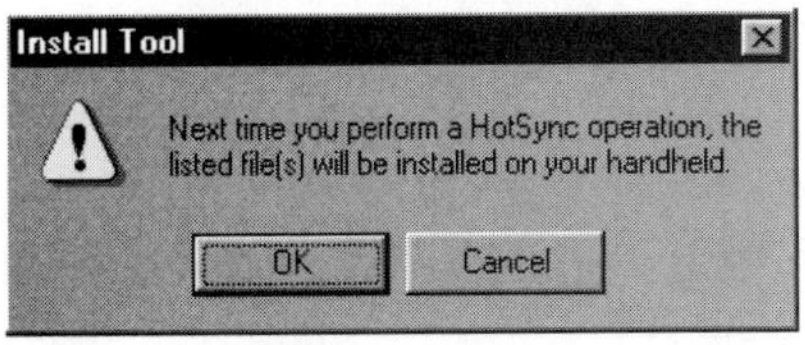

Figure 11.10 Now all you have to do is HotSync, and the program will be installed on your Palm.

System extensions

BackupBuddy (www.backupbuddy.com, shareware $20): BackupBuddy takes up where HotSync leaves off. As you learned in Chapters 9 and 10, HotSync synchronizes and backs up data for the built-in programs but it does not back up anything else. Data that you generate in add-on programs will be gone forever if something happens to your Palm—except if you have BackupBuddy. Think of BackupBuddy as insurance for the data in your Palm. It backs up *everything* in your Palm every time you HotSync (the same one-button process). Windows and Macintosh versions are available.

HackMaster (www.daggerware.com, shareware $5): HackMaster sounds scary, but really it's just a system extension manager that allows control panels to bypass some aspects of the Palm OS and allows other programs to take advantage of this trick. Many Palm add-on programs (called *hacks*) require that you have HackMaster installed. Once you do, any hacks you install reside within HackMaster. Be sure to read HackMaster's online documentation carefully if you install it, because it can cause minor problems with your Palm if some of the hacks conflict with your other Palm software.

SwitchHack (www.deskfree.com, shareware $5): SwitchHack is a good example of a hack—a program that requires HackMaster in order to run. SwitchHack lets you switch among currently running Palm programs with a single Graffiti stroke, making it seem as if your programs are all running simultaneously. It also provides a menu of the ten most recently run applications.

MenuHack (www.daggerware.com/mischack.htm, free): Another hack, this one changes the way menus appear in programs. You know how you have to tap the Menu icon to make the menus appear? MenuHack makes it so that instead of tapping the Menu icon, you tap the top of the program window to cause the menus to appear (the top of the window is usually a banner with the name of the program). This "feels" more correct, since in Windows and Mac programs you click up there on the menu choices. Well worth the price (free).

Swipe (www.doublebang.com, free): Swipe adds six more Big Line commands—you know, the command stroke in which you draw straight up the face of the Palm? With Swipe, you can assign different actions for Big Lines you draw diagonally and across (**Figure 11.11**).

Launcher III (www.benc.hr/lnchiii.htm, free): Launcher III replaces the Applications screen with a more familiar tabbed style window that organizes your programs better. It's much faster to find programs with Launcher III than with the old Applications screen. You can drag and drop icons and tabs wherever you like. It also adds more beaming options and memory and battery info.

Productivity enhancers

AvantGo (www.avantgo.com, free): A wonderful, free Web browser for the Palm that lets you take your favorite Web sites with you for viewing offline with your Palm. See Chapter 14 for a detailed description of installing and using AvantGo.

Abacus (www.dovcom.com/pilot/abacus.html, shareware, $12): A much better calculator than the simple Calculator program that came with your Palm. Abacus is a financial calculator, based on the Hewlett Packard calculator model HP-12C (**Figure 11.12**).

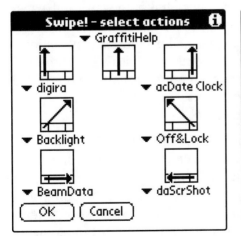

Figure 11.11 Swipe lets you add more Big Line commands.

Figure 11.12 Abacus is a nice replacement for Calculator.

DateBk3 (www.gorilla-haven.org/pimlico, shareware, $20): This is what the Date Book program should be. It has more views, including a vital week-at-a-glance, and you can assign icons to events to make them easy to see in the month or week view. You can even create your own custom icons.

Pocket Quicken (www.landware.com, $39.95): With Pocket Quicken, you have a mobile companion to Quicken 99 (for either Mac or Windows) on your Palm (**Figure 11.13**). Capture checking, credit card, and cash transactions while you are on the go. It requires that you have Quicken 99 or 2000 for Windows or Macintosh. Makes it easy to HotSync your financial data back and forth with Quicken. You can assign your own private PIN number to Pocket Quicken to ensure that only you have access to your financial activity. It also maintains a backup of your transactions each time you HotSync.

ExpensAble (www.landware.com): This one was not released at the time of this writing, but judging by the beta it looks to be another valuable financial Palm application from Landware that will go far beyond the Expense program that comes with the Palm.

TealDoc (www.tealpoint.com, shareware $16.95): One of the best "Doc readers" available, TealDoc has a full list of features. TealDoc supports embedded images, buttons for inter-document and intra-document links, forward and backward searches with advanced search options, changeable fonts, adjustable display options, multispeed forward and backward autoscroll (which turns your Palm into a prompter), and private documents. Makes your Palm work like an electronic book.

AportisDoc (www.aportis.com, $39.95): Another Memo Pad replacement, somewhat like Teal-Doc. Its offers advanced search functions, large fonts, searching, annotating, prompting, and bookmarking capabilities. AportisDoc allows you to not just read but create text documents on Palms, without using large amounts of memory. Like TealDoc, AportisDoc is perfect for

Figure 11.13 Pocket Quicken makes it easy for Quicken users to track finances on the go.

downloading out-of-copyright literature from the Web and reading it on your Palm.

Intellisync (www.pumatech.com, $69.95): Besides BackupBuddy, IntelliSynch is the ultimate HotSync add-on—it allows you to HotSync just about anything. Intellisync enables you to synchronize your Palm directly with your favorite PC-based personal information management, contact management, and group scheduling applications all in one easy step (**Figure 11.14**). IntelliSync provides HotSync support for an impressively long list of software, including Microsoft Exchange 5.0/5.5, Microsoft Outlook 97/98/2000, Microsoft Schedule+ 7.0/7.0a/7.5, Symantec ACT! 3.0.8/4.0/4.0.2, Lotus Organizer 4.1/5.0, Lotus Notes 4.5/ 4.6, Novell GroupWise 5.2/5.5, Day-Timer Organizer 98, Gold-Mine 3.2/4.0, and Eudora Planner 4.0. It also offers intelligent conflict resolution for those times when you make a change to a file in both your Palm and your computer's software.

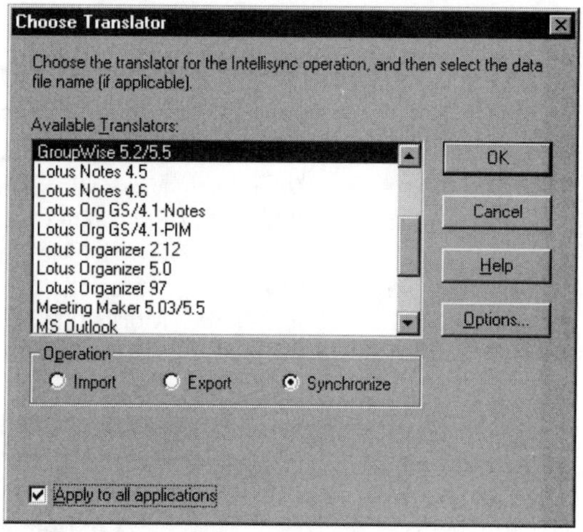

Figure 11.14
IntelliSync offers HotSync support for a long list of software.

Jfile (www.land-j.com/jfile.html, shareware $19.95): JFile is a Palm database program. Although not nearly as complex as Microsoft Access or FileMaker Pro, Jfile does a surprisingly good job. JFile supports field types including popup lists, integers, floating point numbers, checkboxes, and dates. It also has features such as password protection, exporting records to Memo Pad, and easy duplication of database records. Included with Jfile is a Windows application that converts Comma Separated Value (.CSV) files to and from JFile .PDB format databases.

ImageViewer (palm.dahm.com, $12.95): ImageViewer has become the standard for viewing graphics on Palm devices. Use it to view grayscale images, pictures, maps, or diagrams. ImageViewer includes a Windows program for converting graphic files (.BMP, .GIF, .JPG and others) to an ImageViewer format that can be HotSynced into your Palm. One good use of ImageViewer is to scan pictures of loved ones and place them in your Palm.

Travel

Gulliver (www.landware.com, $29.95): Gulliver is a full-featured Palm travel application that lets you manage your travel itinerary with ease (**Figure 11.15**). It handles all the details of business travel and places the information you need at your fingertips. Critical data such as hotel and rental car reservations, flight schedules, frequent flyer ID numbers, airline and airport phone numbers and other information are only a tap away. It's sort of like having a very efficient travel assistant with you at all times. You can even beam your itinerary to other Palm users.

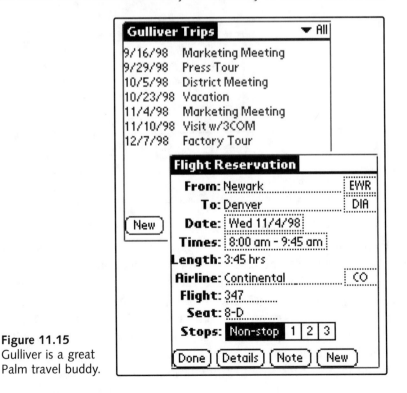

Figure 11.15
Gulliver is a great Palm travel buddy.

QuoVadis (www.marcosoft.com/quovadis/default.stm, share-ware $64.95): Quo Vadis is an amazing mapping program for your Palm. It includes unlimited access to a database of more than 23,000 maps covering the entire United States—even U.S. territiories such as Guam and Puerto Rico. If you travel frequently, you'll find it invaluable as you try to find your way through strange cities and unusual suburban developments (**Figure 11.16**). It's perfect for verifying directions before a trip, picking a place to meet someone, avoiding getting lost, and picking the best route.

Watch out: all those cool maps can suck up your Palm's memory space real quick.

Aramis Travel Guides (www.aramis-inc.com/Pages/Products/cityguide.htm, $17.95 per city): You've probably seen Web sites that function as travel guides to cities. Now you can put that kind of detailed local information into your Palm (**Figure 11.17**). Covers crucial areas such as sightseeing, nightlife, children's activities, accommodations, dining, and information on individual neighborhoods.

SmallTalk (www.conceptkitchen.com/products/pdas00717.html, $79.99): If you only speak English and find yourself in the midst of French, Italian, Spanish, German, or Japanese speakers, you

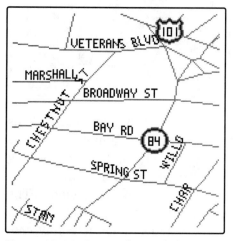

Figure 11.16 Quo Vadis can help you avoid getting lost anywhere in the United States.

Figure 11.17 Aramis Travel Guides are currently available for ten cities, with more on the way.

may wish you had SmallTalk. SmallTalk goes beyond dictionaries and phrase books and uses the familiar flashcard technique. It offers full sentences in categories (lodging, transportation, etc.). You choose what you want to say and hand the Palm to the other person, who is offered a list of appropriate responses. Saves you time and stress trying to communicate across language barriers—not to mention the interest and fun that will be sparked by the presence of your Palm itself.

Fun and games

PocketChess (http://www.eskimo.com/~scottlu/pilot/index .html, shareware $15): PocketChess is absolutely a must-have if you like the classic game (**Figure 11.18**). It is a stellar example of programming efficiency and offers a stunningly competitive game packed into a mere 29K. You can play against someone else or the Palm and choose among eight skill levels.

Figure 11.18 PocketChess is an outstanding example of a Palm game.

OmniRemote (www.pacificneotek.com, shareware $20): This ingenious Palm program lets you turn your Palm into a remote control for your entertainment center (TV and stereo). Setting it up involves beaming your remote(s) at your Palm and creating custom buttons as you build your new Palm remote. The ultimate universal remote, OmniRemote can replace all five of those remotes littering your coffee table. One incredibly cool thing about it is the macros. With one command/button you can turn on the TV, turn on the VCR, turn on the stereo and set it to Video, and start the VCR playing.

HardBall (Included on the Palm Windows CD-ROM or download from www.palm.com/downloads/gameslic.html): HardBall is the classic game Breakout (**Figure 11.19**). You move a paddle back and forth along the bottom of the screen and bat a little ball up toward blocks. The blocks disappear when the ball hits them. When you clear the blocks, a new level starts. It's fun and addictive and it's free.

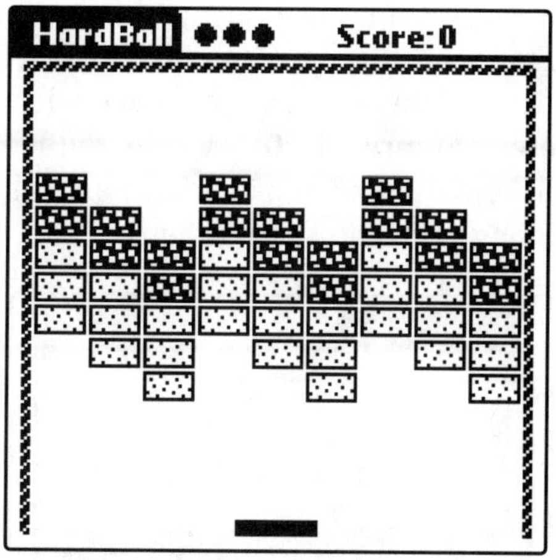

Figure 11.19 The beginning screen of yet another game of HardBall.

SubHunt (Included on the Palm Windows CD-ROM or download from www.palm.com/downloads/gameslic.html): You're a ship floating on the surface of the sea, and beneath evil subs are shooting torpedoes at you. Your job is to avoid the torpedos and bomb the subs.

MineHunt (Included on the Palm Windows CD-ROM or download from www.palm.com/downloads/gameslic.html): This game places you in a minefield. You have to tap dark squares, which might be mines (in which case you are killed) but which might simply be a number instead. A number tells you how many of the squares touching the one you tapped contain mines. So you have to think and use memory and logic to figure out where the mines are before you are blown up.

Puzzle (Included on the Palm Windows CD-ROM or download from www.palm.com/downloads/gameslic.html): If you're like me, this one may remind you of something funny you found once in your Grandma's basement. Fifteen numbered tiles are arranged in 4 x 4 grid. The missing one provides a space for maneuvering the others. The object of the game is to arrange them into numerical order.

Showtimes (jrray.visionart.com/showtimes, free): Showtimes lets you download your local movie listings from Web sites such as Yahoo! and take them with you on the go. First, a custom Perl script downloads Showtime listings from the Web and puts them into Palm database format (.PDB) which you can HotSync to your Palm. Currently, you can use Showtime in the U.S., U.K., France, Australia, Canada, and Portugal. Find out where a particular movie is playing, or see what is playing at a specific theater (**Figure 11.20**). Movie ratings and length, plus theater information such as address and phone number, are displayed along with the show times.

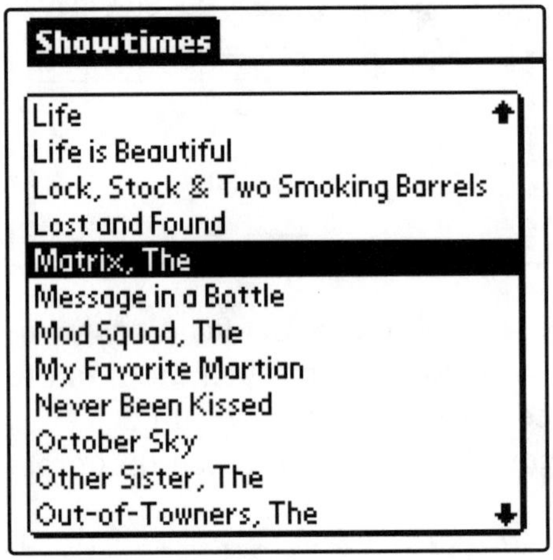

Showtimes

Life
Life is Beautiful
Lock, Stock & Two Smoking Barrels
Lost and Found
Matrix, The
Message in a Bottle
Mod Squad, The
My Favorite Martian
Never Been Kissed
October Sky
Other Sister, The
Out-of-Towners, The

Figure 11.20 ShowTimes is a fun way to check your local movie listings.

This list of software is very incomplete, but it should give you a taste of the universe of Palm programs out there just waiting for you to download, try, and buy. If you like the idea of trying out new Palm software, you should explore the Palm Web sites mentioned at the beginning of this chapter, or turn to the appendix for a longer list.

part four

Connecting with the Net

3Com doesn't say much about the Palm's online abilities, besides the built-in Mail program (which HotSyncs your regular email into your Palm). Nevertheless, armed with a modem and some add-on software, you can use the Palm to connect to your Internet Service Provider, check your email just like your computer does, and surf the Web—all of which are described in the chapters in this part. If you have a Palm VII, read Chapter 15. It will tell you how you can use the built-in wireless transmitter to get an account with the Palm.Net service, with which you can check and send email without a modem, and interact with the Palm Query Applications using a process 3Com calls Web clipping. Finally, the appendix provides you with additional resources that you can use to expand your Palm knowledge beyond the scope of this book.

12

Modems and Getting Online

It's amazing but true: you can hook a modem up to your Palm, connect to the Internet, send and receive email, cruise the Web, or HotSync to your computer remotely. For $129 (Palm III models) or $169 (if yours is a Palm V), you can buy a special 3Com modem specifically designed for use with your Palm. Or for $20 you can by a special connector from 3Com and connect your Palm to a regular external computer modem, which would probably be the cheaper way to go. This chapter covers using the special Palm modem to connect to your Internet Service Provider.

Prices quoted are list prices. You may find cheaper prices online or in stores.

To connect your Palm to the Internet, you need to set up service with an Internet Service Provider (ISP). An ISP is a company that creates an account for you that enables you to use your modem to dial into its computers over a telephone line. It also assigns you an Internet email address, which typically takes the form user@domain.com.

Undoubtedly, there are small, local ISPs in your area, and there are also large, national ISPs such as Earthlink and ATT World-Net which have local numbers for you. You may very well already have an account with an ISP that you use to get your email and surf the Web at home, and if you do, you can use that account to connect to the Internet with your Palm. This chapter takes you step by step through that process.

Palm Modem Basics

You can buy the special Palm modem from your Palm's Accessory Catalog, a copy of which was tucked into the box your Palm shipped in. Call 1-800-881-7256 to order it or buy it from an online store (see the appendix for Palm-related Web sites and other resources).

III The PalmPilot modem (see **Figure 12.1**) is available for all Palm III models (it also works with the older PalmPilots). It's what's known as a 14.4K modem, which means it connects at 14,400 bits per second—not very fast by current standards, but much better than nothing.

V The Palm V Modem (see **Figure 12.2**) works with the Palm V only. It's a 33.6K modem, meaning it connects at a very respectable 33,600 bits per second—more than twice as fast as the PalmPilot modem.

Figure 12.1 The PalmPilot modem fits onto the bottom of your Palm III, IIIx, or IIIe.

Figure 12.2 Your Palm V slides down into the Palm V modem.

If you have a Palm VII, you don't need a modem to connect online for email and other resources because your device has built-in wireless access. See Chapter 15 for all about setting up and using that service and the Palm Query Applications that use it. Note that you cannot currently use the wireless features of the Palm VII to connect to your Internet Service Provider, to surf the Web, or even simply to get your email from your existing account—the wireless access works only with the Palm.Net service. You will receive a new Palm.Net email address when you sign up, something like user@palm.net. But you're not losing anything, because the Palm VII can use a PalmPilot modem just like a Palm III can, and you can use the directions in this chapter to connect to your ISP with a modem and from there you can check your email, get on the Web, and so on.

To connect online with a Palm modem, you need

- A Palm.

- A Palm modem.

- An analog phone line (not a digital line, as is found in most large offices and hotels).

- An account with an ISP.

> **Palm modems and batteries**
>
> Palm modems use batteries ferociously—stock up on lots of fresh ones so you're ready when the juice runs out. Batteries in a Palm III modem will last for around six hours of continuous use. The Palm V can drain its batteries in three hours flat. You can buy a Modem AC adapter from 3Com for $19.95, which will let you plug your Palm modem into a wall socket and save you battery headaches.

There are two kinds of phone lines: analog and digital. Digital lines are often those found in offices and hotels (if you're in a hotel, ask whether you can connect a modem to the line). You'd think, since digital is more modern than analog, that a digital line is what you want, but it's not. You want an analog line. Most typical phone lines, like the one in your abode, are analog. If you try to connect your Palm modem to a digital phone line, it will emit some beeps to tell you, "Hey, this is a digital line," and it won't work.

If you are surrounded by digital lines, look for a fax machine. Fax machines are almost always connected to analog lines. Discreetly disconnect the phone line from the back of the fax machine while no one is looking and insert it into your Palm's modem.

To check your email, you have to install an add-on Palm email program, such as HandMail, or MultiMail (see Chapter 13 for details). To surf the Web, you'll need another add-on Web browsing program, such as HandWeb, ProxiWeb, or AvantGo (see Chapter 14 for details). See Chapter 11 for instructions for installing add-on software and some suggestions on which software is worth installing.

Setting up Your Palm Modem

1. Take your Palm modem out of the box and install the AAA batteries that came with it.

2. Plug one end of the standard RJ11 phone cord that came with your Palm modem into your phone jack, and the other end into the jack on your Palm modem.

3. Snap the modem onto the bottom of your Palm (it fits slightly differently for the PalmPilot and the Palm V modems—see your *Modem Handbook* for illustrations showing how to do this).

4. Turn on your Palm and tap the Applications icon. Tap Prefs to call up the Preferences screen. In the upper right-hand corner of the screen, tap the drop-down arrow and select Network from the list that appears (**Figure 12.3**).

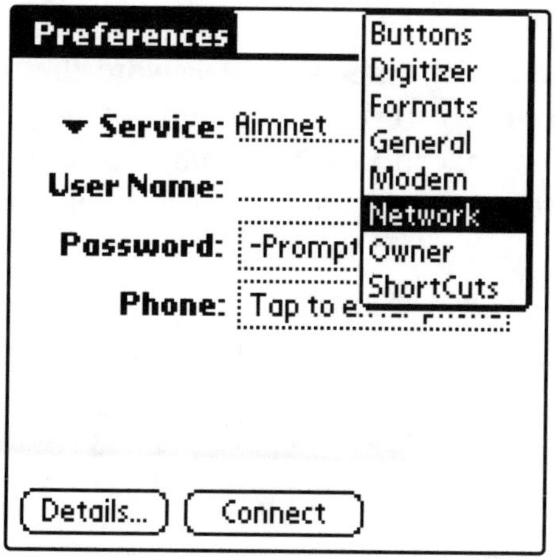

Preferences

	Buttons
	Digitizer
	Formats
▼ **Service:** Aimnet	General
	Modem
User Name:	Network
	Owner
Password: -Prompt	ShortCuts
Phone: Tap to e

(Details...) (Connect)

Figure 12.3 The Network Preferences screen is where you prepare your Palm to dial up your ISP.

5. Tap the Service drop-down arrow to reveal all of the Palm's built-in settings for Internet Service Providers (**Figure 12.4**). If your ISP is among them, tap it and skip to step 8.

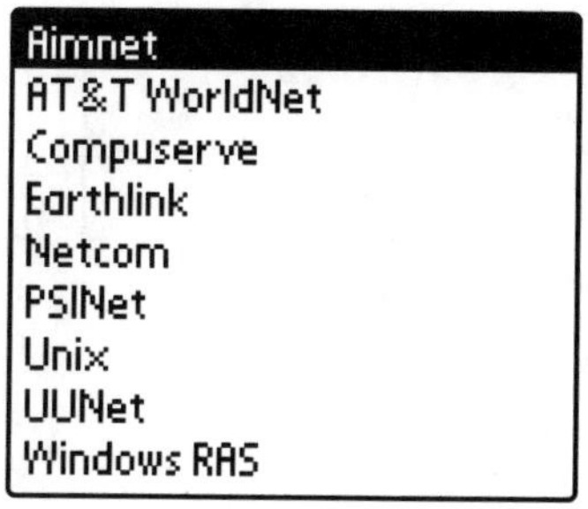

Figure 12.4 Nine of the most popular national ISPs have their names already built into the Palm.

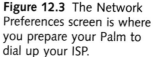

Aimnet
AT&T WorldNet
Compuserve
Earthlink
Netcom
PSINet
Unix
UUNet
Windows RAS

6. If your ISP is not in the drop-down list of built-in setups, you'll have to create a new setup for your ISP. Tap the Menu icon. You may have to tap it twice—once to get rid of the drop-down list and return to the main Preferences screen, and once to make the Service menu appear.

7. Tap New. A new service called Untitled appears. Replace the word Untitled with the name of your ISP.

8. Tap on the User Name line and enter the user name that you use with your ISP. Your user name is almost always the first part of your email address, the part before the @ sign. For example, if you are corbin @sirius.com (I have a feeling you're not), your user name is *corbin*.

9. Tap the Password Prompt box to call up the Password screen (**Figure 12.5**). Enter your password there. It's the same password you use when you connect online with your computer, and it's your email password. Tap OK. You return to the Preferences screen, and the Password filed is marked Assigned.

10. Tap the box that says, "Tap to enter phone." The Phone Setup screen appears (**Figure 12.6**).

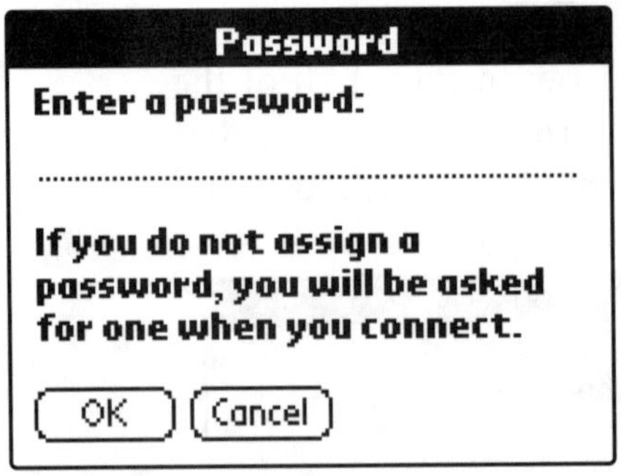

Password

Enter a password:

....

If you do not assign a password, you will be asked for one when you connect.

(OK) (Cancel)

Phone Setup ℹ

Phone #: |...

....

☐ **Dial prefix:** 9,............................
☐ **Disable call waiting:** 1170,.
☐ **Use calling card:**

,,,,,...

(OK) (Cancel)

Figure 12.5 Enter the password you use with your ISP here.

Figure 12.6 Filling in information for dialing your ISP in the Phone Setup screen.

11. Enter the dial-up access phone number for your ISP on the Phone# line. It's probably a local number, which means you don't need to use a 1 + the area code. If you don't know the access number offhand, it's on your computer. Go to your computer and go through the motions of connecting with its modem—the process will show you the phone number at some point.

12. If you have to dial a prefix to get a line (such as 9), put a check mark beside the Dial prefix line and enter the number, followed by a comma (a comma forces a pause of a second or two while the prefix is registered). If you don't know whether you need a dial prefix, look at how your connection on your computer works—if you use one there, you should use the same one here.

13. If you have call waiting on your phone service, put a check mark beside the Disable call waiting line and enter the code that disables call waiting on your line, usually 1170 or *70, followed by a comma.

14. If you want to charge the call to your calling card, put a check mark next to Use calling card, and enter the card number.

15. When you've entered everything you can think of, click OK. You return to the Preferences screen.

16. Tap the Details button to bring up the Details screen (**Figure 12.7**). Select your connection type. Most connections today are PPP connections, but if your provider uses SLIP or CSLIP, select that.

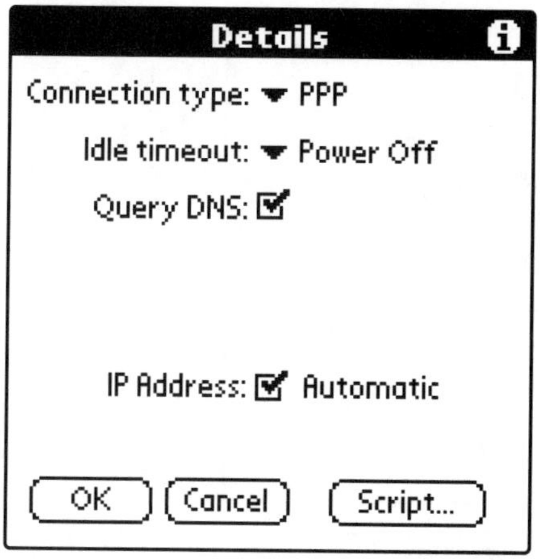

Details ⓘ

Connection type: ▼ PPP

Idle timeout: ▼ Power Off

Query DNS: ☑

IP Address: ☑ Automatic

(OK) (Cancel) (Script...)

Figure 12.7 More network settings to fiddle with before you can connect.

17. In the Idle timeout box, choose how long you want your Palm to remain connected if nothing is happening. Your choices are 1, 2, or 3 minutes, or until your Palm's power is turned off (the recommended setting).

18. Leave the check mark in the Query DNS box. (If your connection ends up not working, come back to this part, uncheck the Query DNS box, and try again).

19. Leave the Automatic check mark in the IP Address box, unless you know that your computer has a stable IP address of its own. If it has an IP address, remove

the check mark and enter the IP address in the lines that appear when you remove the check mark. When everything is hunky-dory, click OK. If you do this, you won't be able to be online with your computer and Palm at the same time, because they will be using the same IP address, which is a no-no.

20. If you know you use a login script, tap the Script button and select your script from the choices that appear (**Figure 12.8**). Choose End to complete the script. If you don't remember normally using a login script, ignore this button. Tap OK, and tap OK again to return to the Preferences screen.

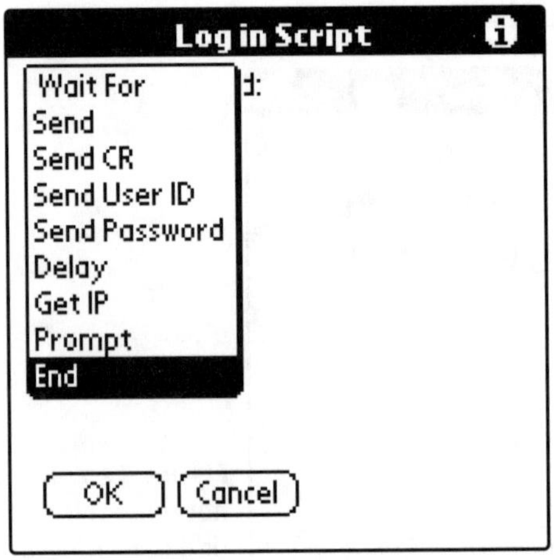

Figure 12.8 Choose a login script from the choices provided, if you normally use a log in script when you connect to your ISP.

21. If you are ready to connect to your ISP, tap Connect. If everything is set up correctly, you should hear the familiar modem screeches and squeals. Your Palm tells you it's dialing your ISP, connecting, and then that the connection is established. When you've connected successfully, the Connect button changes to a Disconnect button, and you'll stay connected until you tap the Disconnect button or turn off your Palm (or until another program, such as an email application, disconnects automatically).

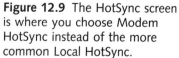

If your modem did not successfully connect, try the process again but change one of the settings you weren't sure about the first time. Change only one setting at a time when you are troubleshooting: that is, change the setting and then try to connect again. If it fails again, change one more setting and try again. It helps to write down the combinations of settings that you've tried. Study the dial-up and modem settings that your computer uses to connect to your ISP and try to duplicate them as closely as possible on your Palm. You may have to contact your ISP for support if you continue to have difficulty—check its Web site (with your computer, of course) for any Palm connection information.

Modem HotSync

Your Palm modem is set up, you have Palm Desktop and local HotSyncing set up on your computer at home, your computer is connected to a phone line and is configured to answer the phone, and you are ready to connect your Palm modem to a phone line and dial into your computer.

If all of that is true, you can HotSync via the Palm modem.

1. Connect your Palm modem to the phone line via the RJ11 phone cord provided (make sure it's an analog line).

2. On your Palm, tap the HotSync icon in the Applications screen to raise the HotSync screen (**Figure 12.9**).

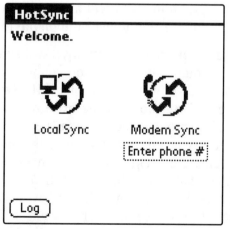

Figure 12.9 The HotSync screen is where you choose Modem HotSync instead of the more common Local HotSync.

3. Tap the box that says "Enter phone #." The Phone Setup screen appears (**Figure 12.10**).

Phone Setup

Phone #: |

☐ **Dial prefix:** 9.
☐ **Disable call waiting:** 1170.
☐ **Use calling card:**

(OK) (Cancel)

Figure 12.10 Enter the information that tells your Palm how to dial your computer in the Phone Setup screen.

If you've already connected to your ISP, as explained earlier in this chapter, you are familiar with this screen. (If not, go back and read the "Setting up Your Palm Modem" section for information on entering information in this screen.)

4. On the line labeled Phone #, enter the phone number that your computer back at home is connected to. Enter it just as if your were dialing it yourself. If it's in the same area code that you are in now, omit the area code. If it's in a different area code, precede it with the numeral 1, followed by the area code.

5. Tap OK. Your Palm will attempt to connect with your computer at home over the phone line.

If your Palm connects successfully, it will automatically perform a HotSync immediately after you connect, just as if it were in the cradle and you were doing a local HotSync. It will be slower than you are used to. Use the extra time it takes to consider how glad you are that such a thing is possible at all. If it wasn't successful, try again, but first reread the first part of this chapter. Modems are tricky things, and hooking up computers to phone lines can be a delicate operation, to be sure. If you simply can't get it to work, you'll just have to HotSync when you get home. In the meantime, treat yourself to a game of Hardball or Pocket Chess (see Chapter 11 for more on these games).

Email

It's exciting to think about: sending and reading email in a little machine that fits in the palm of your hand. How futuristic! As it turns out, because of the speed of Graffiti, the reading part is much more fun than the sending part. Nevertheless, if you always wanted to practice your pithiness, trying to write emails in Graffiti is an excellent way to do that.

There are two ways of sending and receiving email on your Palm, and they work very differently. You can:

- HotSync email back and forth with your computer, which handles the actual connecting, sending and receiving.

- Send email back and forth directly with your Palm, which is attached to a modem.

This chapter covers using email with your Palm both ways. The Palm comes with a built-in email program called Mail, but as you'll find out, Mail only works with your computer—not with the Internet. To do email directly with your Palm, you have to set up your modem (see Chapter 12) and install an add-on Palm email program, such as Handmail or MultiMail, both of which are described later in this chapter.

Palm VII users can get their Palm.Net email through the wireless feature, of course. The user gets a new email account on Palm.Net. The special Palm VII email program is called iMessenger, and it is described in Chapter 15. But if you want to check email on your existing email account, you can HotSync your email or attach a modem to your Palm VII, and it will work just as the other Palm models do.

Palm Email via HotSync

This section explains Palm email using HotSync to transfer email between your Palm and your computer's email program. Mac users must install and configure the MultiMail conduit software, as mentioned. Download and install the software (see Chapter 11 for how to install add-on software) and configure it according to the onscreen directions. Once that's done, you're all set to HotSync email.

If you're a Windows user, you probably set up Mail during the installation when you installed the Palm Desktop software. But you may have skipped Mail setup. To check, double-click the Palm Desktop icon to start Palm Desktop and click HotSync > Setup. The Change HotSync action dialog box appears (**Figure 13.1**). If at the bottom of that dialog box you see something like, "Your mail is currently set up with the following configuration," and it names your email program, then you already set up Mail for HotSyncing and can skip the following section.

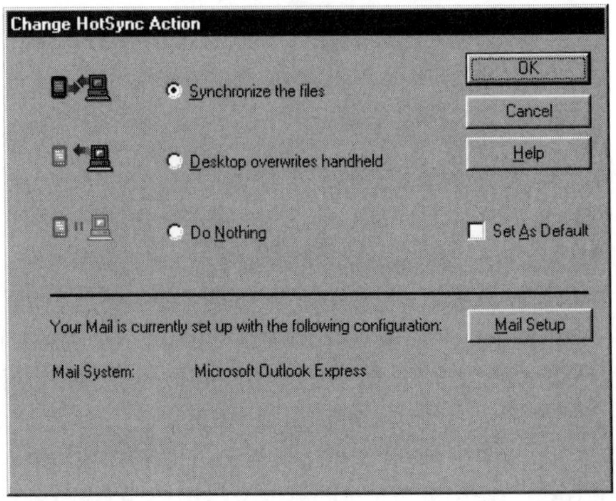

Change HotSync Action

- Synchronize the files
- Desktop overwrites handheld
- Do Nothing

OK
Cancel
Help

☐ Set As Default

Your Mail is currently set up with the following configuration:

Mail System: Microsoft Outlook Express

Mail Setup

Figure 13.1 This dialog box tells you whether you're set up to HotSync your email to your Palm's Mail program.

Setting up Mail for HotSyncing

If you don't see "Your mail is currently set up...," click the Mail Setup button in that dialog box to start the Mail Setup utility (**Figure 13.2**). Select your computer's email program from the list of available programs.

> *If you don't see your email program listed, I recommend that you start using Eudora Light or Outlook Express, both of which are free. You can download Eudora Light from www.eudora.com. Or download the free Internet Explorer package, which includes Outlook Express, from www .microsoft.com.*

With your selected email program in the "Synchronize with" box, click the Next button. You should see a screen like the one in **Figure 13.2**, telling you that Palm Desktop is now configured to HotSync your email. The next time you HotSync, your email will be transferred to your Palm's Mail program. Click Finish. You may have to do a little more configuring in the email program itself, but Mail Setup will tell you what you have to do before it closes.

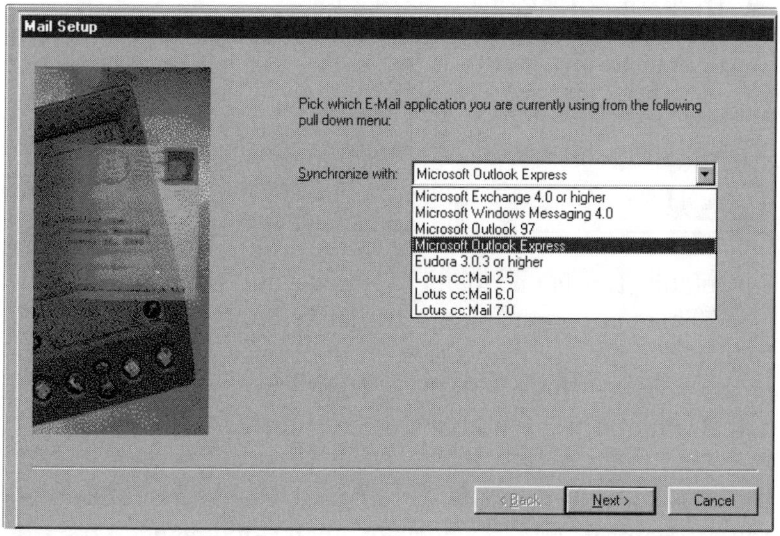

![Mail Setup dialog box. "Pick which E-Mail application you are currently using from the following pull down menu:" with a "Synchronize with:" drop-down showing Microsoft Outlook Express and options: Microsoft Exchange 4.0 or higher, Microsoft Windows Messaging 4.0, Microsoft Outlook 97, Microsoft Outlook Express, Eudora 3.0.3 or higher, Lotus cc:Mail 2.5, Lotus cc:Mail 6.0, Lotus cc:Mail 7.0. Buttons: Back, Next, Cancel.]

Figure 13.2 Way to go—you're ready to HotSync your email with your Palm.

HotSyncing your email

A typical scenario would have you using your computer to check your email at the end of the day to gather up the last scraps of it and then HotSyncing. You could then take your Palm with you and read and reply to your email at your leisure: on the bus, train, or nice comfy bed at home, for example.

If you don't know how to HotSync, go back and read Chapter 9 (Windows users) or Chapter 10 (Mac users).

To HotSync your email, put your Palm in its cradle and press the HotSync button. The HotSync process will start. When it's done, take your Palm out of the cradle, tap the Applications icon, and then tap the Mail icon. You'll see all your emails listed (**Figure 13.3**).

Mail 41 Msgs, 24 Unread	▼ Inbox	
✓ Marjorie B...	Re: GoLive...	8/4
✓ Ted Ganchi...	<No Subjec...	8/4
✓ Marjorie B...	Re: Little P...	8/4
Computer...	FREE Comp...	8/4
✓ Marjorie B...	Re: Little P...	8/4
✓ Tracy Bro...	New militar...	8/4
Sat Sharma	Fwd: FW: Air...	8/4
rflores@p...	Re: Directl...	8/4
✓ Tracy Bro...	Re:	8/4
Marjorie B...	Re: ch 2 figs	8/4
Amy Chan...	Re: party i...	8/4
(New) (Show)		

Figure 13.3 Amazing but true, your emails are in your Palm, ready for reading and replying.

By default, the Palm opens to show your Inbox in the Mail view. There are other folders available in the same place other Palm programs use categories: In the upper right-hand corner of the screen. The other folders are Outbox, Deleted, Filed, and Draft. You'll learn about these shortly.

HotSync options

You can control certain aspects of email HotSyncing in the HotSync Options screen. Tap the Menu icon, tap Options, and tap HotSync Options to bring up the HotSync Options screen (**Figure 13.4**).

All: The default, choosing to HotSync all your email means every email in your computer email program's Inbox gets transferred to your Palm from your computer during a HotSync.

Send only: The HotSync only works from your Palm to the computer. The only thing that happens is that messages in your Palm's Outbox get transferred to your computer email program's outbox (or sent immediately, if your computer is connected to the Internet at HotSync time). Nothing transfers to your Palm.

Filter: Filtering lets you discriminate more precisely among emails and direct HotSync to transfer only those emails that exactly match the text criteria you set (**Figure 13.5**). You can set two kinds of filters by tapping the drop-down arrow that says "Ignore messages containing" (your other choice is "Retrieve only messages containing"). If you choose "Ignore messages containing," then Mail will not transfer mail that contains any words in the Subject line, for example, that you enter on the Subj: line here. If you want to retrieve messages only from coworkers, say, select "Retrieve only messages containing" and enter your company's domain name on the From line (for example, *yourcompany.com*).

> **The Macintosh email problem**
>
> Windows Palm Desktop provides a built-in conduit that lets you exchange email with your computer's email program, including Eudora, Outlook Express, cc:Mail, and others. Not so with the Mac. To use the Palm Mail program with your Mac, you have to buy the MultiMail conduit developed by Actual Software (it costs around $30). You can download it from wwwpalmcentral.com and other Palm Web sites. Once you purchase, install, and configure the conduit, you can HotSync email between your favorite Mac email program and the built-in Mail program on your Palm.

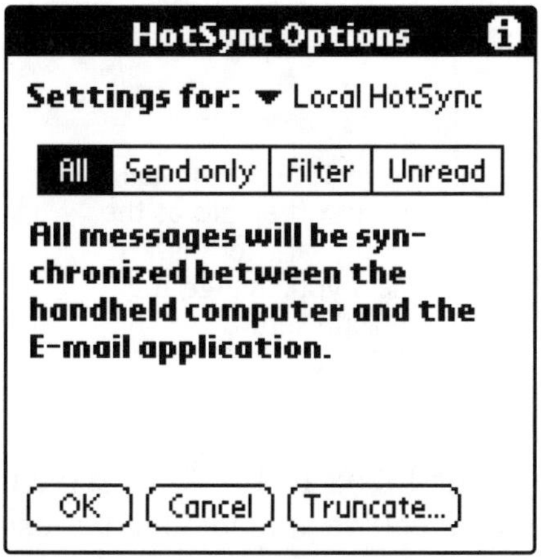

Figure 13.4 Specifying which email gets HotSynced in the HotSync Options screen.

Figure 13.5 Setting up email filtering.

Unless you are always overwhelmed with spam (unsolicited commercial mail), trying to set up effective filtering is not worth the effort, in my opinion. You could accidentally block important messages. And remember, the email is also on your computer, whose email program probably has much better filtering options than Palm Mail does. Better to set up filtering there so that unwanted messages are blocked in the first place.

Unread: Select the Unread box to retrieve only those messages from your computer that you have not read.

Truncate: The biggest email message that Mail can accept in whole is 8,000 characters (characters are letters, numbers, punctuation, and spaces). Mail cuts off the end of messages according to your settings. Tap the Truncate button to reveal the Truncate Options screen, where you set the number of characters an email can have before Mail cuts off the end of it. Because of the limited amount of memory in your Palm, the lower the Truncate character count, the more emails you can store in your Palm (but the shorter they'll be, obviously). If you anticipate storing a large number of emails on your Palm, set the Truncate limit at 500 or 1,000 characters.

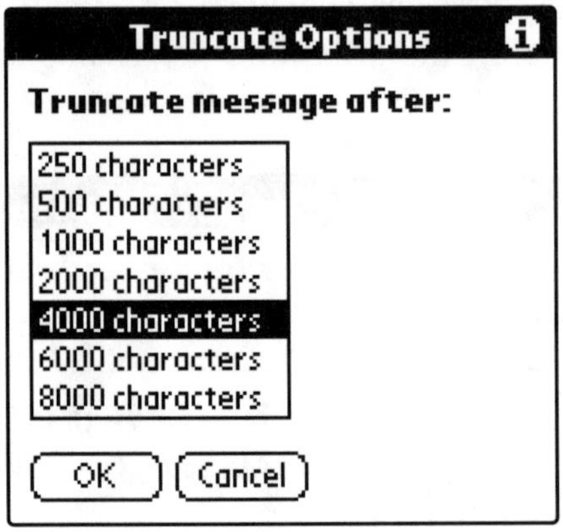

Truncate Options ⓘ

Truncate message after:

250 characters
500 characters
1000 characters
2000 characters
4000 characters
6000 characters
8000 characters

(OK) (Cancel)

Figure 13.6 Palm Mail will cut off emails at the 4,000-character mark unless you change the Truncate setting.

Reading email in Palm Mail

Make sure you're looking at your Inbox in the Mail screen. The check marks you see mean you've already read those emails on your computer. Tap a message's description to bring the message up onscreen in Message view (**Figure 13.7**). Scroll down to read the whole thing. Note that, just as with the email you already know and love, the angled brackets signify text quoted from other emails. In this case, my brother is answering a question I sent him, and my question is preceded by >.

Don't forget the physical scroll button on your Palm. It's great for scrolling through long emails without using the stylus.

Changing the view: As you know, emails have additional information such as date, time, email address of the sender, subject, and sometimes lots of incomprehensible Internet routing gibberish in the header area. You can control whether to view that stuff onscreen or not by tapping one of the two little boxes in the upper right corner of the Message view. The box with just two lines showing restricts the header to the name of the sender and the Subject. Tap the other box showing many lines to reveal the rest of the header stuff (**Figure 13.8**).

Changing the font: As in other Palm applications, you have a choice of three fonts to use when displaying your incoming email. Tap the Menu icon, tap Options, tap Font, and select the font you want (normal, bold, or large).

Hide
headers

Display
headers

Inbox Message 23 of 43

From: Christopher Collins
 Subj: Re: Nuvo?

>What's your piece that's running in NUVO?

It's that Phish review -- I think it may be online, too?
(www.nuvo-online.net)

Here's a rough one:

(Done) (Reply) (Delete) ◀▶

Figure 13.7 Emails on your Palm look pretty much like they do on your computer.

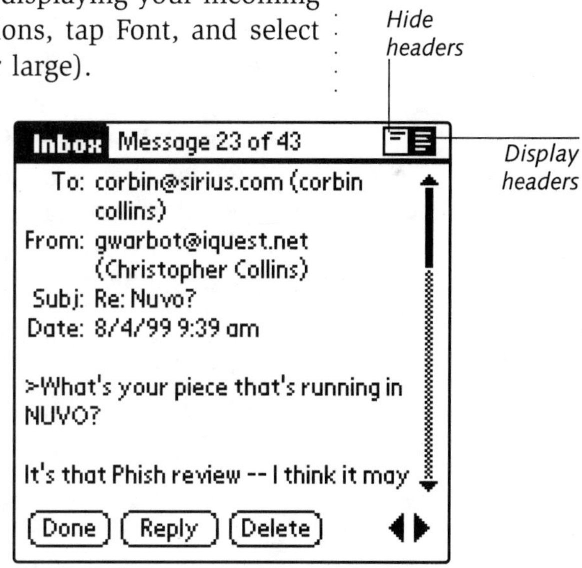

Inbox Message 23 of 43

    To: corbin@sirius.com (corbin
        collins)
 From: gwarbot@iquest.net
        (Christopher Collins)
 Subj: Re: Nuvo?
 Date: 8/4/99 9:39 am

>What's your piece that's running in NUVO?

It's that Phish review -- I think it may

(Done) (Reply) (Delete) ◀▶

Figure 13.8 The same email shown in Figure 13.7 is shown here with the long header box selected.

Filing and deleting: When you're done reading an email, and you don't want to leave it in your inbox, you have two choices (besides replying to it or forwarding it—see the next section for how to reply and forward): You can file it or delete it. To file it, tap the Menu icon, tap Message, and tap File (or write the Graffiti command ╱⎮). Your message will be moved to the Filed folder. To delete a message, tap the Delete button.

When you tap the Delete button, your email isn't actually deleted right away. Instead, it simply moves to the Deleted folder and stays there until you HotSync. If you change your mind about deleting an email, and you haven't HotSynced yet, tap on the folders drop-down arrow (in the upper right-hand corner of the Mail screen), choose Deleted, and then tap the message. It will appear onscreen again and offer you an Undelete button. Tap it. Your email is now restored to your Inbox.

Once you HotSync, all deleted email disappears from both your Palm and your computer's email program. So only delete email in your Palm if you don't care to ever see the message again. If you think you might conceivably need it sometime, file it instead.

Replying to and forwarding an email

As I mentioned earlier, unless you have a GoType keyboard (see the Appendix), writing email on your Palm means using Graffiti. And that means it's pretty slow going. Just get used to the fact that when you write a Palm email, you will be keeping it short.

After you read an email, you may want to send a reply to it or forward it to someone else. To do that, tap the Reply button at the bottom of the screen. The Reply Options screen will appear (**Figure 13.9**).

Figure 13.9 All these choices lie under the Reply button.

Sender, All, Forward: The three Reply to boxes let you reply to just the sender or to everyone who was sent the original email, or to forward the message to someone else. Tap Sender, All, or Forward to make your choice.

Include original text: A check mark in this box will paste the text of the original email into your new email. By default, this option is selected. If you don't want to include the text of the original email, uncheck the box.

Comment original text: Checking this box will put the standard angle brackets in front of the original email's text, just as most email programs do. If you don't check this box, it will be hard for your recipients to tell which is your reply and which is the original email.

Tap OK when your options are selected. You will see a New Message screen with the original email text in it (**Figure 13.10**). If you are replying, the email addresses are already filled in for you.

What about attachments?

What happens if someone sends you an email with an attachment? The attachment stays on your desktop computer, but it is not Hot-Synced to your Palm—only the email that carried the attachment winds up in Palm Mail. You'll see a message alerting you that the email had an attachment that is still on your computer.

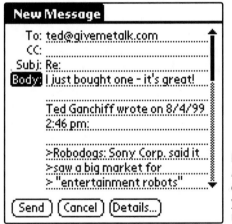

Figure 13.10 The New Message screen has everything filled out for you—just write your reply in the Body: line.

If you are forwarding instead of replying, the To: line will be blank, and you'll have to enter the email address of your new recipient. See the next section for tips on pulling email addresses out of Address Book.

When you finish with your reply, tap Send. You return to the Mail screen, where you can continue reading emails and replying to them. Your email disappears and moves to your Palm's

Outbox. The next time you HotSync, your email will be sent via your computer during the HotSync.

If your computer is connected online when you start your HotSync, your email is sent immediately by your email program—during the HotSync itself. If not, the email is placed in your email program's Outbox and will be sent the next time you connect your computer to the Internet.

See the following section for more on your options when creating a new email.

Sending a new email in Palm Mail

To create a brand new email, tap the New button at the bottom of the Mail screen. A blank email appears (**Figure 13.11**). On the To: line, either use Graffiti to write the email address of the recipient or write the Graffiti command /L (for Lookup) to bring up a list of all the email addresses that you have entered in Address Book. Tap the address, tap Add, and it will be entered on the To: line in the New Message screen.

On the To: line, if you write the first letter or two of the person's last name and then write /L, the Lookup screen automatically scrolls so that names starting with that letter are at the top of the screen. Lookup saves you from having to scroll through every address you have to get to Kathy Zhering's email address.

```
╔═══════════════════════════════╗
║ New Message                   ║
║ ┌────┐                        ║
║ │ To:│ │.......................║
║ └────┘                        ║
║   CC: ........................ ║
║  Subj: ....................... ║
║  Body: ....................... ║
║        ....................... ║
║        ....................... ║
║        ....................... ║
║        ....................... ║
║        ....................... ║
║        ....................... ║
║        ....................... ║
║ ( Send ) ( Cancel ) ( Details...) ║
╚═══════════════════════════════╝
```

Figure 13.11 Tapping New brings up a fresh, New Message screen for you.

CC-ing: If you want to "CC" (carbon copy) other recipients, enter their email addresses on the CC: line. If you want to "BCC" (blind carbon copy) someone, tap the Details button. The Message Details screen appears (**Figure 13.12**). Tap the BCC box to put a check mark in it. When you return to the Message screen, a new BCC line will be there, but only this once—you have to re-create it like this every time you want it.

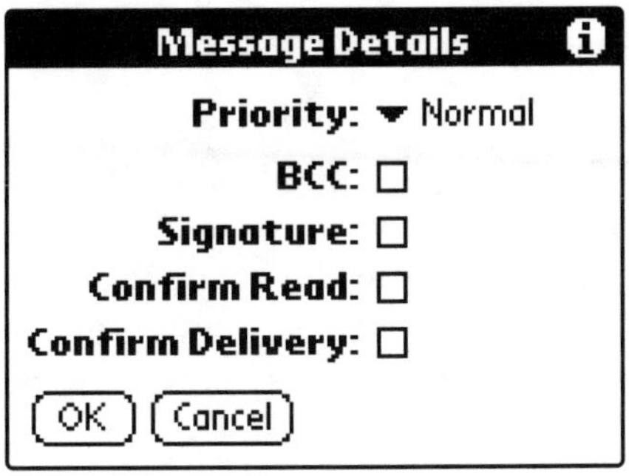

Figure 13.12 The Message Details screen lets you secretly send the email to without any other recipients knowing.

BCC or blind carbon copy sends a carbon copy of the email to someone, but no one else on the list of recipients can see that the BCC'd person also received the email.

Signature: In the Message Details screen, tap the Signature box if you want to include your signature at the end of your emails (see the next section for instructions on creating an email signature).

Confirm Delivery: Put a check next to Confirm Delivery if you want to have an email sent to you when the email is delivered to the recipient's mailbox.

Confirm Read: Put a check next to Confirm Read if you want to receive an email notifying you that the recipient has actually opened the email on his or her computer.

You may not have known this was possible—it means that other people could be checking to see whether you've read the emails they sent you. Junk emailers (also known as spammers) use the Confirm Read trick to verify that an email address actually reaches not just an email address but a live person. That's why you should avoid opening emails that look like spam; if you open them, you'll end up getting more spam. Delete spam on sight!

Saving a draft: If you're interrupted in the middle of writing an email, tap the Cancel button. You'll be asked whether you want to save a copy of it in the Draft folder. Tap Yes. When you return to it, you'll find it there, ready to finish and send.

When you have configured everything you need to in the Message Details screen, tap OK to return to the Message screen. Write your email and tap Send to send it.

Creating a signature

You may be familiar with signatures from your regular email activities. A signature is text that you can append to the end of your messages. Signatures typically contain the sender's name and maybe job title, company, sometimes a phone and/or fax number, and perhaps a choice quotation or axiom.

To create your signature, tap the Menu icon, tap Options, and tap Preferences. The Preferences screen appears (**Figure 13.13**). Write your signature in the space provided. When you're done, tap OK. If you have a check mark in the Signature box in the Message Details screen, your signature will be tacked onto the end of your emails.

Figure 13.13 A signature saves you from writing your name and other info every time you write an email.

Purging

As in other Palm programs, such as Date Book and To Do List, Mail lets you purge. In Mail, you purge your deleted emails without waiting to HotSync. Tap the Menu icon and tap Purge Deleted. You'll get one warning screen that informs you that purged emails cannot be restored. Make sure you understand that there is no going back and then tap Yes.

Showing more onscreen

You may have noticed that the Palm Mail screen is rather cramped for space. There is one thing you can do to increase the space available for showing your email senders' names and the Subject lines of your emails in Mail view. In Mail view, tap the Show button. The Show Options screen appears

(**Figure 13.14**). Remove the check mark from the Show Date box and tap OK. You'll return to the Mail screen, and the date column, which was taking up about 20 percent of the screen, will be gone (**Figure 13.15**).

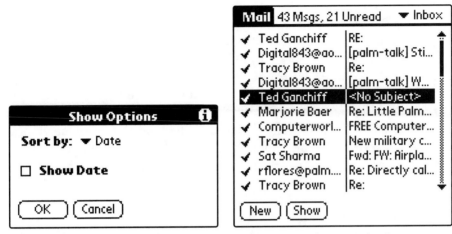

Figure 13.14 Uncheck the Show Date box to remove the date column from your view.

Figure 13.15 The new, dateless, more roomy Mail screen.

Also in the Show Options box, if you tap on the drop-down arrow labeled Sort by, you can choose to sort your emails by date, sender, or subject. Usually email is sorted by date, so the latest emails are at the top of the screen. But sometimes you want to find a message by a certain person or subject.

If the Palm Mail program doesn't blow up your skirt, there are other Palm email programs that let you HotSync email to and from your desktop email, such as Palmeta Mail and Top Gun Postman. You can download these and try them out by visiting www.palmcentral.com and other Palm-related Web sites (see the appendix for more Palm resources).

Palm Email via the Internet

Of course, it's even more novel and exciting to connect to the Internet with the Palm modem, download, and send email without using your computer at all. Before you can do that, though, you have to have an account

Finding email text
Don't forget the ever-useful Find icon. Now that you have email messages in your Palm, Find will find text in them. Tap the Find icon, enter the text you want to find, and Find brings back everything containing that text—including text from your email messages.

with an Internet Service Provider (ISP), and you must obtain and set up a Palm modem (or connect your Palm to a regular old computer modem with a cable you can buy from 3Com). See Chapter 12 for details on connecting to your ISP via the Palm modem.

Several good direct Internet email programs are available for the Palm, among them HandMail, MultiMail, PDQmail, Top Gun Postman, and PocketFlash (for AOL users). I briefly cover HandMail as an example in the remainder of this chapter. I just want to get you going on how to set up, check, and send email in a Palm application, and HandMail is pretty typical in this regard. You should be able to take the spirit of what I describe here and apply it to other Palm email programs to at least get up and running. Go to www.palmcentral.com. to download a demo version of HandMail and the others.

HandMail as an example

For $49.95, HandMail 2.0 and HandMailAOL by SmartCode Software (www.smartcodesoft.com) are nice, well-rounded email programs that turn your Palm into an email machine. Hand-Mail for AOL works with AOL accounts, and HandMail 2.0 works with most other email accounts, including those with ISPs. HandMail works just like email on your computer. You can read and write email while you're not connected and then connect to the Internet with the Palm modem to send and receive.

Unlike most other Palm email programs, HandMail also works with America Online accounts. It lets you preview email before you download it. It also lets you save text as Memo Pad documents that you can send as email attachments to other Palm users. It has more sophisticated filtering options than Palm Mail does. And HandMail lets you download emails up to 50K (roughly 150 screens) in length.

Install HandMail by following the instructions in Chapter 11 for installing add-on software. After you do, tap the HandMail icon in the Applications screen. At the Welcome screen, tap OK.

You have to set up your POP and SMTP information for your email account.

POP stands for Post Office Protocol, and it is the piece of software that pulls your email from your ISP's server and places it on your Palm. SMTP stands for Simple Mail Transfer Protocol, which controls sending your mail from your computer to your ISP's server and from there to the recipients' mailboxes somewhere on the Internet. To use Internet email, you must set up both of these protocols in any email program.

A few email systems use a scheme called IMAP instead of POP. If your email is of the IMAP variety, you should try a Palm email program that supports IMAP, such as MultiMail. HandMail does not support IMAP.

The good news is you've already set up POP and SMTP in your computer's email program, such as Eudora, Outlook Express, or cc:Mail. Go into that program and root around the Options or Setup screens. Write down your POP server name and your SMTP server name. Typically, these take the form (for the POP server) *pop.domain.com* and (for the SMTP server) *smtp.domain.com* or *mail.domain.com*, where *domain.com* is replaced with the domain name of your ISP.

Setting up POP: In HandMail, tap the Menu icon, tap Setup, and tap POP3. You'll see the POP setup screen (**Figure 13.16**). Fill in the POP information you got from your computer's email program, along with Mailbox (your user name) and Password (the same password you use to check email on your computer— tap on the Unassigned box to enter it).

Don't worry about the difference between POP and POP3— they are the same.

Leave the boxes at the top set to "1" (that's your main email account—you can configure up to five different email accounts in HandMail). Put a check mark in the "Leave mail on server" box, at least for the first few times you check email. It will make you feel safer knowing that no matter what happens with your email once it hits your Palm, it's still on the server and you can download it again using your computer if you need to. Your computer should be configured to delete the email from the server once it downloads to your computer.

When you're done, tap OK.

Setting up SMTP: Tap Menu, Setup, and then tap SMTP. The SMTP Preferences screen appears (**Figure 13.17**). Enter the SMTP info you got from your computer into the appropriate fields, just like you did for POP. When you're done, tap OK.

POP3 Preferences ⓘ	SMTP Preferences ⓘ
Mailbox: 1 2 3 4 5	**SMTP:** 1 2 3 4 5
Server: pop.sirius.com	**Server:** mail.sirius.com
Mailbox: corbin	**E-mail:** corbin@sirius.com
Password: -Assigned-	**Name:** Corbin collins
☑ **Leave mail on server**	☑ **Default account**
(OK) (More...)	(OK) (More...)

Figure 13.16 Setting up your POP information in HandMail.

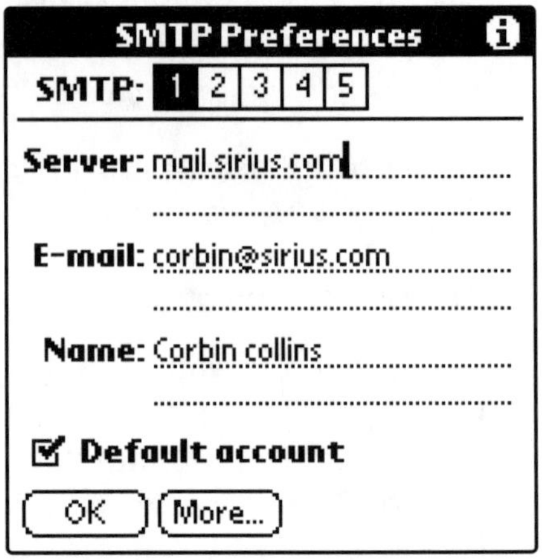

Figure 13.17 Setting up your SMTP information in HandMail.

Using HandMail: Snap the modem on. In HandMail, tap the Mail menu and tap Retrieve. Your Palm will start up the modem, you'll hear those exciting modem sounds, and your email will start flowing into your Palm (**Figure 13.18**).

When the retrieval is finished, you'll see your HandMail Inbox screen, hopefully brimming with email messages from friends, family, and/or colleagues (**Figure 13.19**). Form this point on, it works pretty much like Palm Mail does, with more options and features.

Tap a message to bring up a little selection list, where you pick what you want to do with it. To view it, tap View. To forward it, reply to it, move it to another folder, or delete it, pick the appropriate choice.

Tap the Menu icon, Setup, General to open the General Preferences screen. Make sure there's a check mark next to Auto Disconnect.

HandMail is chock-full of features to learn and explore. It comes with a handy manual in Adobe Acrobat format (to view it you need the free software Acrobat Reader—downloadable from www.adobe.com. And don't forget, HandMail isn't the only game in town. Check out www.palmcentral.com and other Palm software sites for many more choices of email programs (see the Appendix for a list of these sites). Happy emailing.

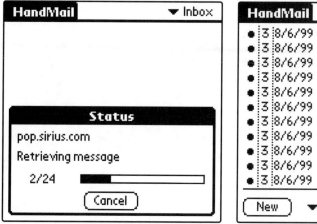

Figure 13.18 Here come your emails!

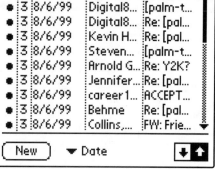

Figure 13.19 HandMail's Inbox screen shows the list of your emails.

Surfing
the Web

It's amazing that you can surf the Web in your Palm, even more amazing than email. It's hard to believe there could be enough room in that tiny device to provide a connection to the Internet and display Web pages. Yet several add-on Web browser programs let you do just that. In this chapter, I discuss using three Web browsers: AvantGo, ProxiWeb, and Palm-scape, each of which works a little differently.

To get on the Web from your Palm, you need the same kind of setup you needed for direct Internet email. That is, you must have an account with an Internet Service Provider (ISP), have access to an analog phone line, have a Palm modem (or a cable to attach your Palm to a computer modem), and you must install Web browsing software.

AvantGo also works without a modem. Ingeniously, it combines HotSyncing with your computer's Internet connection to go out on the Net and grab customized, stripped-down Web sites from the AvantGo Web site. AvantGo calls these "pre-optimized" Web sites channels, *and there are thousands of them. When the HotSync is finished, the Web sites are on your Palm, ready to surf without being connected. As a bonus, the AvantGo Palm software also works as a Web browser you can use to surf the Web directly through your Palm modem.*

You'll find all three of the programs (and more) that I cover in this chapter at the Palm Central Web site (www.palmcentral.com). Other Palm-related Web sites, such as PalmGear (www.palmgear .com) also offer software for download and/or purchase. Use your Windows or Macintosh Web browser to connect to one of these Web sites, find the Web browsing software you want to try, download it to your computer, place the .PRC file in your Palm: Add-on directory, and HotSync the program into your Palm. See Chapter 11 for detailed instructions on installing add-on software. See Chapter 12 to learn how to connect your Palm to the Internet.

If you have a Palm VII, you can lift the antenna and enjoy the Web-like "Web clipping" services provided by Palm.Net (see the next chapter for details). But you don't have to—everything you learn in this chapter you can also do on a Palm VII if you use it with a modem.

You should download ProxiWeb from www.proxinet.com. so that you can create an account that will let you use the software optimally.

This chapter assumes you've been on the Web before with your regular computer. If you haven't surfed the Web before, doing so on a Palm for the first time will be confusing and unimpressive.

ProxiWeb

ProxiWeb (by ProxiNet, www.proxinet.com) is the updated software that used to be called Top Gun Wingman, the first graphical Web browser for Palm devices. ProxiWeb has an impressive array of features and supports fancy Web technologies such as forms, Secure Sockets Layer (SSL, for sending sensitive information securely over the Internet), and server-side image maps.

The main difference between viewing Web pages on your desktop or laptop computer and using ProxiWeb to view them on your Palm, is that at some point a ProxiWare server strips down the content so that all the fancy graphics and animations and frames and so on are gone. To use the security and cookies features, you have to create a ProxiNet account when you download ProxiWeb from www.proxinet.com (do so if you plan to send credit card and other sensitive info over the Web). Just follow the instructions on the Web site for downloading ProxiWeb. When your account is set up (it's easy and fast, and at the time of this writing, still free), you can use ProxiWeb to view Web pages that have been optimized for use in your Palm.

You don't have to register at the ProxiNet site to use Proxi-Web, but if you plan to visit sites that want to set cookies (customized settings stores on your Palm) or send your credit card number online securely, you'll need to register.

Exploring ProxiWeb

Once you've installed ProxiWeb on your Palm, tap on the Applications icon, find the ProxiWeb icon, and tap it. Tap OK to get past the Welcome screen. Now tap the Menu icon, tap the Prefs menu, and tap Security. Enter the ProxiWeb user name and password that you set up on the ProxiNet Web site (**Figure 14.1**). When finished, tap OK.

Figure 14.1 Setting up personal info in ProxiWeb's Security Preferences screen.

You return to the ProxiWeb "home screen" (**Figure 14.2**). Notice the tiny icons along the bottom of the screen. If you've used a Web browser before, they should make sense to you. From left to right, the icons correspond to your browser's functions: back (to the page you just viewed), forward (to the next page among those you've already viewed), open (enter a new URL), reload (call up a fresh version of the current Web page), view cache (select a Web page from a list of those you've already visited), and bookmark (select a Web page from those you've designated as bookmarks).

Figure 14.2 This is how ProxiWeb's home screen looks when you launch it.

ProxiWeb has taken the liberty of giving you some popular sites pre-installed as bookmarks (**Figure 14.3**). Tap the little "B" icon to see them. Tap one of the bookmarks—Yahoo!, for example—and tap the Goto button. You'll see a dialog box like the one in **Figure 14.4**.

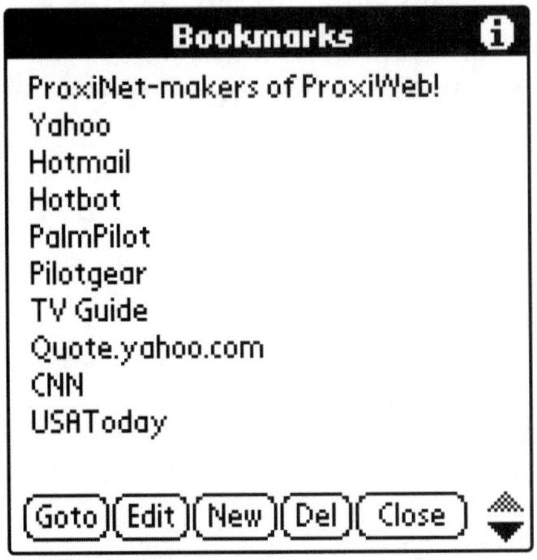

Bookmarks

ProxiNet-makers of ProxiWeb!
Yahoo
Hotmail
Hotbot
PalmPilot
Pilotgear
TV Guide
Quote.yahoo.com
CNN
USAToday

(Goto)(Edit)(New)(Del)(Close)

Figure 14.3 Thoughtfully, ProxiWeb has already provided some "starter" bookmarks.

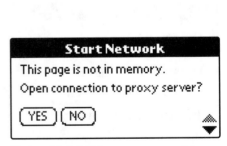

Start Network

This page is not in memory.

Open connection to proxy server?

(YES)(NO)

Figure 14.4 Well, yes, you want to connect and go there—otherwise you wouldn't have tapped on it, right?

*Whenever you ask ProxiWeb to display a Web page that you've never viewed in ProxiWeb before, it asks you the question shown in **Figure 14.4**. To save connection time and your Palm's memory, ProxiWeb wants to always be viewing Web pages that it has stored already. But that's just not how Web surfing works much of the time, and you'll be tapping "YES" at this screen quite a bit.*

If you're not already connected to your ISP, your Palm will start dialing to connect to the server, and you'll hear the modem dial and squeal for a while. Once connected, ProxiWeb loads the page (a percentage indicator appears on the bottom right of the screen).

You may be disappointed by how the page ends up looking. Most Web pages, of course, were never designed to be viewed at 160×160-pixel grayscale resolution. It's hard to tell what's what, frankly. Still, once you get accustomed to the fact that the Web is not very pretty on the Palm, it's still amazing that it works in the first place.

As in any Palm program, when everything doesn't fit on the page (as in ProxiWeb's Yahoo display), it's time to scroll. Don't forget the plastic scroll button on the face of your Palm—it makes for easier scrolling than the infinitesimal scroll bars do. As you scroll down Yahoo!'s home page, you start to understand that the structure has been broken and put together in a different way. Still, you can see some things that start to be familiar, such as the Yahoo! Categories.

Don't be surprised when you have to keep reconnecting every time you want to view a new page: ProxiWeb is so stingy with connection time that it automatically disconnects and terminates the phone call when a page successfully loads from the Internet.

Some neat ProxiWeb features

- When you see a Web page whose information you'd like to save and use somewhere else in your Palm, tap the Menu icon, tap View, and tap Save As Memo. The Web page is automatically saved as a Memo Pad item on your Palm (the title is the URL). Open it in Memo Pad to view it (**Figure 14.5**).

- Tap the Go menu and tap Add Bookmark to save the current Web page as a bookmark. In the Bookmarks screen (shown back in **Figure 14.3**), tap the Del button to delete a bookmark.

- Tap the "open" icon to use Graffiti to enter a brand new URL. A little screen pops up where you can write the URL. Tap the convenient Shortcuts drop-down arrow to select from some common Web address elements, such as http://, www., and .com (**Figure 14.6**)

- If you want to view the behind-the-scenes source HTML of a page, tap the View menu and tap Source.

Memo 1 of 16	▼ Unfiled

http://www.yahoo.com
Yahoo! Messenger
instant messaging
Yahoo! Mail
free email for life
advanced search
Yahoo! Auctions
–
bid now!
Blair
Witch

(Done) (Details)

Figure 14.5 Yahoo! is even more stripped down as a Memo Pad document.

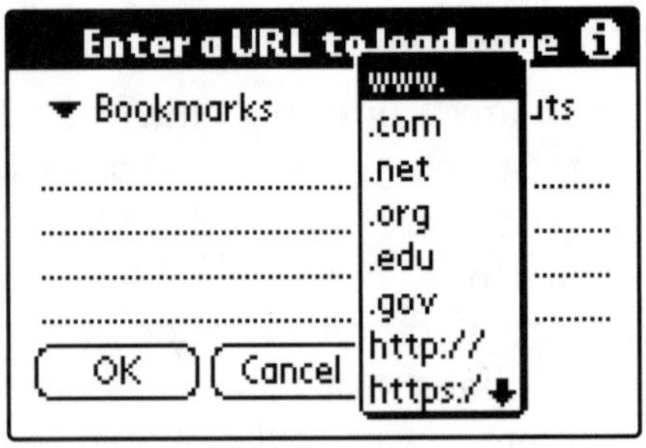

Enter a URL to load page ℹ️

▼ Bookmarks   www.   .ts
                .com
                .net
                .org
                .edu
                .gov
(OK) (Cancel) http://
                https:/ ↓

Figure 14.6 Built-in shortcuts save you from having to write out full Web page addresses.

All in all, although it's incredible that ProxiWeb works at all, I think you'll find cruising the Web with it a bit of a disappointment. It's just not the same as seeing all those fancy graphics in full color on your computer screen, which is how Web pages were meant to be used. However, it's way better than nothing. In a pinch, it's definitely nice to be able to use the Web from your Palm if you have to. If you're traveling and don't want to bring your laptop, it may be the only way to quickly look up the Web info you need.

Palmscape

Palmscape (by Oku Kazuho) is another totally free Web browser for Palms. It's small and fast. On the downside, it doesn't do graphics, it lacks the convenient icons of ProxiWeb and some other Palm Web browsers, and it appears not to have been updated since 1997. The current version at the time of this writing is Preview Release 4.1. You can download it from Palm Central (www.palmcentral.com) and other Web sites.

Install Palmscape like any Palm add-on software (see Chapter 11 for instructions on installing add-on software). Once you've HotSynced it to your Palm, find the Palmscape icon in the Palm's Applications screen and tap it. Palmscape opens to its Welcome screen. Tap the Open button, and the Open URL screen appears (**Figure 14.7**). Using Graffiti, write the URL of the Web site you want to go to (in this case, Yahoo!). When you're done, tap Open.

Palmscape retrieves the Yahoo! home page (**Figure 14.8**). Scroll down to see the whole thing. Like ProxiWeb, Palmscape closes the connection once the page downloads.

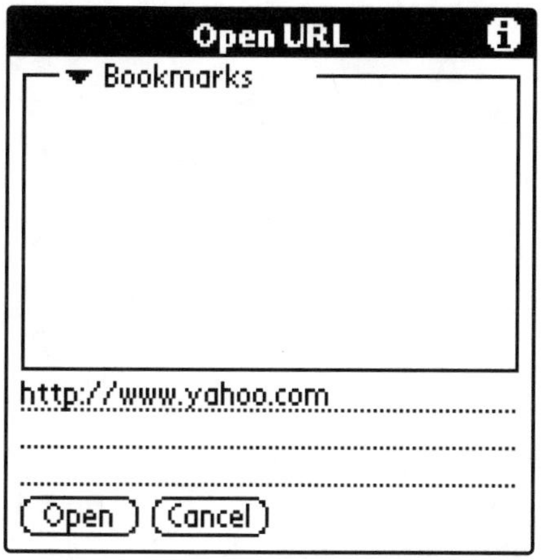

Figure 14.7 Write the URL you want directly into the Open URL screen in Palmscape.

Figure 14.8 What Yahoo! looks like in Palmscape.

The lack of navigation icons means that, for many common Web browsing commands, you have to tap Menu and then select a command from the Go menu (**Figure 14.9**). Note that some commands have Graffiti ShortCuts, which should save you a little time.

Figure 14.9 The Go menu is where you'll find the familiar Web browsing commands.

It doesn't get much simpler than Palmscape. It doesn't support any of the fancy new Web technologies, but for fast, very simple Web browsing, it works just fine.

HandWeb

The sister program to HandMail (see Chapter 13), HandWeb 2.0 is another popular Palm browser. Its features are on a par with Proxi-Web: graphics, forms, cookies, authentication.And like ProxiWeb, it does not support frames or Java. You can download HandWeb from www.smartcodesoft.com.

AvantGo

AvantGo, fromAvantGo, Inc., (www.avantgo.com) has won numerous awards for innovation—and for good reason. It is to the Web what Palm Mail is to email. That is, your computer handles the downloading from the Internet, and then you Hot-Sync the Web pages to your Palm and surf them offline (while you're not connected). The latest version of AvantGo also works as a Web browser all by itself. Like ProxiNet, AvantGo's servers strip away unnecessarily fancy Web stuff that Palms can't view anyway and send you optimized Web sites called "channels" that you view in your Palm. And most impressively, it's all free.

Currently, the AvantGo desktop client that allows HotSyncing of Web pages is available for Windows only. Mac users can use the AvantGo Palm software as a Web browser on their Palm, but they can't use the HotSync feature. Installing the program is also different for Mac users. Follow the MacOS links on the AvantGo Web site for instructions on installing AvantGo without the desktop client software.

Setting up AvantGo

Download the AvantGo setup program by visiting www.avantgo .com and following the links. Run the installer by double-clicking on the AGPalmClientSetup program that you dowloaded. AvantGo installs itself on your computer and displays a message saying that the next time you HotSync, the AvantGo Palm software will be installed on your Palm.

When the AvantGo installation finishes, the software starts up your computer's Web browser (Internet Explorer or Netscape Navigator) and connects to the AvantGo site. If your computer is not connected at the time, though, the connection fails and the installation does not complete.

If your installation fails, you have to manually pick up where it left off. Start your Web browser and go to this URL:

http://www.avantgo.com/setup/install_complete.html ?device = Palm

The AvantGo Web page tells you to put your Palm in its cradle and press the HotSync button (**Figure 14.10**). The HotSync process installs the software on your Palm. You may see an error message informing you that you haven't set up any Mobile Link servers or something. Just ignore that for now and continue the process. Click the Next button at the bottom of the Web page.

On the next Web page, you create your AvantGo.com account. Choose a user name, password, enter your email address, check any boxes that look interesting to you in terms of content (sports, news, entertainment), and click the I Accept button (you are agreeing to AvantGo's terms of use—read them if you want).

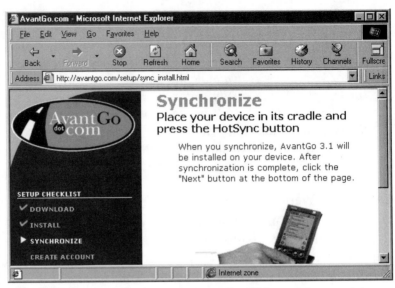

Figure 14.10 Follow the instructions on the Web page to complete your AvantGo installation.

Next, the AvantGo site configures what it calls a Mobile Link server for your computer (**Figure 14.11**). Just read and follow the instructions as they appear in the dialog boxes. When you're done configuring, click Next.

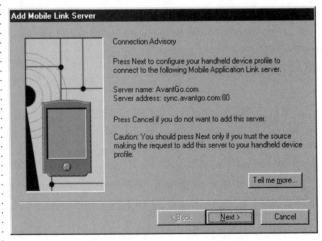

Figure 14.11 Configuring the Mobile Link server.

You have to HotSync again, and the AvantGo server loads some Web pages onto your Palm according to the interests you chose earlier (**Figure 14.12**). Click Next. If all went well, you should see a "Congratulations" message. You are now set up to use AvantGo and surf the channels you selected.

From now on, every time you HotSync, AvantGo interrupts the process and tries to connect to the Web. If your computer is not online at the time, a dialog box appears notifying you that AvantGo can't get to the Web. After a few seconds the notice goes away and your regular HotSync continues (you can also click Cancel to make it go away immediately).

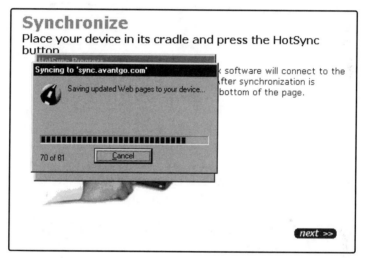

Figure 14.12
HotSyncing over the Web!

AvantGo on your Palm

Find the AvantGo icon in the Applications screen and tap it to launch the AvantGo browser on your Palm (**Figure 14.13**). Tap one of the channels to read it.

For example, if you subscribe to Infospace movie reviews, tap on the Movie Reviews link to start browsing movie reviews. However, as you try to go "deeper" into the channel you'll quickly find that AvantGo didn't download everything already, because instead of movie reviews, you'll see a dialog box like the one in **Figure 14.14**. The next time you HotSync, AvantGo downloads the stuff you want from the channel.

Figure 14.13 The AvantGo home screen shows the channels available for browsing.

Figure 14.14 You may have to connect your computer to the Net and HotSync again to fulfill your request.

You can increase the "link depth" so that more information is downloaded in advance by visiting AvantGo.com with your computer's Web browser. Log in using your user name and password. Your channels will appear. Click on the channel you want to increase the link depth for and wait for the Channel Properties screen (**Figure 14.15**). Increase the Link Depth setting and click Save Channel.

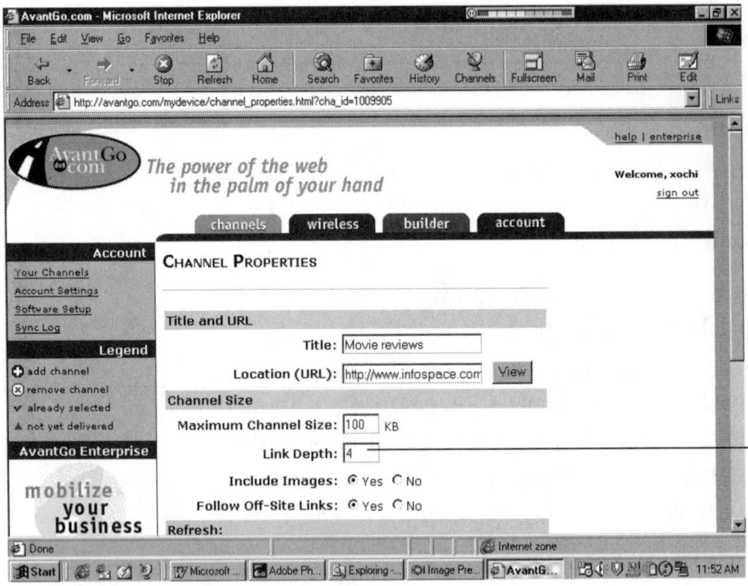

Link Depth setting

Figure 14.15 Increase the Link Depth setting on AvantGo.com.

AvantGo tips

- Remember that increasing the Link Depth, downloading images, and so forth come at a cost: memory space in your Palm. AvantGo is a very cool Palm program, probably the most creative and advanced one there is. But it is a memory hog. If you don't have a Palm IIIx with its 4MB of memory, you will have to be frugal about how much you ask AvantGo to download.

- On the AvantGo Web site, you can choose when to refresh your channels. If you HotSync several times per day, you don't want AvantGo making each one last forever. Have your channels refresh once each day at 6 A.M.

- AvantGo makes an excellent offline newspaper reader. The channels are specifically designed to be properly formatted and easily readable on the Palm. Highly recommended are The New York Times, the Wall Street Journal, and Wired News. One of the things that most people are amazed at is when I read the newspaper on my Palm. If you want to take information from the Web with you on your Palm, I don't think there's any better way to do it than with AvantGo. (Thanks to Michael Bergen for this tip and the previous one.)

- You can view a Web site that doesn't have a channel by clicking on the Account tab in your account screen. Click on Create Custom Channel and follow the onscreen Wizard's instructions. Type in the URL of the Web page you want and fill in any other information it asks for (start with a link depth of 2), and then click Save. After that, when you next perform a HotSync, the page you want will be in your Palm.

- It can be annoying to tap a link only to get a message saying your request will be sent the next time you HotSync. Therefore, AvantGo is much more satisfying if the computer you HotSync with has a constant connection to the Internet instead of a modem connection.

- The AvantGo.com Web site has excellent instructions, help, Frequently Asked Questions (FAQs), and other documentation that will tell you all you need to know to configure it to best suit your needs.

- A great way to use AvantGo is to make all your requests and then at the end of your work day, HotSync to go online and retrieve all the pages you asked for. Then read them on your Palm at your leisure—at home, on the bus, or wherever else you're comfortable reading stuff on your Palm.

15

Palm VII and Palm.Net

The Palm VII is a hint of what computers will be in the future: small, portable, and connected no matter where you are. It's not without its drawbacks, but it's a fascinating machine and extremely innovative. It doesn't need a modem to send email or download online content, because it all happens through a built-in wireless radio transmitter and antenna. When you raise the Palm VII antenna, the device turns on and looks for a nearby Bell South Network station. If it finds one, you hear a little double bleep, which tells you that the device is ready when you are to use the wireless feature.

The Bell South wireless network supposedly covers more than 90 percent of the United States, with strong coverage mostly in cities. Many rural areas do not have access yet. I took my Palm VII on a cross-country drive on I-80 from San Francisco to Indiana. The wireless service pretty much did not work from Nevada to Iowa (I slept through Salt Lake City—it might have worked there). Around Des Moines, I started getting service again, but then it would still cut out in rural areas. If you're in a medium-to-large urban area, you probably don't have to worry, but if not, ask a lot of questions about access in your area before you purchase a Palm VII.

The Palm VII is more than just a wireless device. It's also a full-fledged Palm that can do everything any of the other models can do. But the attraction is, of course, the array of Palm Query Applications (PQAs) that can utilize the wireless function. The device ships with 24 PQAs: 10 are preinstalled and ready to go when your first turn it on. The other 14 are on the Palm VII CD-ROM. You install those by placing the CD-ROM in your computer's CD-ROM drive and installing them like any other Palm add-on software (see Chapter 11 to learn how to install software).

You can quickly tell whether a program is a PQA or not: if it has three little lines shooting out of it to the right (indicating wireless broadcasting), it's a PQA and will use the Palm VII's wireless capabilities.

Naturally, anything this cool has its costs. Palm VII users sign up for accounts with a 3Com service called Palm.Net. At the time of this writing, there is a one-time $19.99 setup fee and two available payment plans: Basic and Expanded.

There are rumors that the Palm.Net payment structure may change in the near future. Check before buying a Palm VII.

Basic plan: $9.99 a month, first 50 kilobytes (KB) free. 50KB comes out to around 30 email messages, 20 stock quotes, 10 sports scores, 10 traffic reports, and 10 weather updates. After you hit your 50KB, you are charged 30 cents per KB.

Expanded plan: $24.99 a month, first 150KB free. 150KB comes out to around 90 email messages, 60 stock quotes, 30 sports scores, 30 traffic reports, and 30 weather updates. After 150KB, it's 30 cents per KB.

That's just a sample usage. If you don't plan to check stock quotes or sports scores, for example, you would get more free emails. Think of each Palm VII screen as equaling around one-third of a kilobyte. So, the basic plan gives you around 150 free screens of information, and the expanded plan around 450. After that, each screen of transmitted material will cost you roughly a dime.

Activating the Wireless Service

Before you can use your Palm VII's wireless features, you have to activate your Palm VII and set up your Palm.Net account. To do that, raise the antenna. The Palm VII will turn on (if it wasn't on already), and the Applications screen will open to the Palm.Net category of Palm Query Applications (the PQAs). You should see around a dozen icons (**Figure 15.1**).

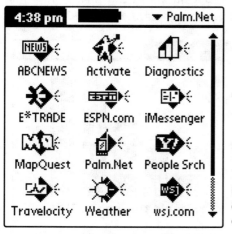

Figure 15.1 The Applications screen's Palm.Net category of PQAs.

Tap the Activate icon and follow the instructions (have your credit card ready). You have to choose between the Basic and Expanded plans. If you are certain you'll be logging a lot of time using the wireless stuff, pick Expanded—otherwise, choose

Basic (you can always upgrade to Expanded later). You'll be asked for billing information and for a user name for your Palm.Net account. Your user name will end up as the first part of your email address at Palm.Net. For example, if you choose Charlemagne as your user name, your Palm.Net email address will be charlemagne@palm.net.

Don't imagine that you can get a Palm.Net account, drop your regular Internet Service Provider, and then somehow get your Internet email through your Palm.Net account on your PC or Mac. You can access your Palm.Net email address only from your Palm VII. So, now you'll have two email addresses.

It may take a few tries to get the activation to work. The signal strength may not be strong enough where you are. Tap the Diagnostics icon to check your signal strength. You'll see a little graph showing the percentage of full strength signal the Palm is detecting from the nearest Bell South station (**Figure 15.2**). If it's low (below, say, 70 percent), try moving toward a window or even going outside. Even at 100 percent strength, the activation can fail. You just have to keep trying. If it just won't work, call Palm.Net Customer Care at 1-888-756-PALM.

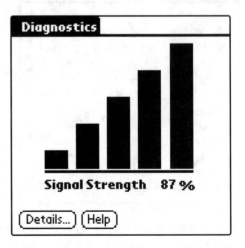

Figure 15.2 Diagnostics says my signal strength is pretty good (leaning out my apartment window in San Francisco).

Tap the Details button for a lot more specific information about the state of the wireless transmitter's signal.

Using the Palm Query Applications

It would be great if you could simply browse the Web through the wireless transmitter on your Palm VII. Well, you can't—not yet anyway. The thing is, most Web pages are *huge*. And don't forget: you are paying by the kilobyte. It's one thing to get unlimited modem access to the Web through your computer and ISP for the price of a local call. That's where Web browsing shines. But the Palm is not a G3 or 400MHz Pentium II, and neither does it sport a 15-inch screen. It's just not designed for that. What it's good at is retrieving short bursts of text that are easy and convenient to read wherever you are—which is where the concept of *Web clipping* comes in.

Web clipping is Palm's term for taking out all the fancy big graphics and JavaScript and tables and animation and so on that make the Web so great on your computer. What you have left is just pretty much the shortened, text version of a Web site, with a few small graphics. As I already mentioned, Palm programs that can do that are called PQAs. 3Com partnered with several big-name Web companies to create the PQAs that ship with every Palm VII.

But what is a PQA, really? The best way to learn is to start trying them. Raise the antenna to open the Applications screen to the Palm.Net category, which is where your PQAs are. Let's go through them alphabetically.

Tap the left-pointing arrow at the top of a PQA screen to go back (it works the same as your browser's Back button). Tap the History drop-down arrow at the top of the screen to revisit something you read a while back. Any button or link that shows three little lines fanning out from it means you will be sending data if you tap it.

ABC News

This PQA is, as you have no doubt surmised, an abbreviated version of the ABCNEWS.com Web site. You get a handful of stories in eight categories (**Figure 15.3**). Tap Headlines to get the top few stories of the hour. Each story is short: a paragraph or two. You can read the entire contents of the ABC News Palm program in a few minutes.

ABCNEWS.com ◀ ▼ History

ABCNEWS.com
READY WHEN YOU ARE

Headlines

US	World
Biz	Tech
Science	Living
Travel	Entertainment

Tour ABCNEWS.com
Copyright © 1999 ABC News Internet Ventures

Figure 15.3 The ABC News home page on your Palm VII.

The Front Page button at the end of stories and headlines takes you back, not surprisingly, to the beginning again (the home screen) where you can choose other stories in other categories.

The pulsating dot that expands and contracts while pages are loading works as a stop button. If you get tired of waiting for a page, tap that dot to make the Palm stop trying to download.

Activate

You already used up this one. After you activate your Palm VII, all you get when you tap the Activate icon is an error message.

Diagnostics

You saw the main Diagnostics screen in **Figure 15.2**, and that tells you the signal strength. Tap the Details button to see a lot more detailed technical info about it, including how well your transmitter is charged and the ID number of the base station where you're getting your service (not that it does you much good to know that).

E*Trade

This PQA (**Figure 15.4**) lets you track your favorite stocks, check on the state of the stock market (**Figure 15.5**), and read a little bit of market news. You can build a customized list of stocks that you want to keep tabs on, called a *watch list*—that way you don't have to keep writing the symbol in Graffiti every time you want to check your stocks. Stock quotes are on the usual 20-minute delay that the Securities Exchange Commission mandates.

To actually *trade* from your Palm VII, you have to apply for an E*Trade account. Tap the "Someday, we'll all invest this way" link on the home screen. You'll see a form to fill out to request an application. E*Trade will mail you—physically—a big application to fill out to apply for an E*Trade account. Once you're accepted (you may not be, depending on your net worth), you can buy and sell stocks from your Palm VII.

Figure 15.4 The E*Trade home screen offers a blank for you to write your favorite stock symbol in for a quick check.

Figure 15.5 Check out the state of the stock market by tapping Markets in the home screen.

ESPN

Never again will you be without sports scores (**Figure 15.6**). The ESPN PQA offers links for news on football, basketball, baseball, hockey, soccer, golf, auto racing, and more. There's also a Top News link at the top of the page.

Tap a sport to read news on that sport, get scores and schedules, and review current team standings. To quickly check scores only, tap the "S" button in front of each sport name.

iMessenger

iMessenger is your new wireless email program that works with your Palm.Net account (**Figure 15.7**). It is totally separate from the regular Palm Mail program and has nothing to do with it— the messages in the two systems never get mixed up. That said, iMessenger works similarly to the Mail program, except that you do actually send and receive email directly with the transmitter. To get email, you have to tell friends and colleagues your new you@palm.net email address.

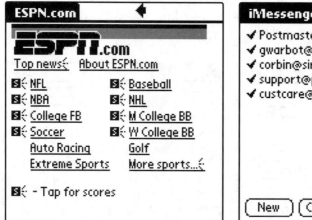

Figure 15.6 The ESPN home screen should make any sports lover salivate.

Figure 15.7 iMessenger is your Palm VII's wireless email application.

Getting iMessenger email out of your Palm VII

Your iMessenger email is not HotSynced, but there are two sneaky ways to get your iMessenger messages into your computer. Get online with your computer and on the www.palm.net Web site, click My Account, click iMessenger Blind Carbon Copy, and then enter your regular email address (not your Palm.Net address). From then on, outgoing (but not incoming) messages you send from your Palm VII are also sent to your regular email address, where you can open them and store them in your computer's email program. The other trick is to use your Word processor to open the file iMessengerDB.bak, which is in your Palm: iMessenger folder on your computer. You'll see some garbled computer junk with them, but your messages are right there in text format.

You have mailboxes called Inbox, Outbox, Deleted, Filed, and Draft. They work just as you think they'll work. You can add a signature to the end of your emails in the Preferences screen. When you delete email, it goes into your Deleted folder, and you can retrieve messages by tapping on them and tapping Undelete. It isn't actually deleted forever until you tap the Message menu and tap Purge Deleted.

Only the 500 characters of an email are transferred to your
Palm VII at one time. If the email is longer than that, you have
to tap the More button to get more of it.

*You're used to email being all-you-can-eat. Just remember,
with the Palm VII after 30 messages or so, you can hit your
monthly limit for the Basic Plan—after that, you're paying
about a dime per email. See the beginning of this chapter
for a breakdown of how the plans work.*

*To save money, enter your regular email address in the
Preferences screen under the Options menu. That way when
people reply to your iMessenger emails, you'll get them on
your regular computer, where email is virtually free. Plus, if
they quote your original message, you'll have a record of
your iMessenger messages as well.*

MapQuest

MapQuest is a handy little application if you do a lot of driving
(**Figure 15.8**). Enter a starting address and a destination address
and tap the Directions button, and Mapquest will give you very
specific driving directions from one to the other. If you want
directions from an airport, tap the Address drop-down arrow,
choose Airports, and enter the city and state.

Figure 15.8 You'll never
have an excuse for getting
lost in America again.

245

Palm.Net

If you're wondering how many kilobytes of data you've burned so far this month, tap the Palm.Net icon to start the Palm.Net PQA (**Figure 15.9**). Tap the My Account button. You're asked for your user name and password (**Figure 15.10**). Enter them, tap the Submit button, and soon you'll see how many kilobytes you've used. If you tap the Customer Support button, you're shown a list of Palm VII Help topics, which may or may not answer a question you have. If it doesn't, tap Contact Us to email your question to the folks at Palm.

Figure 15.9 You can check your account status and get help with questions in the Palm.Net PQA.

Figure 15.10 Enter your Palm.Net user name and password to check your palm.Net account.

Yahoo People Search

If you need to find a phone number or email address for someone, People Search may be your answer (**Figure 15.11**). It's like having a huge phone book covering all of the United States. Just enter the person's first and last name, along with city and state (you select the state from a list). If you want the street address returned, put a check mark beside Show Addresses. Tap the Search button. Yahoo returns a list of names and addresses matching the criteria you entered. For email, tap the Email link on the home screen first and then enter the first name, last name, and domain name.

The information returned by Yahoo People Search can be wrong or out of date in many cases. Or the person you're looking for won't be among the names returned. Don't expect too much from it, but it's usually worth a try— cheaper than a long distance information call.

Travelocity

Use Travelocity to check flight schedules, arrival and departure times, terminal and gate information, and baggage carousel numbers for flights you're interested in (**Figure 15.12**). If you enter departure and destination airports, when you want to fly, and airline (or not), it returns a list of flights that match. You can use that list to pick a flight and call your travel agent (or book it on the Travelocity Web site). If you're a member of Travelocity (go to www.travelocity.com to join for free), you can check information on trips you've already booked.

Figure 15.11 Yahoo People Search can find phone and email information all over the U.S.

Figure 15.12 Travelocity is like having a little personal travel agent.

Weather

This PQA is a microscopic version of the cable television's Weather Channel (**Figure 15.13**). It offers news, weather reports, and forecasts for U.S. cities (**Figure 15.14**). Tap the

My Weather button to get a five-day forecast for your area. How does it know where you are? Creepily (or conveniently, depending on your level of Big Brother paranoia), your location is easy to pinpoint—the PQA just checks to see which Bell South station is providing your access.

If the idea of broadcasting your location every time you flip up the Palm VII antenna bothers you, there's not much you can do about it. Read a bit more in this chapter for information on how to set up an alert whenever you're about to give away where you are.

Figure 15.13 Weather is brought to you by the Weather Channel.

Figure 15.14 Looks like a beautiful day on tap in Indianapolis—but storms tomorrow.

wsj.com

This is the smallest edition of the *Wall Street Journal* you're likely to ever run across. As you can see from the home screen (**Figure 15.15**) it offers three types of news: Business, Markets, and Technology. Tap on one of those links to get a summary page (**Figure 15.16**) containing a few short articles you can download. There is also a special offer to receive the larger, dead-tree version delivered to your home free for two weeks.

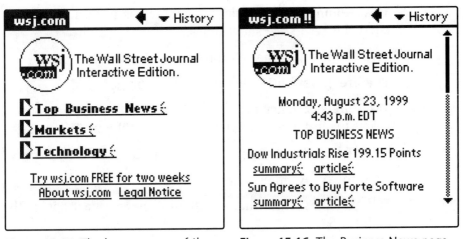

Figure 15.15 The home screen of the Palm VII's Wall Street Journal PQA.

Figure 15.16 The Business News page offers a few business articles.

Other PQAs on the Palm VII CD-ROM

If you choose to, you can install more PQAs from the Palm VII CD-ROM. (You may have already done so.) Here are brief descriptions of each.

ATM Locator: This PQA is from MasterCard. Enter your location information, and you'll get a list of MasterCard-compatible ATM machines in your area.

ATMs—Visa: Same thing except this one's for Visa-compatible machines.

BofA: Bank of America customers can access account information, including balances and transaction histories.

Dictionary: Search for definitions of words, brought to you by Merriam-Webster. Also offers a thesaurus.

EtakTraffic: General traffic reports for 21 cities. You can sign up for an extra service that examines your commute route (to the tune of $60 a year).

Fodor's: Condensed travel information for 100 cities in the world, focusing mostly on dining and accommodations.

Frommer's: Similar to Fodor's, except it is U.S.-centric and offers broader information on entertainment, tourist spots, and shopping.

MoviePhone: Very simple, one-tap access to local theaters—tap a theater to see show times.

OAG Flights: Another airline flight information PQA.

TheStreet: Very brief financial news stories.

TM Wireless: Enter the name of the band, and you can buy tickets to their shows right from your Palm VII from TicketMaster.

UPS: Track your packages shipped via United Parcel Service.

USA Today: Another newspaper PQA.

Yellow Pages: Just what you think it is, except it covers the entire U.S.

In case you're wondering, this is only the beginning. Many more PQAs are available. Visit www.palm.com to download and check them out.

Wireless preferences

The Palm VII gives you one additional Preference category. In the Applications screen, tap the Prefs icon and tap the drop-down Category arrow. Select the Wireless category. If you've activated the Palm.Net service, the Proxy information will already be filled out (don't mess with it) like in **Figure 15.17**.

Put a check mark in the "Warn..." check box if you want to be alerted every time you are about to give away your location, at which point you can say no. The problem is, saying no means not using the Palm VII PQA application at that time. There is no way to mask where you are and use a PQA at the same time.

Figure 15.17 The extra Wireless Preferences screen lets you be paranoid.

Final Palm VII Thoughts

The Palm VII Palm.Net service is amazing and disappointing, in my opinion. On the one hand, it's incredible that this kind of device exists already—it's quite futuristic. But although some of the PQAs are useful and ingenious, mostly they feel like teasers. I'm trying to see the Palm VII as merely a hint of what's to come. Surely in a year or two, we'll think nothing of having instant Web access in our pockets. But the Palm VII isn't quite there yet. Most of all, the pricing structure needs to get in line with what Internet surfers are used to: unlimited access with no per-kilobyte surcharges.

If you're merely toying with the idea of buying a Palm VII, I think you're probably better off buying a Palm IIIx or V and using an innovative software/service such as AvantGo (see Chapter 14). It's much cheaper, the information can go as deep as you want, and you choose which Web sites to Hot-Sync to your Palm.

Palm Resources

If you've read this book, you have a basic understanding of how a Palm works and what you can do with it. So where do you go from here? What are the resources available to you to take you to the next level? This appendix lists just a few of the many Palm-related organizations and products that can help you go much deeper in your Palm knowledge.

Official

Palm Computing (www.palm.com): This is, of course, the official Web site for the Palm. It offers news, lots of product descriptions, software for downloading, information for Palm developers, and links to other Palm-related sites.

User groups

User groups are a great way to meet other Palm enthusiasts. It's one thing to start learning about something on your own, but a user group adds another dimension. I found this book's wonderful technical editor by going to a San Francisco Palm/Pilot User Group meeting. See this book's foreword by Michael Bergen for more on how a user group can enhance your excitement for the Palm.

Palm Computing's list of user groups: www.palm.com/resources/usergroups.html

San Francisco Palm/Pilot User Group: www.sfpug.org

Palms and accessories

PDA Mart (www.pdamart.com): A good place to find deals on all kinds of Personal Digital Assistants (of which Palms are only one type).

Outpost (www.outpost.com): Low prices on lots of consumer gadgets, including Palms and Palm accessories.

Buy.Com (www.buy.com): Another good, affordable online shop for consumer electronics of all sorts, including Palms and Palm accessories.

Computer Discount Warehouse (www.cdw.com): Yet another Web store that offers Palms and accessories at reasonable rates.

20-20 Consumer (www.20-20consumer.com): An independent consumer-oriented price comparison site.

Screen protectors

Concept Kitchen (www.conceptkitchen.com): These folks make little plastic strips that protect your Graffiti area or whole screen from scratches. They also make some of the coolest Palm accessories out there, including the best screen cleaner on the market, called Brain Wash. They also make a sterling silver fingertip stylus and the new Bumper case, which is a rubber shock-absorbent case.

Keyboards

Landware (www.landware.com): This company makes more than just good Palm software—they also manufacture the GoType Keyboard, which is a keyboard that works kind of like a cradle: You place your Palm in it and start typing! Includes software that runs on your Palm. Needs no power. The new GoType Pro keyboard is now available for the Palm V.

Software

All of the following Web sites are large depositories of Palm software and other good stuff like news, information, rumors, discussion groups. You could spend all day downloading great stuff from any one of them (or all of them). You'll find many of the same programs in them, but each offers something unique as well. These are terrific resources that you should definitely bookmark in your Web browser.

- **Palm Central** (www.palmcentral.com)
- **Palm Gear** (www.palmgear.com)
- **EuroCool** (www.eurocool.com)
- **PilotZone** (www.pilotzone.com)
- **ZD Net's Palm Software** (www.zdnet.com/swlib/ pilotsoftware/)

Downloadable books and literature

Programs like TealDoc and AportisDoc let you read books electronically on your Palm. But where do you get these books? You get them here:

MemoWare (www.memoware.com): Craig Froehle's Web site is a collection of literature and other copyright-free material that can make your Palm a powerful information appliance.

Lending Library (www.macduff.net): John Swain's free site is another wonderful place to find great literature you can read on your Palm.

Peanut Press (www.peanutpress.com): They offer current commercial books for sale, and they include their own reader. This is the only place to get current books and literature, instead of copyright-expired stuff. They have a small but nice selection, including science fiction and non-fiction.

Books about the Palm

Palm III and PalmPilot: Visual QuickStart Guide by Jeff Carlson. Published by Peachpit Press. This book is a very well-written, recipe-based, easy-to-use guide to getting the most out of your Palm. It's a great next step if you've finished this book.

PalmPilot: The Ultimate Guide, 2nd Edition by David Pogue. Published by O'Reilly and Associates. This is the undisputed bible of everything Palm. Comes with a CD-ROM containing a massive collection of Palm software.

Magazines

Some of these offer paper editions, and some exist only as electrons.

- **HandJive** (www.handjivemag.com/index.shtml)
- **PalmZone** (www.palmzone.com)
- **PalmPower** (www.palmpower.com)
- **The Piloteer** (www.pmn.co.uk)
- **Tap Online** (www.tapmagazine.com)
- **Wireless Week** (www.wirelessweek.com)

Newsgroups

Here are some Usenet newsgroups that are essentially world-wide bulletin boards of information about the Palm, continually updated. Your ISP probably offers a news server (ask them or check their Web site). If not, you can use DejaNews (www.dejanews.com) to read these newsgroups.

- **alt.comp.sys.palmtops.pilot**
- **comp.sys.palmtops.pilot**
- **comp.sys.pen**
- **comp.sys.palmtops**
- **comp.sys.handhelds**

Random resources

The Palm Web Ring (www.palmcentral.com/webring.html): This is a collection of Web sites that link to each other in special ways. You'll see a toolbar with a button called Random. Click that button to be taken randomly anywhere within the Web ring.

Index

A

Abacus calculator program, 185
ABC News PQA, 241–242
About Applications option, 36
AC adapter
    for modem, 197
    for Palm V model, 6, 23, 24
accessories, 196, 254
Accessory Catalog, 196
Activate PQA, 242
Activation screen, 26
add-on programs, 177–192
Address Book, 79–90. *See also*
    Contacts module
    automatically adding phone
        numbers from, 75
    creating business card in,
        81–85
    creating categories in, 82, 86
    deleting entries in, 83
    finding text in, 87–88
    importing data into, 80, 85
    managing contacts in, 85–88
    marking entries as private,
        83, 141
    navigating in, 86–88
    Palm Desktop version (Mac
        OS) (*See* Contacts module)
    Palm Desktop version
        (Windows), 139–142
    preferences for, 89
Address Book button, 10, 38
address entries. *See* entries
Address Entry Details dialog box,
    82–83
address view, 80
airline information, accessing,
    247
Alarm checkbox, 68
Alarm Preset checkbox, 75–76
Alarm Sound option, 38

alarms
    adjusting volume of, 38
    alarm sounds, 76
    preferences for, 75–76
    setting for events, 67–69,
        162
    To Do List and, 96
America Online (AOL), email for,
    218
analog phone lines, 198
AportisDoc program, 100,
    186–187
App menu, 32–35
application buttons, 9, 10–11
applications, 59–121, 177–192.
    See also specific software
    add-on programs, 177–192
    backing up data in, 24
    beaming, 34
    built-in applications, 34,
        59–121
    categories for, 31–32, 34–35
    deleting, 33–34
    displaying information
        about, 35
    downloading from Web,
        178–181
    installing downloaded
        programs, 181–183
    memory and, 33
    resources for, 255
    system extensions, 184
    using calculations in, 120
    viewing installed programs,
        29, 30
    working with, 30–37
Applications icon, 11, 12
Applications screen, 12, 29, 30–37
Appointment dialog box (Mac
    OS), 161
appointments. *See* events
Aramis Travel Guides, 189

arrows, drop-down, 28
Assigned box, 116
ATM Locator PQA, 249
ATMs—Visa PQA, 249
attachment icon, 166, 171, 172
attachments, email, 213
Auto-off after option, 37
automatic fill option, 113
AvantGo Web browser, 185, 224,
    230–236

B

backing up data, 24, 44, 184
Backlight "Big Line" command,
    39
backlighting, 10, 23, 39
backspaces, strokes for, 48
Backup Buddy program, 24,
    44, 184
batteries, 22–24
    Auto-off after option and, 37
    backlighting and, 10, 23
    Beam Receive option and, 38
    modems and, 197, 198
    for Palm V model, 6, 23–24
    recharging, 23–24
battery indicator, 23
BCC (blind carbon copy), 215
Beam Category command, 104
Beam Data "Big Line"
    command, 39
Beam Receive option, 38
beaming, 17. *See also* IR port
    Beam Data feature and, 39
    Beam Receive option and, 38
    applications, 34
    business cards, 81, 84–85
    categories, 86, 104
    events, 74–75
    memos, 104, 106
    travel itineraries, 188

LandWare Palm Solutions

Mention Peachpit and get a 10% discount when you purchase directly from LandWare.

GoType! / GoType Pro
SRP $79.95 / $89.95

The fastest way to enter information into your organizer

Now you can enter information into your connected organizer as quickly as you can type. GoType! requires no batteries or cables and has been especially designed to consume very little power. GoType! is simple to use; just place your organizer into the integrated docking port and start typing.

goVox Voice Recorder
SRP $49.95

Instantly capture verbal information — anytime, anywhere

goVox adds voice memo recording capability to the Palm III series of organizers by replacing the flip-cover with a stand-alone voice recorder. Custom circuitry provides recording and playback with superior speech clarity. Record up to 99 messages with a total of 8 minutes. Perfect for capturing important facts on the run.

Pocket Quicken
SRP $39.95

Instantly organize your finances — anytime, anywhere!

Pocket Quicken is the standard in mobile financial tracking software that makes managing your finances as easy as turning on your organizer. With an easy-to-use interface and excellent connectivity to the desktop, Pocket Quicken transforms your organizer into a mobile money manager that is flexible, easy to use, and fast.

6290

Gulliver
SRP $29

Access and manage your travel itinerary

Gulliver handles all the details of business travel and puts the information you need at your fingertips: hotel confirmation numbers, phone numbers, flight schedules, frequent flyer ID numbers, and much more. Gulliver streamlines input and access of information with easy-to-use templates and popup menus.

Software for Terra Firma

complete visual overviews, demos, and ordering at www.landware.com
PH (201) 261-7944 • FAX (201) 261-7949 • SALES (800) 526-3977